Cumbria

Cumbria

John Parker

John Bartholomew & Son Limited
Edinburgh and London

Other Titles in this Series:

Available in 1977:
Devon & Cornwall DENYS KAY-ROBINSON
South Wales RUTH THOMAS
The Scottish Highlands JOHN A. LISTER

In preparation:
South-East England OLIVER MASON
North Yorkshire CHRISTOPHER STAFFORD

First published in Great Britain 1977 by
JOHN BARTHOLOMEW & SON LIMITED
12 Duncan Street, Edinburgh EH9 1TA
And 216 High Street, Bromley BR1 1PW

ISBN 0 7028 1004 5

All maps © John Bartholomew & Son Limited

Book and jacket design: Susan Waywell

Printed in Great Britain by
Hazell Watson & Viney Limited,
Aylesbury, Buckinghamshire

Colour sections printed in Great Britain by
John Bartholomew & Son Limited, Edinburgh

Contents

Acknowledgements

Thanks are due to the library staffs of Cumbria County Council – particularly to the staff at Ambleside – to the guides at Dove Cottage for their help with Wordsworth references, and to Ann and Anne for typing the manuscript.

John Parker, Graythwaite, Cumbria,
March 1976

Publishers' Note
The publishers of this guide are always pleased to acknowledge any corrections brought to their notice by readers. Correspondence should be addressed to the Guide-book Editor, John Bartholomew & Son Limited, 216 High Street, Bromley BR1 1PW.

A Note on Editions
Within *Cumbria* there are some quotations from the longer poems of Wordsworth and Keats. In such cases the line numbers that have been given refer to the following editions: *Wordsworth Poetical Works* (1936 edn.) ed. Thomas Hutchinson, revised Ernest de Selincourt
Keats Poetical Works (1956 edn.) ed. H. W. Garrod

Regional Map

Showing the Area Covered by this Guide

Introduction

Cumbria is more a country than county. Sitting outwards at the north-west corner of England between Morecambe Bay and the Solway, and walled on the east by the Pennines, its isolation accentuates a distinct, rugged character that is quite unique. It is impossible to give an objective description. The landscape demands a response and an exploration. Those few people who are repelled by wild scenery might care to give it no more than a superficial glance and may find Daniel Defoe's description of the old county of Westmorland apt: 'the wildest, most barren and frightful of any that I have passed over in England or even in Wales itself; the west side which borders on Cumberland is indeed bounded by a chain of almost impassable mountains'.

Camden, the Elizabethan historian, was more meticulous in his investigation when he visited Cumberland in 1582, and was much taken by its beauty:

> The country although it be somewhat with the coldest as lying farre North, and seemeth as rough by reason of hilles, yet for the variety thereof it smileth upon the beholders and giveth contentment to as many as travaile it. For after the rockes bunching out, the mountains standing thicke together, rich of metall mines, and betweene them great meeres stored with all kinds of wildfoule, you come to pretty hills good for pasturage, and well replenished with flocks of sheepe, beneath which againe you meet with goodly plaines, spreading out a great way, yielding corn sufficiently. Besides all this the Ocean driving and dashing upon the shore affourdeth plenty of excellent good fish.

The description is precise and Camden was probably the first to sing the region's praises.

But it was two centuries after Camden before the land was explored purely for its beauty. Even for some time after the coming of the improved turnpike roads the fell country was outside the ken of ordinary mortals journeying between Lancaster and Carlisle, or round the Solway to Whitehaven. The inhabitants of this wilderness were regarded as strange highlanders occupied in subsistence farming, or mining, or making charcoal. Apparently poor, tough, and independent, they were left to themselves and their mountains. The first tourists liked to pretend that they were courageous in penetrating to the awesome dale heads. While courting the 'horror' of Borrowdale in their carriages they might dutifully keep their voices down lest the reverberations from the sound should bring the crags falling about their heads. 'Horror' was a well-used word in the old guide-books. 'The full perfection of Keswick', states one, 'consists of three circumstances, beauty, horror and immensity united'. The modern traveller, familiar with Wales and the Scottish Highlands, is less horror-prone and will readily appreciate, with Camden, that the Cumbrian wilderness, with its peaks, crags, escarpments, sixteen lakes, and scores of tarns, is leavened by a more luxurious valley cover of woodland and pastures and by a homely pattern of human settlement. The 'mountains standing thicke', the 'pretty hills good for pasturage', the 'goodly plaines', the 'Ocean driving and dashing upon the shore': this is Cumbria, timeless and unmoved.

Mountains apart, Cumbria is an English county containing something of almost everything that is typical of the English countryside, from rich and temperate features to those that are spartan and bleak. The more observant explorer, though, will note a difference: the sparseness of historical remains among the richer farmlands, where one might expect to find them. The explanation is simple: Cumbria was a frontier area for hundreds of years; it was a territory disputed periodically from the Roman conquest to the seventeenth century. For a long period after the final abandonment of Hadrian's Wall half of Cumbria was part of Scotland. And when there were no hard-fought battles, border raids were regular occurrences. Cattle rustling, pillaging, and burning to and fro around the border-line were commonplace. After Bannockburn, Robert the Bruce plundered all the wealth, mainly monastic, as far south as Lancaster. Less-well-organized looting went on for several centuries. Families on both sides of the Border engaged in feuding and robbery and were subject to a very rough, home-grown justice. Compared with many other areas of England, the result has left a historical wasteland. The remnants of this period are mainly the battered walls of castles and fortified houses. Like the borderlands of Scotland, the history of Cumbria is one of bloodshed, rivalries, feuds, skirmishes, and political struggles: a strange mixture of farce and tragedy.

What is known as the English Lake District, and is now Britain's largest National Park, is the central precious jewel in the Cumbrian setting. In attempting to describe the formation and shape of the central fells Wordsworth likened them to a wheel, with spokes radiating from a hub: the hub being the highest land in England. But he then had to admit to two hubs. And it seems that even to accept the radiating valley pattern as nearer to two superimposed wheels, with their hubs some 13km. apart, it would still have to be admitted that the details are somewhat mangled. The 'mountains standing thicke together' occupy only about 1,700sq.km., yet there is so much in so little that it would require a man's whole life-span to explore the area.

The central fells are rugged: the lines of communication across them are principally for adventurous walkers. There is only one easy north–south central road, the A591, fortuitously accommodated by a geological fault crossing the Dunmail Raise (239m.) between the two hubs, as near to the centre of the National Park as one can get. The Raise was once the boundary between England and Scotland; and until 1974 formed the boundary between the old counties of Cumberland and Westmorland; it was also the site of at least one great ancient battle. (The old saying 'Nowt good comes o'er t'Raise', still used by locals, has an ancient and sinister source.)

The geological structure of Cumbria is complicated and interesting. Its complexity is the source of the wide variety of scenic interest, for which the district is unique and famous. In the main area of the Lake District there are essentially three types of rock, giving three types of landscape. In the southern part are the Silurian Slates, which break down fairly easily to give rounded, low fells supporting extensive woodland. In the centre are the hard Borrowdale Volcanics, which show the rugged, craggy, uncompromising lines of the higher fells and peaks. In the northern area are the shales of the Skiddaw Slate Series, an older rock that breaks down into small, flaky fragments, giving straighter, angular outlines to the fells and an illusion of great height. Many of the lake-filled valleys differ from head to foot in their scenic types: Windermere's lower half, for instance, is in the Silurian Slates, and its lovely broadleaf woodlands crowd the rounded skyline and shores; but the northern reaches are backed by a skyline of dramatic volcanic peaks. Derwent Water's head is also in the volcanics, with its foot in the Skiddaw Slates. Ullswater starts in the volcanics, but its middle reaches are in the Skiddaw Slates, and its foot is in the limestones.

The main valleys offer this scenic variety, but there are also minor valleys leading into the main ones, and these in turn are often fed by even smaller valleys. Add to this scenic mixture the one further essential ingredient: the influence of man. Neither farmer, rich landowner, nor forester have changed the essential shape and character of the region, but they have added much to the colour and texture; and the permutations seem almost endless. A brief impression is fine enough, but the explorer's rewards are rich indeed. This explains why the district has such a wide appeal and dedicated following. There is something for every taste: the austerity of the wide-open fell; the challenge of cliff and crag; green ravines loud with falling water; the serenity of still lakes; the friendly hem of a wood; the hospitality of a fell village. The 'Lakers' often find their own particular niche and return to it time and time again. Whole libraries of books have been written about the Lake District, and its literary associations are impressive. Writers who have used the Lake District as their subject or inspiration include Daniel Defoe, Gray, Keats, Shelley, Charles Lamb, Stevenson, Scott, Emerson, Charlotte Brontë, Beatrix Potter, Carlyle, Tennyson, De Quincey, Coleridge, Southey, John Ruskin, and William and Dorothy Wordsworth.

If the centre of Cumbria did not attract all the attention, the rest of the county's landscape would be better known and better appreciated. Outside the centre, Cumbria is largely a rolling country of limestone and sandstone, with cliffs and sandy beaches in the west, and the wild wall of the Pennines on the east. Most of it is agricultural land with a scattering of seemingly timeless, neat, and attractive villages; and around the western and northern rim, from Barrow to Carlisle, is a grouping of more densely populated towns, springing from the mining industries of the last century, yet following a pattern of human settlement strangely comparable with that of Neolithic times.

Cumbria is the second largest county in England and Wales, with a total area of 681,000ha., 224,000 of which are designated as National Park. Until the boundary changes in 1974, what is now Cumbria was divided between the counties of Cumberland, in the north and west, Westmorland, in the east, and part of Lancashire, embracing the southern peninsula of Furness. Westmorland has vanished from the map and its passing will long be mourned in Kendal, its largest town, and in Appleby, its county-town; Cumberland at least retains a semantic affinity with Cumbria. The Furness Peninsula was always part of the county of Lancashire by virtue of its ancient low-tide link with Lancaster across Morecambe Bay. But it, too, is now part of Cumbria. Lancashire, Cumberland, and Westmorland once met at the summit of Wrynose Pass, where the commemorative Three Shire Stone still stands. The new county also took in a small snip of Yorkshire, acquiring Sedbergh and Dentdale.

The total population of Cumbria according to the 1971 Census was 475,831, a significant part of it being the city of Carlisle (71,500) and in the mainly industrial towns of Barrow, Ulverston, Workington, Whitehaven, and Kendal (151,000). The old industries of mining, steel, and agriculture are now supplemented by diverse modern industries. Tourism has expanded in the central areas and in recent years has grown in importance in the outer areas, yet, thanks largely to the National Parks Act, the extensive land ownership of the National Trust, and the commendable restraint and sensitivity of landowners and business interests, it has never become vulgarized.

Cumbria still 'smileth upon the beholders and giveth contentment to as many as travaile it'.

TOP: *The River Ellen near its source: steeply dipping Skiddaw Slates in the foreground*
BOTTOM: *Buttermere, with Honister Pass left background. The southern boundary of the Skiddaw Slate Series takes in Buttermere's northern fells and sweeps westwards at the foot of the lake. The granophyre of Ennerdale is an intrusion covering the west side of Buttermere*

Geology

To understand and appreciate Cumbria's landscape, human history, and natural history it is important to understand something of its geology. To a geologist the rocks of Cumbria, because of their complexity, problems, and variety, are an exciting subject for study. And the non-geologist will find much of obvious interest.

The variety of landscape is immense: the cliffs and crags and screes; the beaches; the tree-clad hillsides; the great green fells; the stone-built villages and towns; the quarries; the network of dry-stone walls. The forms, colours, and textures are infinitely variable, and the story they tell goes back 500 million years. The time-scale is excusably hard to grasp, for after all human presence on earth is less than two million years.

Long before the oldest rocks in Cumbria were raised the earth's crust had been constantly changing – lifting, folding, eroding, receiving outpourings from the core – and the seas were constantly moving, and deepening and shallowing. The process continues of course, but infinitely slowly.

The geologist recognizes that generally the deepest rock strata are the oldest, with the newer levels superimposed above in an identifiable sequence that can be scientifically dated. The central highlands of Cumbria, forming the beautiful Lake District fells, are of the older formation: all the layers of more recent rocks have, over many millions of years, been broken, crumbled, and swept away from the surface. The oldest rocks are in the north and north-west. These are the Skiddaw Slates. In a wide band through the central area the Skiddaw Slate is covered with a volcanic outpouring: the Borrowdale Volcanic Series. In the south and east there are visible remains of the Silurian Coniston Slate Series, which once covered the whole area. And around the rim of the Lake District and covering the perimeter of Cumbria are the later sandstones and limestones, these rocks having been removed from the central areas.

The Skiddaw Slates

These rocks are sedimentary. They were formed from mud deposits in a shallow sea in the Ordovician period (500 million to 450 million years ago). Earth movements affected the types of deposits and resulted in the muds and clays varying greatly in texture and colour. All this hardened under pressure, the deposits being several thousand metres thick. The resultant material is a shale rather than what might more commonly be thought of as slate: slate as the builder knows it is only found in a few places in the Skiddaw Series. Most of the material, being minutely jointed, breaks down into small, thin flakes by the action of water and frost. The high fells of Skiddaw Slate are therefore angular rather than rough and craggy, the stable areas often being extensively covered in heather where the rock has broken down into soil beds.

The obvious and dramatic exposures of Skiddaw Slate tower over the foot of Derwent Water; Skiddaw and Blencathra, the northern fells, dwarf Keswick. Skiddaw is Keswick's sheltering wall, and is often one of the first challenges to would-be fell-walkers. Because of its composition it is almost without dangerous crags and its summit can be gained in good weather even by the novice. Nevertheless it is an impressive bulk, and only 45m. less than the highest point in England.

From Derwent Water the Skiddaw Slate Series spreads south-west and west as well as north. The southern boundary moves south-west taking in Buttermere's northern fells, then sweeps westwards at the foot of Buttermere, taking in the fells between Lowes Water and Ennerdale, forming half of the bed of Ennerdale Water. Some way beyond this the rock is covered by later material, and another exposure only appears much further south of Ennerdale, in the fine bulk of Black Combe, a landmark for mariners as far away as the Mersey. The northern boundary is westward from Back o' Skiddaw, taking in the whole of the Bassenthwaite area, and southward from Cockermouth, taking in Crummock Water and Lowes Water. Further afield in the east, Skiddaw Slate is visible in the Eden Valley in a narrow band on the Pennine ridge; it is particularly noticeable on Murton Fell. Further afield still and going out of the county, but to the west this time, similar rock is found on the Isle of Man.

The varying qualities of the Skiddaw Slate Series are of considerable interest to geologists, particularly where later volcanic activity through the rock has changed its form by intense heat and intrusions. Fossils in Skiddaw Slate are few and are mainly graptolites and trilobites (primitive and extinct sea creatures).

Borrowdale Volcanics

Towards the end of the period of deposition of the Skiddaw Slates, still lying under a shallow sea, there was suddenly some catastrophic volcanic activity. Several volcanic vents opened up in the sea bed. The violent explosions scattered material widely and piled it into consolidated masses: the resulting rock is known to geologists as agglomerate. There was also a great outflowing of lava, forming, as it cooled, hard rock beds varying in type according to the speed of cooling and presence of collected material. The volcanic activity also produced large quantities of settled dust and ash.

Deposits were laid upon deposits to a depth of around 3km. and were later subjected to great pressure. All this violent and complicated activity left the varying types of rock known collectively as the Borrowdale Volcanics, which form the core, and the most dramatic scenery, of the Lake District. The material is hard and is so structured that in subsequent earth movements and erosions it tended to break into large, sharp-angled blocks; and it is a rock that does not break down as easily as the Skiddaw Slates when attacked by water and frost. Consequently the Volcanics form the distinctive, craggy outlines and towering cliffs: Langdale Pikes and all the central fells, including Bow Fell, the Scafell range, Great Gable, Old Man of Coniston, Helvellyn, and the High Street range. From the viewpoints of Orrest Head above Windermere town, or Jenkin Crag above Waterhead, Ambleside, the contrast formed by the great hulks of the Borrowdale Volcanics against a foreground of milder slopes is dramatic and very obvious.

The steep, hard rock-faces offer some of the finest sport for rock climbers to be found anywhere in the British Isles, and their long ridges are a challenge and enticement to fell-walkers.

Volcanic material varies very greatly from place to place and has widely differing qualities. One particular tuff – a rock formed from fine dust – is extremely hard and almost metallic. Its qualities were discovered by Neolithic settlers over 3,000 years ago,

TOP: *The Langdale Pikes, seen from Bow Fell. Borrowdale Volcanic country*
BOTTOM: *Crag of Andesite at Binsey, 5km. NE of foot of Bassenthwaite Lake. Borrowdale Volcanic Series*

and stone axes made from this rock, quarried from high on Langdale Pikes and Scafell Pikes, were exported to far-away parts of the British Isles and even to the European mainland. There is much evidence that eruptions and rapid piling of deposits continued over a long period. The upper, and latest, deposits were in the form of rhyolites, an acidic, light-coloured rock often weathering white; these can be well observed at the head of Kentmere.

Volcanic vents are nowhere very obvious in Cumbria, although Castlehead, near Keswick, is usually regarded as the hardened 'plug' of one of these vents. Capel Crag, east of Egremont, may have been another.

The Coniston Limestone

About 440 million years ago the Ordovician period, which produced the Skiddaw Slates and the Borrowdale Volcanics, was coming to an end. The area became submerged in a shallow sea, while at the same time there were gentle earth movements that forced up the central fells and produced fracture lines and weaknesses. Storm waters rushing down the slopes followed the fracture lines and produced massive erosions. The sea silt formed from eroded material settled into beds, and onto this was added fossil material from shelled creatures: graptolites, trilobites, and brachiopods. This solidified material is known as Coniston Limestone. Little can now be seen, for the subsequent erosion of the covering has left only a narrow band visible, running, at its south-western end, from the Duddon Estuary at Broughton-in-Furness, through Coniston and Ambleside, to the eastern Lake District fells. It does not resemble a typical limestone, being dull grey or mud-coloured. But it was recognized for what it was by the Cumbrian inhabitants long ago: old lime kilns can be seen on the line of the rock by the roadside near Coniston on the way to Ambleside, and one can be seen in a wall recess by the roadside near Waterhead.

The Silurian Slates

The Silurian period followed the Ordovician: this period was still over 400 million years ago, when the only life on the planet was primitive and moving about in warm seas. The land was still in movement and subject to massive erosion from wind and storm.

In the area of what is now Cumbria the sea covered the land, and large deposits of erosion silt were being laid down, forming the rock known as the Silurian Slates. These slates remain as cover over the greater part of southern Cumbria. The build-up of these large deposits was rapid. It is not known how much was eventually eroded away in later times, but today the cover extends to a depth of 4km. The contrast between the Silurian landscape and that of the Borrowdale Volcanics adds much to the beauty of the area at the head of Windermere. The Silurian Slate is of course softer and, being laid down in beds, fractures fairly easily along its bedding plane. It is acidic, but breaks down into reasonable depths of soil and supports good forest cover: the rolling, hilly country east of Coniston Water, now Grizedale Forest, and south-eastwards into what was once Furness is typical. The area covered by the Silurian beds is south-eastwards from the Coniston Limestone as far east as Tebay; its southern parts, around Kendal, Cartmel, and south of Millom, are covered by irregular layers of later deposits.

The oldest of the Silurian Slates can be found along the rock's northern boundary, for here the land took an upwards tilt and the subsequent erosions bit deeper. (Generally, the further south one travels in England the newer the rock.) The Silurian beds have been divided by geologists into six identifiable layers. Only a narrow band of the oldest layer, comprised of the Stockdale Shales, which were put down in deep seas, can be seen; the rock is dark blue or black in the lower deposits.

The fossils contained in the Silurian Slates are mainly graptolites. The upper parts of the beds, as can be seen at Skelghyll, east of Ambleside, are greyer. Above the Stockdale Shales are the Brathay Flags, put down in shallower water: the basic material was fossiliferous mud. The Stockdale Shales and the Brathay Flags cover to a depth of something like 365m.

Above the Brathay Flags are gritty, unfossiliferous deposits comprising the first layer of the upper Coniston Flags (or Coldwell Beds); subsequent layers of this material contain shells and graptolites. The rock type is about 457m. thick.

After this are rocks consisting of massive deposits of gritty silt, largely without fossils, forming the Coniston Grit, about 1,200m. thick. All this material can be seen from south of the Duddon Estuary, north-westwards through Coniston Water and the low fells south of it, through Windermere's head, and through Kentmere and Longsleddale.

Above the Coniston Grit are the Bannisdale Slates, which were built up from alternate layers of mud and grit. This material is usually lead-coloured and contains very few fossils. The thickness of it is something like $1\frac{1}{2}$km. Above the Slates are fossil-bearing grey-green deposits known as the Kirkby Moor Flags. Being uppermost these deposits were later heavily eroded, so it is not known how thick this rock type was. The depth remaining is about 457m.

The combined thickness of these Silurian deposits is about 4km. The best way of finding and identifying the different layers is to examine the old dry-stone walls in the south of the Lake District. Such walls were often made of the material nearest to hand, usually rock quarried on the spot, though near streams and rivers they are frequently made from 'beck-bottoms', rounded stones pulled out of the water: these of course might include some material washed down from other beds.

The Devonian

It can now be imagined that Cumbria was covered with a shallow, heavily silted sea, the slightly domed area of what is now the central Lake District forming the shallowest point. It had remained thus for some forty million years. What followed is known as the Devonian period. Its effect on Cumbria was catastrophic.

In the early part of the Devonian period the earth was shaken by enormous mountain-building earth movements. The Caledonian Uplift pushed Cumbria out of the seas, and the central area was pushed up into a much larger dome. The rocks buckled into folds running diagonally from west-south-west to east-north-east. The various types of rock, soft and hard, bedded deposits and dense volcanics, all behaved differently under this unimaginable pressure. The softer Upper Silurian deposits split along their bedding planes and broke up. The effect on the Skiddaw Slates was more dramatic: the material was easily fragmented and became subject to severe folds, thrusting up through the overlying material; what are now the mountains of Skiddaw and Blencathra are the eroded remains of a massive upward fold – an anticline – and the line-up conforms to the direction of thrust.

The Borrowdale Volcanics offered much greater resistance, and the direction of the upward folds and the troughs – synclines – did not conform strictly to the thrust direction. When the volcanic tuffs were subject to this lateral pressure their particles were rearranged with an effect that produced possible cleavages on lines bearing no relation to the original bedding planes. The whole of the volcanic series developed joints, fracture lines, and faults. Into the subterranean hollows volcanic material from deep under the earth pushed upwards, welling through the surface via the fracture lines and faults, changing the character of the surrounding rock with the heat and vapour, and producing in the process a wealth of minerals.

The Cumbrian Granites date from this period. Granite is a volcanic crystalline material consisting largely of quartz, feldspar, and mica. It was thrust upwards to the surface in 'blisters', the best-known exposure in the county being at Shap, where the quarries provide large quantities of road material; here the rock was pushed through a fault in the Borrowdale Volcanics and Silurian rocks and is some 5km. across. In the western area of Cumbria the area of intrusion was greater, and because the granite contains haematite (iron) it is pinkest in this region. This granite extends from Eskdale, through Miterdale, to the lower end of Wast Water. The granophyre of Ennerdale is another intrusion covering both sides of upper Ennerdale and the west side of Buttermere. The places where the granophyre finishes at Ennerdale can be clearly seen on the shores of the lake: the pebbles change from pink to grey at the Skiddaw Slate junction. The granophyre tends to break down into squarish blocks, making walking difficult. Smaller intrusions of granite occur around Threlkeld, thrust through the faults dividing the anticline of the Skiddaw Slate at its junction with the Borrowdale Volcanic. Further north, on Carrock Fell, the intrusion takes the form of gabbro and granophyre.

The Devonian period, which lasted for fifty million years, was, again, a time of heavy erosion: arid desert conditions built up sandstorms, and there were seasons of heavy rain resulting in flash floods. In the higher, northern, part of Cumbria the Silurian beds, broken by the earth movements, were worn away. The higher Borrowdale Volcanics were also worn down. Vast quantities of material were swept away to distant seas.

The Carboniferous

Following the Devonian period the land was again engulfed by sea in the Carboniferous period (350 million–270 million years ago). This was a shallow sea and for long periods it is probable that Cumbria's higher land was hardly covered at all. During the Devonian period life on the planet had become richer and more varied. The first vertebrates were present in the seas. But, more important, the first primate land plants had developed. The deposits of mud left in the shallow waters of the Carboniferous sea were rich in fossils: corals, molluscs, and crinoids. As the seas became shallower they were colonized by plants that thrived and grew thickly on the muddy shoals; and as the waters fluctuated these plants died to produce peat beds that were in turn buried under great layers of sand and mud. The trapped and pressured peat beds formed the coal measures that have been well exploited in the west of Cumbria, around Maryport and Whitehaven.

The fossil-rich Carboniferous deposits produced a limestone in a sea of constantly changing levels, always deeper to the south and in the Eden Valley area to the east. The remnants of this limestone cover extensive areas to the south of Cumbria and continue in a curving band eastwards from a point east of Kirkby Lonsdale, then north-westwards between Shap and Tebay, then westwards and south-westwards from Caldbeck, by Cockermouth, to Egremont. Another exposure is on the east side of Cumbria northwards from the Dufton Fells through Alston and Brampton. The original covering must have been something like a kilometre thick.

The Carboniferous period lasted for eighty million years and towards its end there were more violent earth movements, the Hercynian Orogeny, which produced mountain chains across Europe and America. The effect was to further complicate the Cumbrian structure, opening old faults brought about by the previous earth uplifts, and again raising the central dome, this time with its centre further south than the original centre around the Skiddaw anticline. Again volcanic material was pushed into the faults and fractures, producing valuable minerals such as copper, in the Old Man of Coniston range, and lead, on the east side of Helvellyn above Glenridding. The origin of the rich haematite veins of south-west Cumbria is thought to lie in this period, although this is not certain.

The Permo-Trias

The uplift was again followed by arid desert conditions, and exposed rocks suffered denudation from blowing sand. As it seems that at this time the equator was little more than 400km. south of Britain, the conditions must have been similar to those in today's Sahara. The Carboniferous deposits were stripped from the central dome; this stripped material, together with fragmented older rocks, accumulated in the lower land around the dome, consolidating into breccia, locally known as Brockram. The results of this process can be seen in the Eden Valley and on the west coast. In places the Brockram was covered in magnesium limestone formed by evaporation of salts in shallow seas, and in other places was covered by red sand. The rock formed from the sand is known as the New Red Sandstone to distinguish it from the Old Red Sandstone of the Devonian period, of which there are no Cumbrian deposits. On detailed examination this New Red Sandstone can be seen to consist of 'millet-seed grains', sand particles rounded by the action of the wind. The sandstone is much in evidence in the north and north-east of the county (the fine cliffs of St Bees Head are of this material) and on the western coast around Barrow and Walney.

A great wedge-shaped area of sandstone with Brockram sweeps north-westwards from Appleby. Many Cumbrian towns are built from this easily-worked material, including Penrith, Barrow, and Whitehaven. Furness Abbey and the old castles of Cumbria have great sandstone walls.

This time of arid, drifting deserts lasted for ninety million years.

The Jurassic and Cretaceous

Next in geological time come the Jurassic and Cretaceous periods, which lasted for 110 million years. Life on the planet had advanced much further and there was lush vegetation, often supporting huge land reptiles such as dinosaurs. These creatures certainly lived in the still sub-tropical Britain – traces have been found in southern England – but the periods did not leave any mark at all on Cumbria. During the Cretaceous period there was another inundation by seas, and great thicknesses of chalk were deposited all over the world; but there are no traces in Cumbria of any deposit. This poses a problem, though geologists suggest that the area was covered but lost all traces of chalk in subsequent erosions.

The Tertiary Influence

In the last sixty-eight million years of geological history, known as the Tertiary period, there were further vast changes to the earth's structure, producing a land form that is essentially the same as the one we see today.

About sixty million years ago there was another great mountain-building period, during which the Alps, Himalayas, Andes, and Rockies were formed. Again the central dome of the Lake District was lifted, this time to something only a little greater than the present height. The centre of this uplift was around Sca Fell. The newer surface on the dome probably had a fairly smooth outline: evidence for this can be seen in the present-day drainage pattern, which has been superimposed on the exposed rock from an earlier system. The water falling on the original upper dome generally radiated on the lines of the rivers as we now know them: the Cocker, the Greta, the Kent, the Rothay, the Brathay, the Duddon, the Esk, the Calder, and the Liza. As the newer rocks wore away the running water wore into the deeper rocks, modifying only where it ran into geological faults and lines of less resistant material. The result at the end of the Tertiary period, something between one million and two million years ago, was a hill and drainage pattern much like today's but considerably more rounded; the water has subsequently cut V-shaped channels and trenches. The land was green with lush vegetation, the climate much like that of the present-day Mediterranean, and animal types we now associate with the sub-tropics roamed freely. Britain was still physically connected with the European continent.

Then came the next catastrophe. The world climate underwent a great change for reasons that are still the subject of scientific argument and conjecture. A severe cooling-down period resulted in the great enlargement of the polar ice caps. Great depths of snow and ice accumulated in Britain. The Quaternary period had begun.

The Ice Age

A series of ice sheets – moving, pressing, grinding, plucking, and up to 760m. thick – was the final tool to sculpt the Cumbrian landscape, leaving the shapes that we know today. The last two million years are a modest fraction in geological time: it may be assumed that we are still in the Ice Age, in an interglacial period.

The inexplicable change in climate came about one and a half million years ago. The sudden fall in temperature in the northern hemisphere meant large accumulations of snow that the summer sun was unable to melt. At its maximum the large polar ice sheet built up to such huge dimensions that it covered Scandinavia and Russia and the continent of America as far south as present-day Illinois. Probably most of the British Isles was covered except for the land south of a line between the Severn and the Thames Valley. The ice moved southwards in the same way that alpine glaciers move today. Glacial ice differs from frozen-water ice: being built up from snow falls it is granular; it therefore flows easily, though slowly, from a high point to a lower point; and not only from high land, but from a 'pile-up', a snow dome, from a point of greater accumulation to a point of lesser accumulation. The valley floors filled first, the ice following the established drainage channels, but gradually and inexorably the valleys filled to the brims and the ice swept over the ridges. In Cumbria only the tops of the Lake District mountains broke the surface of the great ice sea. Ice scratches can be seen today 760m. up on the rock of the Scafells.

There have been three scientifically identified glacial periods. A warmer period followed the first climatic change, and then the first glaciation took place, about 210,000 years ago. About 130,000 years ago there was a second glaciation. And the last glaciation began about 55,000 years ago. Scientists are hampered in their research by the fact that later glaciations wipe out much of the evidence of the earlier advances. The last advance, which lasted until about 8,000 years ago, was the least extensive.

The effect of glaciation on landscape is obvious when the mechanics are understood. The flow of ice down a valley moves faster at its higher layers along the centre of the flow: this area, unhampered by ground friction, slides easily over the slower ice. The bottom of the ice picks up a great deal of rock debris, and this mass of material moving under the severe pressure of the ice above acts as an enormous grater, carving out the floor, crumbling, crushing, and sweeping up the softer material, breaking up the harder material and taking it forward as added cutting-edges, and sliding over the harder bed-rock to smooth and polish it. The edges of the glacier also pick up material as they slide downwards, and these edges cut into the valley walls: gradually the walls may be undermined and large portions will fall onto the ice to be carried downwards with the glacier. The process of wall crumbling is accelerated by frost action. As the glacier advances valleys might be straightened and side-spurs removed. Higher side-valleys, less affected by the main ice flow, might be undercut and left hanging.

All this activity would fluctuate according to the seasons and the amount of snow fall. The highest activity would be at the upper levels of the glacial dome and this area would be less subject to periodic thaws, if they came. For this reason the typical glaciated valley head, subject to longer periods of undermining ice and the plucking action of frost, is steep-walled and hollowed. It is what is generally termed a corrie, Gaelic for a 'cauldron'; in Wales or the South-West it is a cwm or a coomb. In Cumbria it can be referred to as a cove, an old English name for a hollow; examples are Nethermost Cove and Brown Cove, on Helvellyn, or Great Cove, on Crinkle Crags. It can also be a comb or a combe, as with Ling Comb, above Buttermere, and Black Combe. The plucking action at the valley heads can be so great that the wall separating each cove can be worn into slender ridges: mountaineers refer to them as arêtes. Some of the arêtes in alpine areas are almost knife-edges. Striding Edge, on Helvellyn, is the Lake District's best-known arête; it offers an exciting route for well-equipped walkers. The opposite arm of the cove, Swirral Edge, is another arête. though one less challenging. The Helvellyn cove is a good example of a glaciated valley head, and contains another feature typical of a corrie: a small lake, or what is commonly known in the Lake District as a tarn.

A tarn is formed by the descending ice grinding out a bowl-shaped hollow in the cove; the depth of such a tarn might be increased by the deposition of waste material forming a dam. Indeed, the depth of the tarn might be greater than appearances would suggest: Blea Water, below High Street, is 63m. deep. There are a number of valley-head coves holding tarns, and they can be readily seen on a map. On Old Man of Coniston there are Goats Water, Levers Water, and Low Water; there are Angle Tarn below Bow Fell; Stickle Tarn below Pavey Ark in Langdale; Codale Tarn and Easedale Tarn above Grasmere; Bleaberry Tarn above Buttermere; Scales Tarn on Blencathra; Grisedale Tarn below Fairfield and Dollywaggon; Blea Water and Small Water below High Street. The observant will note that these typical corries with their tarns are mainly on the north and east of the mountain summits, for it is there, in the lee of the prevailing wind, that snow would be blown and would accumulate, and indeed still does in hard winters; and it also happens that this position gets the least benefit from the sun and the thawing winds.

As the glacier ground out the main valley floor the water from the becks of the side-valleys, which, as mentioned, were also often left hanging, poured down to the floor of the dale in a series of waterfalls. It is not necessary to look far after heavy rain to see the effect in almost every valley. There are some fine examples to be seen in the splendid views over Buttermere, Sour Milk Gill being particularly striking. Some of the falls, such as Stock Ghyll Force at Ambleside or Aira Force at Ullswater, have become standard tourist attractions. There are hundreds of examples of falls to delight the fell-walker: there is the renowned Dungeon Ghyll in Langdale, or Taylor Ghyll Force at the head of Borrowdale, or Piers Gill in the Scafells. After heavy rain the valley heads are loud with the noise of falling water; and when gales are funnelled up the narrow ravines it is sometimes possible to see the upward currents of air picking up the waterfalls and transforming them into fountains.

The grinding out of the valley floors by the glaciers has produced Cumbria's greatest attraction: the lakes. The disposition of the lakes shows the radiating pattern of the ice flow from the central dome. The descending glaciers scooped out the lake beds from the floor, some of the hollows, such as in Wast Water and Windermere, being cut to below sea-level. The lakes were originally melted water from the last Ice Age, the outlet being blocked by accumulated debris. The larger lakes consist of several linked basins, a feature particularly noticeable in Windermere and Ullswater.

If the rock type and the degree of hardness were similar everywhere one would expect the glaciation to have a uniform effect. Of course the rock types in Cumbria vary enormously, influencing both the original drainage pattern in places and the super-imposed glaciation pattern. The glacial flow might also be deflected or accelerated by tributary flows. Windermere's glacier, for instance, began in a direction roughly south-south-east but was probably deflected southwards below its upper reaches by the ice sheet entering from Troutbeck; losing momentum at mid lake, and riding over what is probably harder rock, the ice's grinding action was shallower and this is where we can now see the islands. At a lower point another ice sheet entered from Esthwaite, adding impetus to the glacier and pushing it through the narrowing valley to gouge out another rock basin to a depth below sea-level.

The morphology of Ullswater might be rather more complicated. The glacier, fed by a number of sources to its south, pushed north-north-west and was deflected to the north by the ice from the Helvellyn range. At the point of the deflection the lake turns suddenly east-north-east and deepens. A glance at a geological map shows that the lake bed is following the line of older rock, the Skiddaw Slate, which is softer and more yielding than the hard Borrowdale Volcanic rocks towering over the southern banks. This must mean that the ice followed the old drainage channel, the hard volcanic over-mantle being broken up and removed by earlier erosions. The lake almost finishes at Skelly Neb, where it is only 15m. deep; but the slowing ice was supplemented by an ice sheet entering from the hard volcanics of Martindale and Fusedale, and another rock basin was carved out.

The effect of glaciation upon Ennerdale is clear: the glacier first had to plough through the hard granophyre, but later met the yielding Skiddaw Slate; these condi-tions produced a narrow lake head and a splayed-out lake foot.

All of the lakes must have been influenced by the rapid erosion that followed the glaciation. The ice swept away all the vegetation serving to stabilize the fell sides; so, from softer rocks particularly, large volumes of waste material were swept into the lakes by swift-flowing melt-water and storm torrents. In some cases this material was of sufficient quantity to divide a lake. Derwent Water and Bassenthwaite, once one large lake, occasionally revert to their original state in times of very heavy flooding; the flat land in between them is covered in Skiddaw Slate debris. Buttermere and Crummock were also once one large lake, and are now similarly divided by silt.

It is easy to imagine that glaciated valleys not now holding lakes could well have held them at one period: perhaps the dams of rock debris were breached, or the lakes silted up. It is possible that there was a lake at the head of Borrowdale, between Ros-thwaite and Seathwaite. The flat floor of Langdale also suggests the possibility of a shallow lake, at least between Middle Fell and Chapel Stile. After exceptionally heavy rain a temporary 'lake' tends to form there.

As the glacial ice tore at the valley sides it became covered by rock avalanches, and as the centre of the ice moved faster there was an inward-flowing current spreading debris over the whole surface. The flow of ice northwards from Cumbria's ice cap, blocked by the huge mass of ice pushing south from Scotland, turned east and west. The upper rock surface in the northern part of the county was considerably reduced by these colliding pressures: Cumbria's rocks were pushed away for long distances and deposited in other parts of Britain. Clay formed from Cumbria's finely-ground 'rock flour' covers much of

Lancashire. Boulders of Shap Granite can still be seen on the Yorkshire coast. Smoothed boulders of the Borrowdale Volcanics can be found on the Cheshire plain. These misplaced rocks are known as erratics and examples can be seen about Cumbria. Volcanic boulders, for instance, can be found perched on Carboniferous Limestone pavement; blocks of Langdale material can be found on the southern Silurian Slates. Sometimes the erratics, left stranded by the retreating ice, are found delicately balanced on other rocks. The Bowder Stone in Borrowdale might be a good example.

Apart from the shape of the landscape, other evidence of glaciation can be found. On hard rock outcrops the scratch marks left by the heel of a glacier can be seen. Sometimes the rocks are worn smooth on one side, on the side that would be facing the moving ice, and on the other side are sheer and rough. This effect is known as *roche moutonnée*. There are also the moraine heaps: mounds of material left by melting ice. When they are high and more or less symmetrical they are termed drumlins. Examples are found in various places in the relatively flat land of the Lune Valley. Some drumlins are symmetrical enough to look man-made.

In certain places there are extensive areas of land covered by a large number of peculiar, irregular hummocks. These are terminal moraines, left at the ends of glaciers when piles of debris were mixed with melting ice. Hollows – known as kettle holes – within some of these mounds show where ice-cores within the debris melted. Looked at from above, the formation of these moraine fields is striking. One of the more obvious examples of such a field is at the summit of Dunmail Raise. The presence of relatively high moraines – there are others on Stake Pass and at the head of Mickleden in Langdale – have caused some debate; the most convincing theory is that they were left by glaciers that appeared *after* the very large glaciations. There is evidence to suggest that after the three major glaciations there was a cold period lasting for about five centuries: thus around 9000 BC Cumbria's ice dome would again have developed, though on a much more modest scale than previously.

Between each glaciation the vegetation made recoveries only to be swept away again. After the cold period of *c*. 9000 BC the recovery progressed without disturbance. The alpine and the tundra vegetation and the grasses and sedges were followed by forest, which eventually established itself on the mountain sides to a height of 750m. The land became more stabilized and greener. Still connected by a land bridge to the Continent, Britain was repopulated with many animals. And the conditions were ripe for the repopulation by man of previously inhospitable areas.

History

If there was any human settlement of Cumbria before or during the Ice Age all signs have been removed by massive glacial erosion. Evidence found suggests that first settlements were established on the west coast, in about 4500 BC, and it is possible that there were a considerable number of these settlements: various artifacts so far discovered are from quite a widespread area. The flint arrow-heads, harpoons, and knives suggest settlement by Mesolithic cultures: hunters and fishermen. Flint is only found in chalk and as there is no chalk in Cumbria it is highly probable that the flint for weapons was picked up from glacial drift on the western shore. Hunting must have been fairly profitable at this time: there is evidence that the country was thickly covered in forest to the fell summits. Expeditions and summer settlements may have reached well into the interior, and possibly from the east as well as from the west: Mesolithic finds have been identified in the western Yorkshire Dales.

The next settlers to arrive were the Neolithic (New Stone Age) people, some thousand years later. In the New Stone Age culture there was a high degree of technical progress and the basis existed for a developing civilization. Neolithic man was an agriculturalist, he kept domestic animals, he made pottery, he wore woven garments, his stone tools were made to startling degrees of precision, and he had the means to move blocks of stone, some of them enormous, to build stone circles. The purpose of the stone circles remains a source for speculation: it is widely assumed that they had a religious function; it is also possible that they were used as a kind of calendar.

Neolithic man engaged in commerce. There is some interesting evidence for this in Cumbria, where an important industry flourished in the hills. Among the central Borrowdale Volcanic rocks, at high levels, there are veins of a very hard, very fine-grained tuff; like flint, this material flakes when broken and can be skilfully worked into a very sharp edge. In 1947 a typical chipping floor of a stone-axe factory was found at the head of Stake Pass in Langdale; and this led to the discovery of a larger site below Pike o' Stickle. Among the great mass of chippings a number of rejected axes were found. Further sites have been found since and it is quite likely that more will be discovered. The largest site so far investigated is on a large level area south-west of Scafell Pike: below the surface detritus are a large quantity of chippings; the activity on this site must have been considerable. Completed axes have not been found on the chipping floor and evidence indicates that the rough-outs were taken from the fells to sites on the coast, where they were finally finished and polished with sandstone. From the coast the axes were exported to other parts of the British Isles: numbers of Cumbrian axes have been found in the south-east of England, as well as in parts of Scotland, Ireland, and the Isle of Man. The factory sites are bleak and windswept, but the climate was kinder in Neolithic times and the sites were then only just above the tree-line. It is possible that the sites were temporarily abandoned in winter.

Archaeologists are prone to caution when dating prehistoric artifacts, even with modern radio-carbon techniques; but it is thought that the Cumbrian factories were probably at the height of their activity between 2800 BC and 2000 BC, although the work began earlier and finished later (production continued under Late Neolithic groups).

It is probable that Neolithic settlement was increased by new arrivals over the years, both by sea and from Yorkshire. There was a new phase of settlement towards the end of the Neolithic period, around 2000 BC, marked by the arrival of the Beaker culture. The name comes from the new settlers' use of well-made pottery vessels, and from their habit of burying the vessels with the dead. The people who used the Yorkshire route into Cumbria had a different decorative design on their pottery from that used by those settlers who arrived by sea. The Beaker Folk are probably responsible for most of the burial mounds scattered widely about the county from the Eden Valley westwards. They still depended a great deal on hunting for food, and findings of well-made arrow-heads of flint have been associated with this culture.

Many of the stone circles found all over Britain (once called 'Druids' Circles' but now known to have pre-dated the Celtic settlements by many centuries) are thought to belong to the Late Neolithic period. Stonehenge itself is thought to have been built at that time on the site of an earlier bank-and-ditch structure. Examples of stone circles are found all over Cumbria, in various states of preservation. If their purpose is a source of speculation, so is their method of construction. Some of the stones are massive. Long Meg and Her Daughters, near Little Salkeld, is the largest circle in the county and among the largest in the country: it is 365m. in circumference and contains 59 stones, some of the stones, including Long Meg, having a girth of about 4½m.; Long Meg stands some 5½m. high. Castlerigg, close to Keswick and in a dramatic setting, is the Lake District's best-known circle. It is some 30m. in diameter and contains an oblong inner enclosure on its eastern side. Swinside circle, in a private farm field on the north-east side of Black Combe, is a little smaller but more symmetrical and better preserved; its remoteness protects it from the attention lavished on Castlerigg. The Shap stones would have been impressive had the structure not suffered so much damage. A double avenue of stones ended in a stone circle, but the railway has partially destroyed the arrangement.

The remains of circles show concentrations on both the western and eastern sides of the county. This no doubt coincides with the settlement pattern of the time, the central areas being too rough and ill-drained to support agriculture, and probably serving as hunting areas only. Arrow-heads of this period have been found in Langdale.

During the Stone Age comparatively large areas of the natural forest were cleared for cultivation: this was made possible by the development of the stone axe. An ingenious, and now well-established, scientific method of studying the botanical history of an area is based on analysis of core samples; this system has been highly developed by the Freshwater Biological Association at their Windermere headquarters. The system rests on the knowledge that plant pollen is composed of a hard material similar to coal, is well preserved in peat and clay, and can be identified microscopically. Using radio-carbon dating it is possible to assess the ecological pattern of an area from which the core was taken. It has been shown that generally tree pollen declined rapidly from the period of the Neolithic settlements and that there was an increase in the amount of grass pollens and evidence of some cereal pollens. There are of course variations in the pattern. In some areas the forest cover never regenerated following the introduction of grazing animals and the deterioration of soils; in other areas it has been shown that forest regenerated following successive clearances.

The remains of a Neolithic settlement, with finds of tools and implements, a quern, a canoe, and considerable quantities of pottery, were found in the late nineteenth century at Ehenside Tarn, near Beckermet on the coastal plain, during drainage work. A careful study indicates a continuous occupation of over 600 years from about 3300 BC. One can imagine that there were many such sites in the fertile areas of coastal Cumbria and in the Eden Valley, but very many centuries of cultivation since has destroyed all evidence.

Bronze Age and Iron Age

It is not possible to state with certainty when, in any given area, the Bronze Age superseded the Late Stone Age. It is even less possible in a comparatively remote area with very difficult lines of communication. Stone instruments continued to be made and used, if not exported, for some considerable time after more sophisticated metal articles were commonly available in areas of southern England, areas far more favourably placed to receive immigrant craftsmen from Europe. The culture associated with the Bronze Age would have been slow to permeate through to remoter areas. Settlers in Cumbria continued to follow the two main entry routes: from Ireland to the west coast, and from Yorkshire into and through the Eden Valley in the east. The finds relating to settlers in the eastern area seem to indicate that they were more advanced than those from the west. The bronze objects found in both the east and west of the county were most probably imports. Finds have not been numerous, but have been widely scattered. Most of the weapons found appear to have an Irish origin.

During the Bronze Age the practice of cremation became general. Archaeologists have gained some knowledge from excavation of burial chambers containing urns of ashes. One such excavation near Coniston by W. G. Collingwood in 1909 proved to be one of the more interesting: the chamber contained a fragment of charred woollen cloth, one of the earliest examples found in Britain, reckoned to be about 2,960 years old.

The Iron Age culture was probably slow to penetrate isolated Cumbria. The communal settlements characterized by stone walls, for instance near Urswick in south-west Cumbria and at Ewe Close and further sites near Crosby Ravensworth in east Cumbria, are Late Bronze Age. There are traces of many other settlements of this kind in Cumbria; and there may be other sites still to be identified. The settlers responsible for these stone-built cattle enclosures and hut circles were of a different stock to the much earlier Neolithic settlers. It is conceivable that they may have been as much puzzled about the origin of the area's stone circles as ourselves.

Organized in tribes under powerful chiefs, these settlers were given to war, and, perhaps not unnaturally, became skilled in making forts. Some of the structures to be found on the hill summits of Cumbria are difficult to date, but are thought to be of that period. The largest and most impressive fort is on Carrock Fell, a fell in the extreme north-east of the Lake District. Various theories have been advanced to explain its purpose: one suggests that it was an important, if peripheral, stronghold of the Brigantes; the obvious gaps in the walls, it is further suggested, are an indication of Roman policing measures designed to cripple the fort, possibly carried out during Agricola's first northern campaign. The size of the fort, 2ha., is quite uncharacteristic of the other hill-forts in Cumbria tentatively ascribed to the Iron Age, and suggests a high degree of corporate activity for its construction. Carrock Fell, by way of contrast, serves to emphasize the smallness of the other enterprises in the region.

The Romans

The Brigantes had submitted to Roman rule by 47, but the tribe – perhaps more properly thought of as a loose confederation – made difficulties and was in open revolt at times. The Romans chose to rule their northern territories from York and their first penetration of Cumbria was probably via Stainmoor into the Eden Valley, after Petillus Cerialis had crushed an open revolt by the Brigantes (sometime before the end of his governor-ship in 74). The next governor, Frontinus, was too occupied with the Welsh tribes to strengthen the Roman grip on Cumbria, and it was left to his successor Gnaeus Julius Agricola to consolidate and improve the position in this hostile area. Agricola marched north from Chester in 79, passing through west Lancashire, establishing marching camps and forts: sometimes, as at Watercrook, Kendal, walling with turf and erecting wooden buildings, but later replacing with stone. As the forces advanced north to Carlisle a similar progress was being made on the east coast and the next stage, which followed quickly, was an east–west link with Carlisle from the mouth of the Tyne. From this consolidated base-line the Roman invasion continued into Scotland, and in 84 the legions overwhelmingly defeated the Caledonian confederacy at Mons Graupius, near Inverness.

Agricola's successors strengthened the Roman hold on Cumbria: his forts were im-proved and more were built, particularly during the reigns of Trajan (98–117) and Hadrian (117–38). The fort at Ambleside (Galava) was rebuilt and a road was built westwards to the amazing site high on Hard Knott (Mediobogdum) and on to a Roman port at Ravenglass (Glannaventa). During this period there must have been a large num-ber of campaigns and marches, rapid building, and the clearing of interlinking roads. These roads ran northwards on three lines through Cumbria, west and south along the Cumbrian coast, and direct across the central fells. Some twenty forts were built in Cumbria during this period. The concentration testifies to the troubles that the occupiers had to face from the Cumbrian tribes. The lack of military finds in the south-west part of Cumbria lends some support to the suggestion that the tribes in this area may have made a pact with the Romans.

Tacitus, summing up events in Roman history between AD 68 and the death of Domitian, wrote: *perdomita Britannia et statim missa* (the conquest of Britain was com-pleted and then let slip). His bold statement hides the intricacies of imperial strategy that compelled Domitian to remove a legion and refuse auxiliary reinforcements, but it underlines the implications that such a strategy had for Britain. When Hadrian became emperor there was war in Britain once more. The building of Hadrian's Wall – one of the most striking monuments to Roman military engineering – was intended partly to define the new frontier and prevent raids from the north and partly to prevent collusion between northerners and the Brigantes – a significant source of trouble in the past. The wall was begun in 122 and was finished by Hadrian's death in 138. It consisted of stone and turf, fronted by a large ditch, stretching for eighty Roman miles across the narrowest neck of northern England between the Tyne and the Solway. Set into this wall at inter-vals of one Roman mile there were milecastles, and between these were two turrets, evenly spaced. Further elements in the wall were the garrison forts, the vallum – a formidable ditch to the rear of the wall, normally 7m. wide and as much as 3m. deep – and the military way, the lateral road behind the wall. The course of the wall made full and skilful use of the natural heights above north-facing cliffs in places on the Whin Sill, a volcanic ledge above the limestone plains. In the north-west the Cumbrian section was further defended by three outpost forts at Bewcastle, Netherby, and Birrens, and there were wall forts built at Birdoswald, Castlesteads, Stanwix (Carlisle), Burgh-by-Sands, Drumburgh, and Bowness. Further down the coast of Cumbria forts were built and strengthened at Beckfoot, Maryport, Burrow Walls, and Moresby. It has until recently been thought that to the west of Carlisle the Romans depended upon a defensive system of milecastles and towers (still traceable) together with a patrol and signalling system. This theory has been challenged by excavations in 1975 that revealed traces of parallel ditches west of Bowness. Hadrian's defensive line may have continued along the vulnerable Solway coast as two deep ditches and a wooden palisade between milecastles.

Work on Hadrian's Wall continued to strengthen the structure: wherever possible any section of the wall that had been constructed of turf was rebuilt with stone during the second century. At the same time the forts behind the wall were strengthened. Cumbria was under military law, garrisoned with something like 10,000 men.

In 138, upon the succession of Antoninus Pius, the wall was abandoned as the Romans under Urbicus advanced into Scotland. To consolidate his position there Urbicus built a second wall between the Forth and Clyde estuaries – the Antonine Wall. Although Hadrian's Wall was abandoned, the road systems in Cumbria were improved and the Romans relied upon supplies from the local agriculture.

The Roman involvement in Scotland gave the Brigantes an opportunity. Around the middle of the second century they rose in revolt and attacked the Roman installations. Gnaeus Julius Verus was sent with reinforcements and Hadrian's Wall and the forts were reoccupied. There were further troubles towards the end of the century, and when some troops were withdrawn to fight in Gaul, Hadrian's Wall was breached: many forts were violently destroyed and the wall itself was extensively damaged.

Severus ordered an eviction of the tribes and reoccupation of the forts and the wall. A successful campaign, followed by repair work, was made by governors Lupus, Pudens, and Senecio. In 208 Severus arrived in person to campaign in Scotland. He died at York in 211. A further campaign in 211 brought the war to a conclusion and the British frontier remained at peace until 296. Villages that had grown up alongside the Roman forts and settlements grew in importance and the local people were to some degree influenced by *Romanitas*. Carlisle had become an important town. But towards the end of the century there was a new threat; this time from Saxon invasions.

As well as external dangers, Britain had to contend with internal weaknesses intensified by power struggles. Carausius, commander of the Classis Britannica, took refuge in Britain and established himself as emperor, but was killed by Allectus, his finance minister, in 293. Allectus assumed Carausius's rôle, but three years later Constantius, sent from Rome to assert Rome's authority, defeated Allectus and recovered Britain. The wall-garrison, brought south by Allectus, seems to have been sent back to its old station.

In 367 the wall, which had always been impregnable when its garrison was there, was attacked by strong combined forces and either overrun or taken in the rear. Three years later Theodosius was able to consolidate his position and the wall and forts were retaken and repaired. In 383 forces were again withdrawn from the North when Magnus Maximus made a bid to gain the throne. The wall held for a time but the Roman civil struggles and the combined attacks from the sea and land had their inevitable effect.

By the early fifth century the Roman fighting units had been withdrawn – in fact all effective forces had long ago gone to Gaul or Italy – and the Emperor Honorius ordered that the British defences were the responsibility of the Romano-British inhabitants. It was the beginning of the end of the Roman civilization. The wall was finished, even though the Border troubles were to continue for centuries to come.

There are many questions unanswered about the Roman occupation of Cumbria. Some of the Roman roads that must have existed have not been traced. The route from Brougham (Brocavum) to Ambleside (Galava) via the fell road on High Street needs to be traced at its southern end from Troutbeck. There must also have been a route from Watercrook (Alauna) to Ambleside, and south from Watercrook to Lancaster.

The Anglian and Norse Colonization

After the withdrawal of Roman influence little is definitely known of English history over the next few centuries. Broadly speaking, the Angles settled in the east of Britain and the west of the country was occupied by the Celts. As Anglian settlement was pushed westwards the Celts were isolated after 615 in south-west England, Wales, north-west England, and south-west and northern Scotland. The Welsh and the north-western Celts called themselves Cymry (hence 'Cumberland' and 'Cumbria'). With Galloway and southern Scotland, Cumbria was part of the kingdom of Strathclyde. In the absence of any other evidence, the extent of Anglian penetration into Cumbria can only be guessed at through the evidence of place-names. There are many Celtic place-names in Cumbria: the more obvious ones include the Celtic element *pen*, meaning a 'head' or a 'hill'. There is a hill at the foot of Dunnerdale named simply Penn; but the element also occurs in such place-names as Penruddock and Penrith. *Glyn* occurs in Glenridding, Glenderamakin. *Blaen*, a 'summit', occurs in Blencathra, Blennerhasset, Blencarn, Blencow. Some of the main river names are Celtic – Cocker, Irt, Mite, Derwent – as are the names of some of the fells. Helvellyn's origin is obscure but the Celtic sound of it is unmistakable. A student of dialect would detect a suggestion of Welsh in the Cumbrian even today. Most Cumbrian shepherds can count sheep in the old Celtic form, as has been done for generations: '*Yan, Tyan, Teddera, Meddara, Pimp*'; this ties in closely to the old Welsh, Cornish, and Breton. Most native Cumbrians will say '*yan*' for 'one' or '*yance*' for 'once'.

The Angles were agriculturalists and they would have settled in the more fertile areas of Cumbria by preference. Place-names ending in *ham* or *ton* are characteristic: Addingham, Hensingham, Brigham, Dearham, Whicham, Broughton, Dalton, Stainton, Alston. A study of local material compiled by the English Place-Name Society will show that place-names of Anglian origin occur for the most part around the fertile plains of Cumbria. Little other evidence of the Anglian presence remains; but there are two exceptional Anglian stone crosses, beautifully preserved, that are among the best in the country. The late-seventh-century Bewcastle Cross attracts many visitors; but hidden away in west Cumbria in Irton churchyard is another, smaller, but also superb, cross of the ninth century.

In the late eighth century Anglian hegemony was threatened by the increase of Viking raids on the east coast. These Danish raiders came well inland to take over much of eastern and central Britain, but the absence of a great number of Danish place-names in Cumbria suggests that they did not go much further west than the Eden Valley, though in the latter half of the century it is recorded that Halfdan the Dane destroyed Luel (Carlisle). Under Roman rule Carlisle had been a beautiful town; as late as 685 St Cuthbert, Bishop of Lindisfarne, had been impressed by the Roman walls and had marvelled at the fountain. But after the Danes sacked the town it is said to have lain in ruins for 200 years.

The Viking raids and settlements in Cumbria generally had a Norse, rather than a Danish, origin, and the impression they made was very considerable. The Norse Vikings had moved into the Orkneys and Shetlands in the mid eighth century. They then established themselves down the Scottish west coast, on the Irish coast, and on the Isle of Man. And from these bases they made raids on the Cumbrian coast. One of the few references to the raids is made by Symeon of Durham, writing in the eleventh century, when he refers to a nobleman, Eardulf, and Tilred, Abbot of Heversham, fleeing across the Pennines from Viking raiders in the early tenth century. But, perhaps later, the Viking movements were not hostile. Place-names show that they began to settle well inland, yet the Anglian place-names in the west survived, so the towns must have survived too, some of them in close proximity to places with names of Norse origin. Furthermore, many of these Norse–Irish and Norse–Manxmen were converts to Christianity. A very remarkable slender Norse cross of the late tenth century, worked in the Danish Jellinge style and bearing – among other decoration – symbols of Christianity, is beautifully preserved in the churchyard at Gosforth, not all that far from the Anglian cross at Irton.

Some recorded Norse history also suggests that at least some of these Vikings might have been refugees. The Norse inhabitants of the Isle of Man, proving recalcitrant, were 'visited' by Harold Fairhair, the Norse king, and a large force of longships, but the King found that many of the inhabitants had fled. It is not recorded where they had fled to. Cumbria would have been an obvious choice.

Norse settlement was very extensive, and the number of place-names of Norse origin is remarkable. There are various indications to suggest that the Viking settlers came via Ireland: the churches they established were dedicated to Celtic saints, such as Patrick and Columba; some of the place-names contain the Celtic element *serg*, meaning a summer pasture; some of the decorative stonework found also shows the influence of Celtic design.

The purely Norse names are quite obvious: the dales (*dalr*), the fells (*fjall*), the becks (*bekkr*), the tarns (*tjorn*), the forces – waterfalls – (*foss*). The many 'thwaites' in Cumbrian place-names refer to the Norse clearings in the forest (Rosthwaite, Satterthwaite, Braithwaite, Seathwaite). It was in this period of Norse settlement that much of the forest of Cumbria was heavily depleted. A Norse–Irish element in place-names is *saetre*, a shieling or summer pasture: Arnside, Hawkshead, Seatoller, Seat Sandal, Ambleside (Amal's shieling). There are also place-names referring to the Norse use of areas: Swindale is the dale of the swine, Grizedale or Grisedale is the dale of the pigs. *Blea* is Norse for blue, *how* for hill. There are numerous other examples of Norse words.

As the Vikings usually made their dwellings of wood there is not a great deal of tangible evidence relating to their occupation. The Viking wheel-head crosses and hogback tombstones can be seen in many of the churchyards and churches of Cumbria; some of them in the eastern part of Cumbria have a Danish origin, but most, and all those to the west, show the Norse–Celtic design. Other remains include some burials that have been excavated, notably those near Appleby and at Cockermouth. It is not certain whether the peculiar mound at Fell Foot Farm, Little Langdale, is a Thingmound, a terraced hillock where the Norse settlers met to settle disputes; if the mound had an agricultural use, as some observers suggest, its significance is lost. Stone enclosures in various places, which may be Viking shielings, need further investigation.

Norse influence is evident in modern Cumbrian dialect, and other customs and traditions – the open-air sports, for example – are attributed to the same source. Much of this is no doubt romantic speculation: there are many unanswered questions. It has been argued that the existence in Cumbria of bank-barns – two-storey barns usually built on a slope, allowing cart delivery of hay to an upper floor for dropping to animals on a lower floor – shows that some of the Viking settlers came direct from Scandinavia, where such barns are common. Bank-barns are concentrated in Cumbria and are not found in such numbers anywhere else in the British Isles.

The last king of Cumbria, Dunmail, was defeated by Edmund, King of Northumbria, in 945, on what is now called Dunmail Raise, the summit of the pass between Grasmere and Thirlmere. Cumbria was then given by Edmund to Malcolm, King of the Scots.

The Norman Conquest had little immediate effect on Cumbria: most of the region was considered to be a debatable, disputed area between England and Scotland. The Domesday Book only makes reference to small areas in southern Furness and in the valley of the River Kent. Twenty-six years elapsed after the conquest before a Norman king (William Rufus) challenged the authority of Dolfin, son of Gospatric, and took Carlisle, afterwards sending in Saxon settlers to cultivate the land. Cumbria was divided by William into several baronies, and castles were built to hold the area: these were at first of wood on earth mounds defended by ditches, but were later rebuilt in stone. The castles were strategically positioned in such places as Appleby, Brougham, Penrith, Kendal, Egremont.

It was the administration of the Norman abbeys rather than that of Norman secular government that played a significant part in Cumbria's history. To the barons much of the wild land of Furness was unprofitable to them. What better way to secure a safe place in heaven than by offering land to the Church? The twelfth century was the great abbey-building century, and saw the beginnings of such Cumbrian abbeys as Furness, Holme Cultram, Calder, Shap, and the priories of Lanercost, Carlisle, St Bees, Conishead, and Cartmel. The Cistercians were great agriculturalists. They knew how to exploit forests and minerals and organize fisheries. Their ownership of Furness, Calder, and Holme Cultram revitalized the countryside. They began to acquire more land in the dales, Furness taking the lion's share, including the land between the lakes of Windermere and Coniston, Borrowdale, upper Eskdale, and low Furness and Walney Island. Not only the Cumbrian abbeys held land in Cumbria: Fountains Abbey and Byland Abbey, Yorkshire houses, were also landowners in the region.

The Border

For many centuries the history of the Border was the history – or the significant part of it at any rate – of Cumbria.

Although during the Anglian and Norse settlements much of the Cumbrian end of the Border was formally part of the Scottish kingdom of Strathclyde, it was the subject of keen bargaining and campaigning. Little is known of its early history; but the tribes, blood-mixtures of Celt, Romano-British, and Norse–Irish, were no doubt principally concerned and occupied with stratagems aimed at acquiring the best land.

On the accession of William Rufus in 1087 the Norman hold on the Border was improved and the castles strengthened. The Scottish kings at this stage encouraged Norman settlement in their country. The Scottish religious houses were built, and the peace was broken only by skirmishes: some of these skirmishes undoubtedly had a political motivation but most were probably only political in the most parochial sense. It would be highly anachronistic to look for a spirit of 'nationalism' among the barony: most formed their alliances using personal loyalties and expediency as guidelines.

David I of Scotland took the northern shires back into Scotland in 1137, but, defeated in 1138 at the Battle of Standard, near Northallerton, and with the brief exception of a raid into England in 1149, he put aside all further designs on English territory. David died in Carlisle Castle in 1153. He was succeeded by his grandson, who, at the age of twelve, ascended the throne as Malcolm IV. Henry II of England, taking advantage of the minority, made various demands upon the new king, who was compelled in 1157 to surrender Northumberland and Cumberland together with three castles, one of which was Carlisle. William the Lion, Malcolm's younger brother and successor, sought in turn to take advantage of the conspiracy hatched against Henry II by that king's three sons and crossed the border in 1173. Failing to take Carlisle, he devastated border towns before being forced to retreat. Undaunted, he returned a year later with a strong force, said to number 80,000, and took Carlisle, although the castle held out against a three-month siege. The siege ended when William was defeated and captured at Alnwick. The resultant Treaty of Falaise, which put Scotland under English tutelage, was adroitly sidestepped by William when, in exchange for money for Crusade, he extracted from Richard Coeur de Lion the favourable Treaty of Canterbury (effectively a repudiation of Falaise).

On the death of William the Lion in 1214 Alexander II was crowned at Scone. From his position as an English baron in respect of his English fiefs he was inexorably – and perhaps not unwillingly – drawn into the events leading to Magna Carta. The borders inevitably suffered from the consequent hostilities. On one of Alexander's raids some of his followers burnt Holme Cultram Abbey, but, records the Chronicle of Melrose, those who escaped the vengeance of God, by which 1,900 were drowned, were punished by Alexander. Carlisle Castle was eventually taken by Alexander, but the defeat of his ally, the French King Louis, at Lincoln forced him to make his peace with the young Henry III and to restore Carlisle.

The chroniclers have left us the impression that the reign of Alexander II's successor, Alexander III, was one of wise government and general prosperity. It is probably an impression that is substantially correct. But some of the chroniclers, writing with a knowledge of the subsequent calamities – the disputed succession and the English wars – no doubt heightened the account.

In 1291 Edward I of England was asked to adjudicate between rival claimants of the Scottish throne: not one to miss so obvious an opportunity he demanded of the claimants that they recognize him as the superior and direct lord of Scotland. Naturally all the claimants found it expedient to comply. But in 1296, largely as a result of Edward's claim, John Baliol, the successful candidate, ordered his armies into Cumberland.

Cumberland towns, including Carlisle, were burned, but the Scottish forces failed to take Carlisle Castle. Edward's retribution was swift and Baliol was soon his prisoner.

A year later the Scots had their revenge. William Wallace, acting in the name of the imprisoned – and later exiled – Baliol, defeated the English at Cambuskenneth Abbey and Stirling; and once again the Scots were across the Border. And once again they failed to take Carlisle Castle. But they plundered and burned down through the Eden Valley and well into the Lake District. Edward pushed north again in the following year: he wasted the Scottish border towns and took Wallace prisoner. Wallace was subsequently charged with, among other things, invading 'the counties of Northumberland, Cumberland, and Westmorland, burning and killing "everyone who used the English tongue," sparing neither age nor sex, monk nor nun'. Wallace was convicted of treason and hung, drawn, and quartered.

Wallace's death did not end Edward's troubles: he now faced a new adversary, Robert the Bruce. Weary and ill, Edward marched north to meet his new foe, but at Burgh-by-Sands on the Solway coast Edward died. Seven years later Robert the Bruce decisively defeated the English at Bannockburn; and in the wake of this rout the Scottish forces devastated the area south of the Border more thoroughly than ever before, pillaging and burning as far south as Furness and Lancaster, and sacking the abbeys and priories.

Rarely in the future were the Borders to suffer so badly; although peace was not a state easily compatible with the spirit, position, and tradition of the region.

Life in the Border Marches was subject neither to English nor to Scottish law: the Law of the Marches was something separate. It is not known when this 'arrangement' was first made: the earliest extant record relating to the Law refers to a conference of 1248 between six English and six Scottish knights, held by royal commands to correct, 'according to the ancient and approved custom of the March, such matters as required to be redressed'. It is not inconceivable that the 'ancient . . . custom' settled Celtic, or Norse, quarrels.

The Law had to be invoked to deal with the endemic crimes of raiding and rustling. From spring to harvest the Cumbrian families farmed; in the summer they lived, like their forbears, in the shielings of the high lands; in the winter they returned to their homes, and on suitable evenings the men would mount their light horses and go raiding.

The Border ballads have romanticized the reivers' way of life. But as often as not the raids were extremely vicious: houses were burned with their occupants, whole cattle herds, household effects, and clothing were stolen, and hostages were taken. The Border reivers introduced a new word into the English language: 'blackmail'. (The meaning has changed a little since; it was originally a 'black rent', the equivalent of a protection racket.) The raiding was largely indiscriminate: questions of 'race' or 'nationality' were superfluous; Scot attacked Scot and Englishman attacked Englishman readily and frequently.

The arrangements made to contain these troubles split the Border into three units. The Western March, always the most troublesome, was 'West of Bewcastle Waste'. One section of land running northwards between the River Esk (north-west of Carlisle) and the River Sark, as far as what is now Langholm, was recognized as 'Debatable Land', a sort of no-man's-land. For each March, Wardens, one from each side of the Border, were appointed. The position of the Warden was an unenviable one: the men under his command were more often than not outnumbered by raiders, the territory was difficult to manage, and, always in the middle of acrimonious feuds, he was loved by no one. The duty of the Wardens extended to the preservation of the Border: they were expected to keep a constant watch on it and to organize its defence in time of war (beacons were the recognized method of announcing a summons to arms). The Wardens were the King's men and were expected to maintain a rudimentary intelligence system in the Border lands. But mention of all these rôles should not obscure the fact that the main and nagging duty was to suppress crime, pursue wrongdoers, guard against raiders, and restrain reivers. A Warden, perhaps not unreasonably, was well rewarded, not that this prevented some of the less scrupulous holders of that office from using their position to enrich themselves. Among the more eminent Wardens on the English side were Warwick the Kingmaker, John of Gaunt, and Richard of Gloucester.

Wardens on different sides of the Border did not always coexist as happily as they might have done: the position was, after all, a political one and no doubt it was occasionally expedient not to discourage Border unrest. Indeed, it is rather surprising that the system worked at all and lasted for so long.

Reiving was a way of life. In times of relative prosperity raiding might be a kind of vicious sport, in lean times it was often a grim struggle for subsistence. The families – or more properly clans and tribes – concerned held their own territories and guarded them jealously. On the Scottish side the Kerrs and Humes occupied much of the Middle and Eastern Marches, the Elliots, the Scotts, and the powerful Armstrongs were pre-eminent in the Western March, and the Maxwells and Johnstones were powerful in the area bordering the Solway. On the English side of the Western March were the Grahams – whose loyalties were fickle – and the powerful, if smaller, families of the Dacres, Salkelds, Lowthers, and Curwens. The picture is not quite as clear-cut as it may seem: for although marriage across the Border was unlawful it was not uncommon. There were Armstrong enclaves on both sides of the Border and smaller families such as the Bells and Halls had 'north' and 'south' branches that recognized no border.

The families would raid anyone worth looting, but there were also bitter feuds. And the feuding was not always confined to cross-border clashes: in Cumbria there was a long-standing feud between the Dacres and the Armstrongs and on the Scottish side of the Border the Johnstones and Maxwells feuded for generations.

The Border Law allowed that the Border might be crossed by riders on 'hot trod', that is in pursuit of their stolen goods; but it allowed only for recovery, not reprisal. To find the devious routes of the thieves swiftly it became a common practice, on the English side at least, to employ 'sleuth' dogs. (This might well be the origin of the popular Cumbrian sport of Hound Trailing, in which hounds race on a drag scent laid down by a runner.) The dogs were highly prized and could change hands for as much as £10.

Though writers and poets have romanticized the reivers, some historians have branded them as vicious and unprincipled villains. The truth, conventionally enough, probably lies between the two extremes.

The end of the reivers came during the reign of James I (VI of Scotland). James, determined to rid himself of the nuisance of the Border and to bring both England and Scotland closer together (he had plans that involved the substitution of 'South Britain' and 'North Britain' for 'England' and 'Scotland'), appointed Lord Hume as lieutenant of the three Scottish Marches, with Sir William Cranston as deputy, and gave George Clifford, Earl of Cumberland, responsibility for the English side.

In November 1603 they started their work by hanging, among others, members of the Elliot and Armstrong families. The following years were grim ones for the Borderers: the law was rigidly enforced and dispossessions multiplied. Iron gates, it was decreed, were to be pulled out and made into ploughshares, only working horses – not riding ponies – were to be kept, every parish was to have official informers and searchers: the list of restrictions and injunctions goes on. The Graham family – a source of trouble over many generations – was harshly persecuted and many of its members were transported to Ireland.

By 1606, the year in which a Border Commission was appointed, most of the families were broken. In 1609 a mass hanging of 'thieves' at Dumfries, supervised by Commissioner Dunbar, effectively put an end to the Border reivers.

Whatever the cost – and that should not be underestimated – James seemed to have brought a measure of stability to the Border. But it was of course a stability that could not endure through the turbulent events of his son's reign. The gazetteer entry on Carlisle alludes to some of the more dramatic incidents of the Civil War in Cumbria.

The Act of Union of 1707 offered a legal underwriting of the relative tranquillity that had followed the Civil War. But Carlisle, at least, was not entirely happy: the legislation meant that it was no longer possible to exact a toll on produce and cattle crossing the Border from Scotland. Compensation of £2,641 perhaps lessened the sting.

The Jacobite risings of 1715 and 1745 affected Cumbria, but not particularly uniquely. Again, the entry on Carlisle outlines the way in which that city was affected by the sad, muddled campaign of '45.

Traditional Trades and Industries

Wool

The native sheep of Cumbria are herdwicks. The herdwick is a small, tough, white-faced animal able to withstand the extremes of weather and temperature on the Cumbrian fells; it produces a tough, very coarse wool of the type now used in the manufacture of carpets. The origin of the breed is not known for certain. The story that the first animals were washed ashore from the wrecked ships of the Spanish Armada is probably apocryphal. Similarities to Scandinavian breeds have been used to support a suggestion that the sheep were brought over by Norse settlers.

The woollen industry has long played a vital part in the Cumbrian economy. Kendal 'cottons', a coarse woollen cloth, was well known in the sixteenth and seventeenth centuries. Strings of pack-horses brought the wool into Kendal from the surrounding markets, and from Kendal it went to all parts of Britain. Kendal town's motto remains 'pannus mihi panis' (wool is my bread). The whole operation was a cottage industry, the wool being carded and spun, and often woven, in the farmhouses. Water-powered fulling mills, though, were very common: the parish of Grasmere had as many as eighteen in the sixteenth century.

The industry declined in the early seventeenth century when the southern markets came to favour the finer cloths from Spain. It revived to some extent late in the century, but the coarse wool never fully regained its appeal and many of the fulling mills were put to use as sawmills, bobbin mills, or paper mills.

Evidence of the old cottage industry remains in the shape of 'spinning galleries', covered working areas open to light and air on the sides of some of the old barns.

After the '45 rebellion Carlisle's woollen industry, not relying too much on the coarser wool of the fell sheep, increased in importance when a company of Hamburg merchants set up a number of woollen mills.

Mining

Lead mining was carried out around Alston during the Roman occupation. Some of the mines around Coniston were certainly worked during Norman times. But accurate dating of mines is uncertain as later operations cut away the evidence of the earlier workings.

In 1564 the Company of Mines Royal was set up. The Company had powers to search for all types of metals, the Crown being eligible for a tenth of all gold, silver, and copper found. Keswick became a mining town and in 1565 received some fifty German mining experts, who set up their little colony on Derwent Island and lost no time in commencing operations. Goldscope Mine, in Newlands Valley, was opened in April 1565; this soon became highly profitable. Another successful site proved to be the Caldbeck Fells. But there was a wide scattering of mines all over Cumbria.

From the early seventeenth century, water power was used to haul ore to the surface, to pump out unwanted water, and to crush the ore. Water power was also used to work the bellows at the Keswick furnaces.

Huge quantities of charcoal were needed for Cumbria's furnaces and the woodlands created employment for many dalesmen in the 'coal trade'. The woods were heavily exploited and peat was also extensively used. By the early eighteenth century, when copper mining declined, the woods had been devastated.

The Woodland Industry

The monks of Furness made good use of the woodland in their care. Products included saddle-trees for pack-horses, cartwheels, cups and dishes, barrels and baskets, and the all-important charcoal. Charcoal was always needed in quantity for the smelting of iron and the other metals mined in the area; the demand continued until the nineteenth century. Bark, for the tanning industry, was also a valuable woodland crop.

Cumbrian charcoal was used in the manufacture of gunpowder, another local industry. The last gunpowder works, the Elterwater works, closed in 1930.

By the nineteenth century the woodlands were being properly managed and coppiced, growing shoots being allowed to develop from the old stools (stumps), and cutting in rotation had been introduced. The conservation saved the woodlands of southern Cumbria; but much of the old woodland of the north has been permanently lost.

The Iron Industry

The production of iron was one of Cumbria's earliest industries. It is not known when bloomeries were first started but they were certainly very common by the sixteenth century, so much so that a royal decree made them illegal because of their inexhaustible appetite for charcoal (possibly at the expense of the Mines Royal).

A bloomery was a crude method of iron smelting: the ore was transformed into workable iron by heating it in the presence of carbon (and thus removing the oxygen). A hearth was often dug into a bank and ore, wood, and charcoal were placed in alternate layers; after lighting, the heat was increased by the use of leather bellows. Solid malleable iron was produced: it could be hammered into various tools and then tempered to give a harder cutting edge.

Signs of these bloomeries can be found in many parts of the Lake District, particularly on the shores of Coniston Water and Windermere. Lake shores were favoured as it was easier to transport the ore to the woods by water than to take the much bulkier quantities of fuel to the ore.

Literature

To the literary-minded the Lake District is Wordsworth. The non-literary will not feel his presence at all. There are, thankfully, no Wordsworth tearooms; even the gift shops of Grasmere, the great number of which would have drawn some bitter sonnets from the bard, do not contain Wordsworth souvenirs. The poet rests here in peace. Grasmere at dawn, before the A591 traffic desecrates the silence, is much as he saw it:

> The innocent brightness of a new-born Day
> Is lovely yet.

(*Intimations of Immortality*, XI 198–9.)

No one who knows his Wordsworth can walk about the Lake District without lines and verses springing to mind; and in a quiet place a person can still learn

> To look on nature, not as in the hour
> Of thoughtless youth; but hearing often-times
> The still, sad music of humanity.

(*Lines Composed above Tintern Abbey*, 89–91.)

Wordsworth's literary output was prodigious and much of his work centred on, or in some way involved, the Lake District. Readers must turn to pages other than these for a discussion, or even a listing, of his works (*Poetical Works* (1936 edn.) is a standard collection), but *The Prelude* must be specially mentioned. This poem, subtitled *Growth of a Poet's Mind*, contains some of Wordsworth's finest poetry; it is obligatory reading – rarely are obligations so pleasant – for a connoisseur of the Lake District. The Penguin edition (1971), containing the text of both the 1805–6 version and that of 1850, is valuable.

Dove Cottage, where Wordsworth wrote his greatest works, is on the edge of Grasmere. Miraculously it has been well preserved: it is in the hands of an imaginative trust and is open to the public. Wordsworthian relics, including original MSS, are kept in a nearby museum. The Wordsworths lived in Dove Cottage from 1799 to 1808: Dorothy Wordsworth wrote much about their life there in her *Journals*.

Wordsworth's birthplace at Cockermouth, and Rydal Mount, where he spent his later years, are also open to the public.

Samuel Taylor Coleridge (1772–1834) was a companion to Wordsworth when the latter lived in Somerset, and it is thought to be Wordsworth's encouragement that helped Coleridge to write *The Ancient Mariner*. Coleridge followed Wordsworth to the Lake District in 1800, rented a part of Greta Hall at Keswick (now part of a school), and, undaunted by the five-hour walk to Dove Cottage, frequently visited his old friend.

In 1803 the Southeys – Coleridge had married the sister of Robert Southey's wife – also moved to Greta Hall. Robert Southey was a prolific writer and the income from his works supported Coleridge's family as well as his own. Contrary to his original intentions, Southey stayed in Keswick for the rest of his life. Coleridge, on the other hand, his health broken by an addiction to opium and his poetic impulse clearly flagging, left for Malta in 1804; he returned in 1805 but left the Lakes for good in 1810.

Southey (d. 1843) is buried in Crosthwaite churchyard: the inscription on his monument – a statue provided by public subscription – was written by Wordsworth.

The Lake District's fame among admirers of landscape was increased by the presence of the poets. In 1802 Charles Lamb came to Keswick to see his great friend Coleridge and was much affected by the place. Thomas De Quincey (1785–1859) took Dove Cottage when the Wordsworths left and, to the chagrin of the Wordsworths, particularly Dorothy, married a local farmer's daughter. De Quincey's life at Dove Cottage is described in his *Confessions of an English Opium-Eater*; his residence lasted, fitfully, until a final departure from the Lakes in 1830. The lives of, in particular, Wordsworth and Coleridge are subjectively, but brilliantly, portrayed in De Quincey's *Recollections of the Lakes and the Lake Poets*, a collection of articles that originally appeared in *Tait's Edinburgh Magazine* between 1834 and 1840.

John Keats (1795–1821) was an enthusiastic visitor to the Lakes and is recorded as having climbed Skiddaw. It was probably Castlerigg Stone Circle that inspired the lines:

> like a dismal cirque
> Of Druid stones, upon a forlorn moor

in *Hyperion* (II 34–5). Percy Bysshe Shelley (1792–1822) lived in Keswick for some months during 1811–12. Sir Walter Scott was a regular visitor to the district, though he was not entirely happy with the abstemiousness of the Wordsworth household and took his drams at the Swan Hotel. Scott's novels *Guy Mannering* and *Redgauntlet* include Cumbrian settings, and his *The Bridal of Triermain* is set in St John's in the Vale, though he misnamed Blencathra 'Glaramara'; the slip was corrected in later editions to 'stern Blencathra'.

Some of the gentry of the counties were keen to entertain the Lake poets, although it may perhaps be suspected that not all were keen for purely altruistic reasons. Mr Bolton, owner of Storrs Hall near Bowness (now an hotel), royally entertained Scott, Wordsworth, Southey, and Professor Wilson. Professor Wilson (1785–1854), who ranked high among the authors of his day, lived at Elleray, under Orrest Head, Windermere. He wrote profusely under the pseudonym of Christopher North, often in *Blackwood's Magazine*, and did much to popularize the Lake District.

Harriet Martineau (1802–76) lived at The Knoll, Ambleside (now a private residence), for thirty years, and was visited there by a number of her illustrious contemporaries, including George Eliot, Charlotte Brontë, Emerson, Matthew Arnold, and John Bright. Her *Complete Guide to the English Lakes* (1855) is one of the better-known guides to the area. Felicia Hemans (1793–1835) lived at Doves Nest, above Low Wood, near Waterhead, Ambleside. She was a respected poet, but is now remembered, if at all, only for her poem *The Boy stood on the Burning Deck*.

John Ruskin (1819–1900) lived at Brantwood – on the east side of Coniston Water – from 1871 until his death. Poet, art critic, philosopher, one of the giants of his day, his influence on the worlds of art and social philosophy endures. His secretary W. G. Collingwood wrote a number of books that have become local 'classics'. *The Lake Counties* and *Lake District History* were written after much original, painstaking, and energetic research.

LITERATURE

James Spedding devoted much of his time in the Lake District – he lived at Mirehouse on the shores of Bassenthwaite Lake – to writing *The Life and Letters of Francis Bacon*. Among his visitors were Thomas Carlyle, Edward Fitzgerald, and Tennyson; Tennyson was much taken by Spedding's house and in his description in *Idylls of the King* of the carrying away of Arthur's body on the ghostly barge, he drew upon his recollections of the shores of Bassenthwaite.

In his later years Sir Hugh Walpole (1884–1941) settled in the Lake District, buying Brackenburn, a house overlooking Derwent Water from the slopes above the south-west shore, in 1923. His 'Lake District novels' still have a following and the settings for *Rogue Herries*, *Judith Paris*, *The Fortress*, and *Vanessa* are authentic. The hamlet of Watendlath is easily recognizable as the home of Judith Paris; Walpole stayed there when writing the novel.

Beatrix Potter, creator of Peter Rabbit, Benjamin Bunny, Pigling Bland, and others – all beautifully illustrated in her children's books – was a most enthusiastic 'Laker'. Her small house at Hill Top, Sawrey, between the Windermere ferry and Hawkshead, is open to the public. It contains much of her work. The Potter enthusiast can walk about the lanes around her home and see many of the scenes that she copied for her books. Beatrix Potter bought a great deal of property in the area and left 1,620ha. of land to the National Trust.

Arthur Ransome, another Lake District resident, lived near Coniston and used settings from Windermere and Coniston Water for his children's books in the 'Swallows and Amazons' series.

The Lake District is one of the most written-about areas in Britain; and as a source of inspiration for writers it can have few rivals. It is no mere chance that this is so.

Red deer

Natural History

The great variety of landscape and scenery is one of the principal attractions of Cumbria; the variety of natural habitats is commensurately great.

Camden described Cumbria's climate as 'being with the coldest as lying farre north'. In this, if in little else, he was less than accurate. Winter temperatures compare with those of the south and south-east of England, though the summer temperatures are cooler. But it is not, strictly speaking, possible to generalize about the Cumbrian climate: it varies from valley to valley. The dominant influences are the Atlantic winds and the Gulf Stream; but the mountains affect all. Average annual rainfall at Grange-over-Sands is 102cm., but is 250cm. in the central fells. The annual number of days with air frost in Grange is on average 30; further inland at Ambleside it is 62; but on the fells it can reach around 160. There are of course frost-pockets – land influenced by exposure to high winds – and temperature averages are raised in locations near lakes. All this as well as the landscape affects the localized natural habitats.

The Coast

Cumbria has a long coast line: between Walney Island and Workington facing the sea, but facing into Morecambe Bay in the south and Solway in the north. Both bays offer much to the naturalist. There is a wealth of fauna in the sands of the tidal flats and this wealth attracts great numbers of sea birds. Morecambe Bay shrimps are a famous delicacy, and at one time one of the great sights of the bay was the horse-drawn shrimp carts heading into the sands from Flookburgh until the horses were shoulder-deep in water. There are now fewer shrimpers and tractors are used.

The main food for the wading birds and the flatfish are small crustaceans, ragworms, lugworms, and cockles. At high water flounder, or fluke, plaice, and dab feed on the sand-flats. The fluke, able to tolerate variations in water salinity, is particularly plentiful in the estuaries. The outer reaches are favoured by other species: codling, whiting, whitebait, and soles; and, of the smaller fish, rock gobies.

The bays attract a variety of waders, ducks, geese, gulls, and terns. At low tide they move in in their thousands: the great shining flats reflect their movements and their calls stir the vast spaces. The most characteristic sounds are the pure ringing cry of the oystercatcher and the flute-like call of the curlew, both heard all the year round. The oystercatcher, with legs and beak of vivid orange, and black and white plumage, is usually the bird that aspiring ornithologists first learn to identify. The knots and dunlins arrive in great flocks, changing direction with military precision, alternately showing pale undersides and dark tops as they turn, and dropping to feed as if by command. Red-shanks are also common: their beautiful triple-whistle call and the red of their legs and beaks clearly identify them. The mussel-beds, particularly in winter, are the haunt of the pretty turnstones.

In early summer, from April onwards, the largest native duck, the shelduck, moves in; and in great numbers. Mallard are also usually present. Wigeon and teal feed on the sands in the autumn; and the red-breasted merganser and the goosander can also be spotted. In winter flocks of geese – greylag, pinkfooted, and barnacle – assemble, particularly in Solway. The bean goose and the whitefronted are occasionally seen.

One of the few English nesting sites of the eider duck is on Walney Island. In the winter and spring the drakes are magnificent in their jet-black and snow-white plumage. The spring crooning cry of the drake, delivered with a jerk of the head, is one of the most exciting sounds of the coast; it can be heard from a considerable distance, even when the bird is out of sight. The eiders nest on the South Walney Nature Reserve (Cumbria Naturalists' Trust), a reserve that also holds the largest assemblies of lesser black-backed gulls – distinguished from the greater by their yellow legs – and herring gulls in Europe. The site is shared with greater black-backed gulls and ringed plovers, and attempts are being made to re-establish breeding colonies of terns.

The largest black-headed-gull colony in England is on a nature reserve on the sand-spit north of Ravenglass; the gulls share the site with sandwich terns. Access to the reserve, only approachable by boat, requires a permit from the owners, Cumbria County Council. The rare natterjack toad also inhabits the reserve, living on sand insects, and digging into the loose sand in hot weather.

Eider ducks

The cliffs of St Bees Head are of great interest to the ornithologist. Fulmars, kitti-wakes, razorbills, guillemots, and herring gulls favour the sandstone ledges. Birdwatchers need to beware of being cut off by the tide.

A wide variety of maritime plants favour this coast. One of the more localized types, the rock samphire, can be seen at Humphrey Head. (The egg-shaped fruit was at one time pickled.) The bloody cranesbill is common in many places: a prostrate pale-pink form (*Geranium lancastriense*) is found on Walney Island and nowhere else.

LEFT *to* RIGHT, TOP *to* BOTTOM: *Razorbill; black-headed gull; fulmar; kittiwakes with chicks; guillemots; dunlins*

Rivers and Streams

The rivers and streams offer an extremely wide variety of habitats; type of habitat is of course influenced by the speed of the moving water, the amount of enrichment, and the temperature. A hand magnifier is essential if the fauna is to be properly examined. At high sources, where the water is very pure and cold, life is of course less abundant. Common in many habitats is *Gammarus pulex*, the freshwater shrimp. Also common are stone-fly larvae, of various kinds, and snails. One interesting creature is Polycelis, the flat-worm, of which there are several species: they are usually seen as small black blobs under stones, but they elongate themselves like leeches when they move.

A charming predator of the small water fauna is that ubiquitous black and white bird, the dipper. It is a fascinating bird to watch from the vantage point of a bridge as it submerges and 'walks' on the river bed, using the force of the water on its wings to hold itself down.

Salmon can be seen fighting their way upstream in the winter and trout can be seen at any time. Eels are extremely common and were once a major export from the Lake District to the London market. They were caught in wickerwork traps. Eels are also much sought after by otters, although the otter, once very common in Cumbria, has suffered a considerable decline in numbers. The sport of otter-hunting has declined too, though in recent years the hounds have instead been put to hunting mink in places where escapes from mink farms have successfully established themselves and bred. Otters are thankfully not extinct in Cumbria, but naturalists who know of their locations usually prefer to keep the knowledge to themselves.

Lakes and Tarns

The lakes and tarns vary tremendously in 'productivity'. Very pure lakes, such as Wast Water or Ennerdale Water, are fed by streams directly from the fells and collect little lower-level drainage; they are also deep (Wast Water is 80m.). Such lakes carry insufficient nutrients to encourage life. By contrast, shallow lakes, such as Esthwaite or Rydal Water, take mineral-rich drainage from agricultural land and human settlements and sustain a comparatively large community.

The amount of plant life in the shallow margins of the lake varies with the type of water, and particularly with the type of bed: mud and silt obviously offer a richer habitat than rocks. The commonest plant of the shallows is Isoetes, the quillwort, a rosette-formed plant with quill-like leaves. In the deeper shallows the long-stemmed plants of the pondweeds grow, some broad-leafed and some linear (Potamogeton species), and some with whirls of narrow leaves on long stems, such as the Canadian waterweed (*Elodea canadensis*) and the very local and rare Esthwaite waterweed (*Elodea nuttallii*). Many of the plants are of course invisible to the naked eye: these are the microscopic algae, an important part of the 'chain of life' in water and the food of a number of the invertebrate animals.

In the richer lakes, such as Windermere, Grasmere, Rydal, or Esthwaite, the examination of a stone from the lake bed usually reveals a number of animal species. The freshwater shrimp Gammarus is commonly found. *Asellus aquaticus*, a water relative of the wood louse, is usually present, together with many tiny snails and small blobs that reveal themselves as small leeches and flatworms when they move. The caddis, mayfly and stonefly larvae, and tiny red water-mites are also frequently in evidence. Scraping the bottom of a rock into a white receptacle filled with water reveals such forms of life more clearly; when in the receptacle they can be conveniently studied under a glass.

The richer lakes usually hold perch, pike, eels, and trout. The clearer lakes usually offer habitats only to trout and char. Trout commonly grow to around 20cm. in the smaller lakes, but can grow to 60cm. in the larger lakes. The trout arrive as 'sea trout' from the sea via the rivers and their food is chiefly aquatic insects and crustacea. Char is an alpine relative of the trout and is found outside Britain as far north as 82 degrees. They cannot exist in a temperature above 15°C., so their Cumbrian habitat is in the cold water of the deeper lakes. They are interesting fish because, living in isolated groups, they have over very many centuries developed local characteristics: they have, for instance, light spots on a dark background, rather than the dark on light as in trout. They are found particularly in Windermere, but also in Coniston Water, Wast Water, Ennerdale, Buttermere, Crummock Water, and Thirlmere. Windermere char was once a much-prized delicacy favoured by the nobility of the seventeenth and eighteenth centuries: the fish was often potted or made into char pie. The char dishes specially produced to hold the delicacy are now collectors' items.

Perch is the commonest coarse fish of the lakes and tarns, preferring the richer lakes but also occupying some of the clearer ones. It feeds on plankton and lake-bed animals and has a great capacity for survival. Some found in Windermere have been reckoned to be fifteen years old. The size is generally up to about 30cm. The humpy back and the stripes readily identify the fish.

Pike, a fish with a torpedo shape and a large jaw, are sometimes called 'freshwater sharks' and are indeed carnivores, their main food being mainly trout, char, and perch. They are in most of the lakes, but, unaccountably, not in Ullswater. They prefer weeds and reed beds. Occasionally specimens of up to 13kg. in weight have been landed.

A very rare fish, found only in Ullswater, Red Tarn on Helvellyn, and Haweswater, is the schelly (*Coregonus laveratus*). It is a silver fish and is sometimes called the freshwater herring. At one time it was netted in huge quantities in Ullswater, the nets being placed across the narrowest part of the lake (hence Skelly Neb). It feeds on plankton and is not often seen; but occasionally, for unknown reasons, large numbers of small fish of the species are found dead on the lake shore. Like herrings, the fish move in shoals. The fish reaches about 31cm. in length.

Another rare fish, found only in Derwent Water and Bassenthwaite Lake, is the vendace (*Coregonus albula*); it is very similar to schelly but has a pointed head. The fish is rarely seen; largest specimens found so far have reached 20cm. in length.

Roach and rudd are coarse fish and have a preference for weedy areas in still bays. They are present, and apparently increasing, in Windermere and Esthwaite Water. They are thought to be a recent arrival, introduced by anglers leaving their live bait after a day's fishing.

Among the smaller fish to be found in Cumbria are the minnow, which manages to live even in the higher tarns, the three-spined stickleback, the miller's thumb, or bull-head, which can be found under stones in the lake shallows, and the stone loach, to be found in Esthwaite.

Wildfowl generally prefer the reedy, shallower lakes to the larger, deeper ones.

Probably the commonest birds are coots and moorhens. The former is a black, long-legged bird with a white bill and forehead (hence 'bald as a coot'). The moorhen is similar in size and general shape to the coot, but is brownish-black with a beak red at its base and has a predilection for feeding on shore around lakes.

Winter is the best time to observe ducks. Mallard, pochard, tufted ducks, goldeneye, shelduck, red-breasted merganser, and teal can be seen. Mute swans are common at all times of the year and they are tame when not with young, often invading picnic parties and reaching for food through car windows. The quieter lakes are visited from the Arctic by whooper swans. Their cry, and the sight of them behind the reed beds of Elter Water (*Eltervatn* is Old Norse for 'Lake of the Swans'), with their straight necks and the dignified high set of the head, is an exciting experience.

Heron populations fluctuate but the bird is usually common. They are often missed, though, because of their tendency to stand motionless among reeds in the shallows. Cormorants are not uncommon. A fish-feeder, the cormorant, standing erect with large head on a snake-like neck, looks rather like a creature from prehistory. It often holds out its wings to dry, giving the appearance of an heraldic eagle. It has an ungainly walk, and, whether fishing for eels or perch or sunning itself, is fascinating to watch. It can dive to a depth of over 10m. These birds are known to nest in the Solway Estuary.

The great crested grebe nests on Esthwaite and Blelham Tarn. The remarkable displays and posturings of these birds in early spring are worth watching, the birds facing each other with heads shaking and crests erect. The little grebe, or dabchick, is more common and nests on small waters, including the hill tarns.

Greylag geese, Canada geese, and, occasionally, barnacle geese frequent several of the lakes, and often graze the lake-shore fields.

The Dales and Fells

All of Cumbria was once part of one great forest. There are now only a few fragments that are arguably survivals of natural forest. At Keskadale, high on the Newlands Pass in the central Lake District, is a small oak wood that is possibly one of these fragments. Although some areas in the southern Lake District have always had tree cover, all the present woodlands have been planted. Some of the most beautiful of the woods, such as those by Derwent Water, or those on the shores of Windermere, were planted by land-owners for aesthetic rather than practical purposes. But these are the exception, not the rule: in the southern Lake District timber has long been regarded as an important crop and has served one kind of industry or another for many centuries. Grizedale Forest, with other forests at Broughton Moor and in Upper Dunnerdale, carry on this tradition in the care of the Forestry Commission. Many of the hardwoods also remain, notably at Graythwaite Forest, and on various National Trust properties.

In the southern area of Cumbria the two native deer, the red and the roe, still thrive as they have done since before human settlement. The heavy red-deer stags can be heard roaring their challenge across the quiet lakes on still, late-autumn nights. Lacking natural predators since the extermination of the wolf, a culling operation is necessary if the deer are not to expand their population beyond the available food supply. This is effectively done by the skilled management of the Forestry Commission. The herds are unfortunately threatened from time to time by organized poachers.

The roe deer are common, and often invade gardens around Windermere. The roe is much smaller than the red, and moves about in family parties. It is possibly our most beautiful native animal: it is extremely shy and relies on speed for safety; its inclination to run headlong when alarmed means that many are killed when crossing roads.

The red squirrel still occupies the broadleaf woodlands. There are no grey squirrels in Cumbria and their continued absence allows the red squirrel a greater chance of survival. Even so, the position of the red squirrel is delicately balanced: its ideal habitat, Scots-pine woodland with hazel undercover, is slowly disappearing. The animals are often seen in the Windermere woods and are plentiful in Borrowdale.

The stability of the badger population is also less satisfactory than it could be. Badgers have been persecuted for many years by badger diggers, but the animals are now generally recognized as harmless and are protected by law. Being nocturnal they are not often seen, but are common in places.

The plants of the woodlands are mainly those that are acid-tolerant. The woods on limestone offer a wide variety of plant cover. The glory of the Cumbrian woods, and growing in many moist places, is the daffodils; they survive in masses in spite of past depredations by the public. The keen botanist will seek out the rich variety of mosses, liverworts, and lichens, some of them rare (they can be found particularly in the Borrowdale woodlands).

The fells from the point of view of the naturalist might well be considered 'deserts'. Denuded of the old forest, which protected and maintained soil covering, subjected over the centuries to heavy grazing by sheep, having to endure sweeping rain, alternating frost and thaw, and conditions of quick-drying, the land is leached of nutrients and subject to soil-creep and erosion. The soil is thin and acid. Where it has any depth at all it is often covered by bracken; the great increase in recent years in expanses of bracken is a worry to the hill farmer: grass cannot grow properly under bracken, and the fern is inedible to stock.

Commonest plants of the thin acid soil are bent-grasses and fescue. Nardus, the thin, tough, wiry grass, is very common as it is scarcely touched by sheep: in it can be seen the pretty but tiny yellow flowers of the tormentil and, in patches like snow, half-buried in the grass stems, the minute but clustered flowers of the heath bedstraw. The wetter parts of the fells are occupied by various mosses, particularly spagnum and hair mosses; and there are two common but interesting small plants: the sundew and the butterwort; both these plants obtain nutrients that are unobtainable in the soil by catching and absorbing insects. The sundew has round, sticky leaves onto which small flies adhere: the leaves then close around them; the white flower is rather insignificant and on a long stem. The butterwort bears a rosette of light, tongue-like leaves lying close to the ground: when insects crawl or land on the plant the leaves curl round and absorb them. The flower is pretty, violet, and on a long stem. Cotton grass, with distinctive white fluffy heads, is also common in some wet areas.

Shrubs on the lower fells usually consist of gorse and, in some localities, large areas of juniper. Bell heather and ling favour the rather deeper soils, such as those found on the Skiddaw Slates or the Silurian rocks. Bilberry is everywhere, though those who like the fruit have to find plants out of the reach of grazing sheep, and, of course, must get to the specimens before the birds.

The most common fern in rocks on the Cumbrian fells is the mountain parsley fern, or mountain polypody. In spring its new-green is bright and almost translucent. Often growing with it is the alpine lady's-mantle; these two plants together flourish to an extent not found anywhere else in Britain.

The richest fell habitat for plants, including the uncommon alpines, are the flushes in the gullies and steep fell sides. These are wet areas fed by springs that have collected valuable minerals in their descent through the rocks. Among the rich mosses are sedums, several species of saxifrage, the globe flower, and flowers usually associated with woodlands.

Of the fell animals, the largest is the red deer: the sole fell herd is protected in a reserve on the Martindale Fells. They are lighter in body than the woodland red deer, having adapted to the tougher conditions. Foxes are very common, but usually only seen by chance: their numbers are controlled by the Cumbrian hunts. Obviously the fox hounds can only be followed on foot in this wild terrain.

The characteristic bird of the fells is the raven. Ravens can often be seen riding the wind currents on the crag faces, and their deep-throated 'kruk kruk' cry is often the only sound to break the silence of the fells.

The smaller birds include the meadow pipit, which nests quite high on the fells, and the wheatear. The tiny wren is also often present, particularly around gullies and in block-scree.

Of the falcons, the kestrel is very common, but, except in mild weather, is not usually seen in its hovering flight high over the fells. The falcon of the fell is the peregrine: peregrines are not as rare as they were, but are still uncommon. They sometimes favour the crags used by rock-climbers in the wildest and most inaccessible areas of the remoter dale heads.

Golden eagles were exterminated in Cumbria as a breeding bird in the eighteenth century. Wandering birds have visited since, but reported sightings are not too reliable as large buzzards, common in Cumbria, are often mistaken for eagles; indeed, one can almost suggest *usually* mistaken for eagles. The buzzard is a beautiful bird with a rare mastery of effortless flight; but an eagle is heavier looking, with more prominent head and beak when seen at a distance; when seen closer there is no mistake. In the early 'seventies the eagles returned to nest in Cumbria and it is fervently hoped that they will stay.

National Park
and National Trust

William Wordsworth, in the concluding part of his *Guide to the Lakes* (1835 edn.), under the chapter heading 'Changes, and Rules of Taste for Preventing their Bad Effects', expressed concern about the lack of sensitivity shown by certain new landowners in the Lake District and hoped that some control could be exercised to prevent them ruining the landscape: 'In this wish the author will be joined by persons of pure taste throughout the whole island, who, by their visits (often repeated) to the Lakes in the North of England, testify that they deem the district a sort of national property, in which every man has a right and interest who has an eye to perceive and a heart to enjoy'.

Wordsworth was not by any means alone in his concern about the potential spoliation of the countryside. Nor was the concern limited to this country: the first act of conservation of any importance was the creation of Yellowstone (USA) in 1872; it was at that time the only national park in the world.

National Trust

In Britain the first action came from a trio of friends and idealists: Robert Hunter (1844–1913), Solicitor to the Post Office and the servant of public causes, including the Commons Preservation Society; Octavia Hill (1838–1912), a formidable social reformer; and, lastly, Hardwicke Rawnsley (1851–1920). The Vicar of Crosthwaite and a canon of Carlisle, Hardwicke Rawnsley was one of those rare all-rounders. He was an athlete at Balliol and was reckoned to be the troubadour of the college. He was a writer and aspiring poet, a world-wide traveller, impassioned lecturer, preacher, and historian. He climbed the Cumbrian hills and campaigned for the protection of footpaths. He gave active support to many causes. But most of all he campaigned for the preservation of the countryside. Together the three founded an organization whose object was to acquire land, or funds to buy land, for the benefit of the public. After gaining much support the organization was duly registered under the Companies Act on 12 January 1895 as 'The National Trust for Places of Historic Interest or Natural Beauty'.

The first Lake District property was bought by public subscription in 1902. Brandelhow Woods, by the shores of Derwent Water, was acquired and declared inalienable. Gowbarrow, by Ullswater, was acquired in 1906. Manesty, by Derwent Water, was acquired in 1908. Support for the Trust grew and, thanks to the energy of, and the respect earned by, Canon Rawnsley, fifty properties were gained in Borrowdale. Farms were added to the Trust ownership by the generosity of Beatrix Potter, G. M. Trevelyan, the historian, and Sir Samuel Scott. Some of the high fells were also acquired. Part of the Scafells and Great Gable were given to the Trust by the Fell and Rock Climbing Club of the English Lake District as a war memorial after the 1914–18 war.

In 1976 the National Trust owned sixty-seven Lake District hill farms and several lowland farms, together with a stock of 17,500 sheep. It is here that the Trust plays an important and unique role: it conserves a whole local way of life and ensures the continuing existence of the flocks of tough Herdwick sheep, a breed that belongs to the Lake

District and to nowhere else; the Trust also ensures that the farmhouses are modernized without being spoiled and that the farms are made viable.

In 1961 the commons of Lord Lonsdale, amounting to 6,880ha., were leased to the Trust; the total area of the estates now under the Trust's protection (1976) amounts to 32,380ha. The Trust owns 280 cottages and houses, and, unless unfit for permanent habitation – in which case they are rented as seasonal holiday cottages – they are let to local people.

Only a few historic houses in the county – those mentioned below – are owned by the Trust. Acorn Bank, near Temple Sowerby, is a convalescent home, but visitors are welcome to the garden, famous for its great variety of kitchen herbs. Sizergh Castle, south of Kendal, the home of the Stricklands, is open to the public on a number of days each week. Hill Top, at Near Sawrey, the small home of Beatrix Potter, is over-visited at times. Townend, Troutbeck, near Windermere, is a typical statesman's house of the seventeenth century. Wordsworth's birthplace on Cockermouth's main street is another of the Trust's properties. Hawkshead Courthouse has been made into a museum of local life.

The best-known property of the Trust is the beauty spot of Tarn Hows, between Hawkshead and Coniston. Its popularity has led to much wear and tear and the land is now under a programme of restoration.

The National Trust is the largest landowner in the National Park. Its administrative offices are in Borrans Road, Ambleside, and there are National Trust information centres in various parts of the county. The Trust continues as it began, as a charity depending on generous public subscription. In the mid 1970s membership stood at 540,000.

National Park

The history of the establishment of national parks in England and Wales is a dreary one of frustrated campaigns hindered by apathy and national crises. Although there were earlier campaigns for their establishment, the first organized campaigns came in the 1920s. In 1929 a committee under Lord Addison, set up to enquire into the feasibility of national parks, came to encouraging conclusions. But the country was in the middle of an acute depression and the attention of the government was distracted. Rather ironically it was largely the unemployed, seeking energetic exercise in the countryside, yet denied access to many hills, who increased the pressure for the provision of national parks. Following protests about slow progress by government, outdoor organizations founded a Standing Joint Committee for National Parks to maintain the impetus for parliamentary action.

After the Second World War John Dower was authorized to make a report on the need for national parks; and in 1947 the Hobhouse Committee was set up to decide how to implement the Act envisaged in the Dower report. There was much in the Committee's report that was not accepted but progress was made and the result was the National Parks and Access to the Countryside Act of 1949. A passage in the Hobhouse report summarizes the spirit behind the Act: 'It is just because this is a densely populated and highly industrial country that the need for National Parks is so pressing. People need the refreshment which is obtainable from the beauty and quietness of unspoiled country'.

In 1952 the Lake District National Park was designated, and was the largest of the ten parks decided upon. (The others are Dartmoor, Exmoor, the Pembrokeshire Coast, Brecon Beacons, Snowdonia, the Peak District, the Yorkshire Dales, the North Yorkshire Moors, and Northumberland.) The total area of the Lake District National Park is 224,000ha.; and the total area of all the National Parks is equal to about a tenth of the area of England and Wales.

In a British National Park the land is not owned by the nation. It is, rather, a special area of natural beauty receiving careful protection. But where public access is barred to important areas of fell or lake shore a National Park authority has the power to negotiate access agreements, or it can make an access order. In the Lake District, because there has long been free access to the fells, no negotiations have been necessary, and there is already much free access to many of the lake shores.

The twofold duties of a National Park are to preserve and enhance the natural beauty of the area and to promote its enjoyment by the public. Since the designation of the Lake District National Park the Park Planning Board has maintained a strict control of development within its area. The sensitive might spot mistakes; but on the whole the measure of the Board's success is in what one cannot see. The area has remained largely inviolate, while the local industries have been allowed to continue. Supported by amenity societies, such as the Kendal-based Friends of the Lake District, one of the Board's greatest successes was in gaining strict control of Manchester Corporation's measures to extract water from Windermere and Ullswater. Its greatest failure was in failing to prevent the A66 road improvements through the centre of the National Park: the 'improvements' included building a new road out into Bassenthwaite Lake's shore-line and an elaborate crossing of the lovely Greta Gorge. The decision in 1973 of Mr Geoffrey Rippon, then Secretary of State for the Department of the Environment, to proceed with the scheme, after his inspector had admitted to a public enquiry that the alternative route to the north of the National Park was feasible, was greeted with wide-spread dismay. In a debate on the issue in the House of Lords, which fills twenty-six pages of Hansard, only one peer, the Government spokesman, spoke in favour of the Minister's decision.

Among the provisions for 'helping the public to enjoy the amenities' are the In-formation Services and the Warden Service of the National Park. In 1966 the National Park Planning Board acquired Brockhole, a large house on the shores of Windermere between Windermere town and Ambleside. And in 1969 the house and grounds were opened as the first British National Park visitor centre. Permanent displays, a continuing lecture programme, and an information room introduce visitors and student parties to the amenities that the Lake District has to offer.

The National Park Information Service has permanent information centres at Bowness Bay, Ambleside, and Keswick. There are also a number of mobile information units. An evening lecture service operates from the Bowness and Keswick centres during the season. The information literature on offer covers a wide field, including such topics as natural history and suggested walks.

The National Park Warden Service operates in the field, and there are patrols on lake shores, on the fells, and in public access areas. The wardens are required to help and advise the public on routes, mountain and water safety, and the country code, to attend to complaints, and to be generally helpful. They also run courses in fell-walking for young people and leaders, and, with Brockhole and the Information Service, courses on map reading. The Warden Service also leads a series of guided walks. The professional wardens are assisted by some 200 voluntary wardens who make themselves available at weekends.

Following the reorganization of local government in 1974 the Lake District National Park Special Planning Board established its headquarters at County Hall, Kendal; it is the intention ultimately to acquire a headquarters nearer the centre of the National Park.

Having parallel intentions, the National Trust and the National Park naturally work very closely together, with the aim of retaining the beauty and the freedom of the region so that 'every man has a right and interest who has an eye to perceive and a heart to enjoy'.

Mountain Safety

No one can venture onto the fells without putting himself at some risk. It would be wrong to exaggerate the risk: thousands of people every year enjoy safe fell-walking in Cumbria. But the accident figures rise annually and the local mountain-rescue teams now turn out for rescues, on average, twice every week. This is a greater frequency than in any other mountain area in Britain. It is not that people are more careless, it is just that there are far more people fell-walking in Cumbria than ever before.

All members of mountain-rescue teams are keen fell-walkers and climbers, and every one of them must have very mixed feelings on seeing the growing lines of walkers heading for the popular fells. It is of course easy to appreciate that the perspiring explorers are seeking 'adventure'; and it is equally obvious that a certain amount of risk is a vital ingredient in the mildest excursion. There are people on the fells who are quite aware of the conditions and the 'rules' and very rarely come to grief; and there is a small minority of would-be mountaineers who, blissfully ignorant, often become stretcher cases; but in between there is a large grey area out of whose ranks come most of the accident statistics. A thousand a year? No one can tell you what the total accident rate is: the rescue teams must only pick up a minority of the total. Many walkers and climbers with sprains, cuts, or bruises – even broken bones – reach the valleys with the help of friends and passers-by. And fell-walkers getting lost? There must be many hundreds, but the worst that most suffer is a descent into the wrong valley. (The local taxi firms do quite well out of lost walkers.) But at regular intervals people are caught by nightfall and have to be looked for, particularly in wet or cold weather when death from exposure becomes a possibility. Cold is one of the most frequent causes of death on the fells.

For the fit and active with a taste for fine landscape and a head for heights, fell-walking is an ideal form of recreation. But like any other form of physical recreation it requires some basic skills.

The footwear. Poor footwear is the largest single cause of mountain accidents, minor or major. Only a person with a very long apprenticeship and experience of walking (or running) on very rough, steep ground could get away with wearing anything other than fell boots. The fell shepherd wears curved, long-wearing, iron-shod boots – or he might wear clogs – that would cripple a lowlander. An athlete who has specialized in fell-racing will manage very well with special light running-shoes: it is a matter of knowing where and how to place one's feet. But the vast majority of people, including experienced mountaineers, must wear strong boots (not wellington boots) with ankle support and well-coated rubber soles. Even then, it is necessary to know the limitations of these boots: wet, greasy rock, muddy slopes, and hard ice must be watched for. Nailed boots, rare nowadays, are superior on wet ground.

Fell boots need not necessarily be expensive and indeed the expensive type with steel sole stiffeners are only necessary if the buyer intends to walk in hard snow and ice or tackle rock climbs. To avoid blisters boots should only be worn with thick woollen socks or stockings. Boots can be hired from some dealers.

Windproofs. The wind-speed on the fell summits can be from two to two and a half times as strong as that on the valley floor. This is not often readily appreciated. A mild spring day in the dale might tempt many people to seek the viewpoints; but on the heights there often blows a freezing east wind. Thick woollen sweaters cannot protect a body from cold without a windproof. An anorak, coming down well below the waist, is the popular answer. Trousers or breeches also need to have some windproof qualities. Cotton 'jeans' are only for midsummer, and even then the prudent will carry light overtrousers in case the wind freshens.

Waterproofs. No one should venture onto the mountains without waterproofs. Modern garments, jackets and overtrousers, can be quite light and take up little rucksack space. Fell-top weather in Cumbria is notoriously changeable. Rain thrown horizontally by strong wind can be both unpleasant and dangerous: it is the commonest cause of exposure.

It is possible to obtain a windproof that is also rainproof. Whether it is a good idea to wear one is a matter of opinion. Garments of this kind can cause perspiration and one can get wet from the inside instead of vice versa. The position can be eased if the jacket has a full-length zip.

Fell-walking Equipment

To enjoy fell-walking in comfort and safety there are some vital items of equipment that should be carried.

Map and compass. The map scale should be at least 1:50,000. Ideally the compass should be one with a protractor scale attached, but this is not vitally necessary. What is necessary is that the owner should know how to use the instrument. The skill is easily learned.

The rucksack. To carry the essential while leaving the hands free, a rucksack is necessary. It should not be too small: a small rucksack stuffed drum-tight with gear makes for acute discomfort.

Food. A good supply of food is sensible. 'Iron rations' to be eaten only in emergencies are also a good idea. Food containing sugar or glucose, which produce energy quickly, are of most use.

Extra clothing. A spare sweater to pull on if the weather becomes cold is not only a comfort, it could be a life-saver in an accident.

Other items might include a torch with a spare battery and spare bulb – vital at all times other than the long days of summer, and even then a good idea. Without a torch, and delayed beyond sunset for one reason or another, it could prove necessary to 'sit it out' until dawn. It is unpleasant and, in bad weather, dangerous.

A whistle, perhaps tied to a rucksack cord, can be invaluable in an emergency. Six blasts at intervals is the international mountain distress call. The answer, when helpers can see the caller, is three blasts.

A first-aid kit need not be elaborate, but carrying one is a good idea. A few triangular bandages, some lint, elastic dressings, aspirin, safety pins, and scissors would suffice.

A plastic bag big enough to crawl into in an emergency weighs very little and most mountaineers carry them.

Winter extras. Winter fell-walking is for experienced walkers only. Warmer clothing, with woollen hat and gloves, and extra warm clothing in the rucksack, are obviously needed. If there is snow and ice an ice-axe is necessary and it is vital to know how to use it to cut steps and how to stop a slide on ice. Ropes, and experienced companions to rope to, are necessary if any serious ice-climbing is tackled.

The Basic Safety Rules

The safety rules for fell-walking are just common sense. But even the sensible and intelligent are sometimes forgetful.

Leave your route description with someone. Failure to do this might mean that if a walker breaks a leg no one will have a clue where to start looking for him. If the walker is unduly delayed (e.g. forced to descend into a different valley from that intended) word should be got back to 'base' so that a rescue team is not called out unnecessarily. If 'base' is not on the telephone, a message to the police will save undue alarm.

Plan the route carefully. The commonest mistake is to try to do too much in the available time. Allow about 4km. per hour and add one hour for each 500m. climbed.

There should be a second plan prepared in case the original plan has to be abandoned because of bad weather. The local weather forecast should be consulted even if the weather seems fine: a local telephone forecasting service has been organized by the Tourist Board and the National Park for the Lake District area (Windermere 5151).

Group Leadership. The leader of any group or family should keep it together at all times. This means moving at the speed of the slowest member, and even turning the whole group back if a member is not able to continue the walk.

The Mountain Rescue Organization in Cumbria

All mountain rescues are arranged and coordinated by the police in response to the 999 emergency service.

Between the wars there was little call for mountain rescue. The comparatively few cases were dealt with by the police, with the support of local shepherds, quarry men, and any climbers or walkers who happened to be about the area at the time. The only 'stretcher' available in those years would probably have been a farm gate.

After the last war there developed an enormous interest in walking and climbing and this, with the large increase in car ownership, led to greatly increased numbers on the fells, a lengthening of the holiday season, and much more weekend activity. Local climbers in Coniston and in Keswick were the first to see the new need for organized rescue and they formed the first teams. They were mainly concerned with climbing accidents on the Coniston and Borrowdale crags but inevitably they found themselves both dealing with such accidents *and* organizing searches for missing walkers. In Langdale accidents to climbers could be dealt with fairly smoothly because there were always climbers staying or camping at the valley head, and they would rally to a call from the hotelier at the Dungeon Ghyll Old Hotel, himself a well-known climber. But as incidents increased over a wider area, the need for further rescue teams became clear.

There are now teams at Cockermouth, Keswick, Penrith, Patterdale, Kendal, Langdale/ Ambleside, Coniston, Millom, and Wasdale. These are supported with back-up teams such as the Furness Search Team – a Sedbergh team – and the Outward Bound Schools at Eskdale and at Ullswater. These teams all cover the Lake District. The Pennines are covered by the Penrith and Kendal teams, the latter team having special equipment for dealing with falls in old mine workings. The Cave Rescue Organization based in the Yorkshire Dales is also available to deal with caving accidents. An RAF rescue helicopter can be called in to help whenever an incident involves a risk to human life.

Accidents at a known location are usually dealt with swiftly and efficiently. Each team knows its area well and can reach the casualty, and evacuate him, by the quickest routes. All the teams have fell-walking doctors as team members, or on call. To equip a team with medical gear, ambulances, stretchers, radios, and specialized crag-rescue gear is a very expensive business; and, although the teams obtain some support from local authorities and from their central body, the Mountain Rescue Committee, a considerable proportion of the money is raised by the team members themselves. The Continental practice of charging the rescued for the rescue has been suggested as a possibility in Cumbria, but the teams have so far opposed this. Many of the rescued, of course, make voluntary donations.

The greatest problem facing the rescue teams is the increase in the number of walkers and climbers getting lost. It is particularly difficult if the person missing left no particulars of a route before setting out. The rough fells of Cumbria make for extremely difficult searches, particularly in high summer when bracken can be shoulder-high. The need to coordinate the teams into a common organization to deal with such emergencies was realized in the 1950s and the Lake District Mountain Accidents Association was formed. The Association meetings are held regularly to discuss common problems and to organize mountain-safety publicity. Following a very long search for a missing walker in 1960, the 'large-search' technique was reviewed and the result was the formation of a Mountain Search Advisory Panel, consisting of police officers and leaders from each rescue team. The panel is rapidly convened by the police when a local rescue team needs the urgent assistance of a large body of searchers; it then makes decisions on the setting up of search headquarters, the number of teams to be called in, and the organization of leadership and search areas. Specially-trained search dogs are increasingly being used and it is the normal practice to deploy these early while the ground is fresh. If the weather is dangerously bad, or the days short, it is often thought wise to deploy very large numbers of personnel. If necessary, searchers can be called in from Lancashire and Yorkshire; and the RAF rescue services can be asked for support.

Much is being done, both locally and nationally, to promote mountain safety and everyone is hopeful that ultimately this will tend to reduce accidents. Restrictions, by any authority, on the movements of fell-walkers would be unthinkable: a sense of freedom is a main aim and attraction of the pastime. National Park Wardens' mountain-safety patrols deliberately keep a low profile.

Short-stay Guide

This page is intended for the person whose time in Cumbria is limited to a few days. What, out of all that is described in this book, is most worth visiting? The question is an invidious one, but below are some unashamedly subjective thoughts on the matter. The items are listed in alphabetical order, not order of preference.

The list would become interminable if fells, dales, tarns, and lakes were added as individual items. The visitor travelling to even a few of the places mentioned below will sample at least some of Cumbria's scenic beauty and variety.

Not all of the items in the list are the subject of a separate gazetteer entry: it is suggested that the index will provide the most convenient way of tracing descriptions.

Archaeology
Bewcastle Cross
Castlerigg Stone Circle
Gosforth Cross
Hadrian's Wall
Hardknott Fort
Irton Cross
Long Meg and Her Daughters
Roman bath house (Walls Castle), nr.
   Ravenglass

Buildings (ecclesiastical)
Carlisle Cathedral
Cartmel Priory
Furness Abbey
Lanercost Priory

Buildings (secular)
Brough Castle
Brougham Castle
Carlisle Castle
Dove Cottage, Grasmere
Holker Hall
Levens Hall
Muncaster Castle
Sizergh Castle

Townend, Troutbeck, Windermere

Museums and Visitor Centres
Brockhole National Park Centre
Grizedale Wild Life Centre and Museum
Hay Bridge Deer Museum and Reserve,
   Bouth (by appointment)
Keswick Museum
Museum of Lakeland Life, Kendal
Lowther Wild Life Park
Ruskin Museum, Coniston
Tullie House Museum, Carlisle
Wordsworth Museum, Grasmere

Villages
Crosby Ravensworth
Dent
Great Salkeld
Hawkshead
Kirkby Lonsdale
Milburn

Waterfalls
Aira Force, Ullswater
Lodore Falls, Borrowdale
Stock Ghyll Force, Ambleside

Gazetteer

Abbreviations

NP for National Park
NT for National Trust

Entries in the gazetteer

The first figure of the map reference supplied to each
entry refers to a page number in the map section at the
back of the book. The subsequent letter and figure give
the grid reference.
Population figures are based on the 1971 Census

Abbey Town 5B6 (*pop.* 785)

Abbey Town is a hamlet, the bulk of whose buildings are constructed of stone 'quarried' from the ruins of Holme Cultram Abbey. The remains of the abbey, representing only a fragment of its former glory, are used as the parish church (ie the major part of the abbey's nave, without the aisles). Abbey Town is an exciting arts centre: programmes include classical music, jazz, dance, drama, and poetry. A festival is held in June.

HOLME CULTRAM ABBEY was founded in 1150, when this part of Cumbria was in Scotland, by Cistercians from Melrose Abbey; the land was given by King David. During construction the area was taken – and the grant to the abbey confirmed – by Henry II. The abbey's lands were extensive; iron and salt were produced but wool was the main source of wealth, and the abbey enjoyed an export trade through the nearby port of Skinburness.

From the outset the abbey suffered from border raids. No doubt Edward I's use of the place as a military base during his successful Scottish campaigns – the abbot was seconded as a member of the King's Council – increased its attractiveness as a target for revenge. After Bannockburn, Robert the Bruce robbed all the Cumbrian church establishments, and, even though Robert's father was buried in the abbey, Holme Cultram fared no better than the others.

The abbey was dissolved in 1538, but the church was allowed to remain standing as a parish church: its endowment formed part of Queen Mary's benefaction to the University of Oxford, one of the conditions being that the University should supply a parish priest. The church, in an area vulnerable to Scottish raids, fell on hard times. Its tower fell in and its roof fired. Special efforts at restoration were made in the early eighteenth century: it was decided to reduce the size of the building by removing the aisles and the east end, and walls were built up between the twelfth-century piers. Further work was done in the late nineteenth century and in this century.

Of particular interest in the church are the old pulpit, a fine Norman west doorway, and a porch, with dogtooth moulding, of 1507. Monuments include one to the Earl of Carrick, Robert the Bruce's father, and another to Abbot Rydekar (d. 1434). Carvings include a carved niche, probably of the fourteenth century, and a carving of Henry VII. Further excavations are taking place in the area.

A tourist information centre has been established in the church building.

Allcock Tarn Rydal Fell 3D4

Allcock Tarn is a small, part-artificial tarn on the fell to the south-west side of Heron Pike, east of Grasmere. It is in the ownership of the NT and is a popular objective for Grasmere walkers. The usual climb is from the green above Dove Cottage (qv): a track leads through a gate

high on the green's left-hand side (Brackenfell, NT). The zig-zag path offers good prospects over Grasmere.

The tarn is quite small and is not spectacular, but the views from above the dam, taking in the fells of Coniston and Langdale, and the Helvellyn range, are excellent.

Allonby 5B6 (*pop.* 425)

Allonby is a village on the road between Maryport and Silloth in a shore area under statutory protection following its designation as an Area of Outstanding Natural Beauty. There are sand dunes and an extensive beach. Allonby made an early bid for the tourist trade, being developed with that object in mind in the eighteenth century; at that time it enjoyed a reputation for good sea-bathing. Sea-water baths were opened in 1835 but have long since closed. Among the holidaymakers in 1857 was Charles Dickens. The only real attraction is the Solway: there is little in the town itself.

Joseph Huddart (1741–1816), the hydrographer and innovator of ships' safety measures, buried at St Martin's-in-the-Fields, was born in Allonby.

Alston 4F1 (*pop.* 1,915)

Alston sits at the north shoulder of Cross Fell at a height of 281m., and, with its inclined cobble streets has an unusual alpine atmosphere, slightly marred by heavy vehicle traffic on the A686 (Newcastle–Penrith) and the A689 (the Wear Dale route to east coast). It has a tight, proud, and friendly community typical of the isolated Pennine villages, and a refreshingly pleasant nineteenth-century shopping street. Much of the building material of the older houses is of limestone and millstone grit; roofing slates are often made of the easily-split millstone grit, a material that gives the roofs a heavy, bulky appearance.

Alston was once a famed mining town and the area remains of great interest to geologists. Lead was first mined in Roman times and continued to be mined, interrupted only by the border raids, until a decline in the seventeenth century. During that century the Alston manor came under the ownership of the Radcliffes. But the ownership was short-lived: James Radcliffe, the last Earl of Derwent Water, lost everything, including his life, after supporting the 1715 Jacobite rising. In 1734 the estates came under the ownership of the Commissioners of the Royal Hospital for Seamen, at Greenwich, and mining activities revived. A peak was reached in the nineteenth century when not only lead, but silver, iron, zinc, and copper were mined, and, with the minerals, flourspar and barytes. In 1821 total mine revenues exceeded £100,000. Some of the principal mine owners were Quakers, and their influence prompted some enlightened experiments in workers' welfare: education, disablement funds, and sick relief – measures that became a model to others – were introduced. (The Quaker Meeting House is on the main street.) Cheaper foreign sources of metals brought the industry to a decline in the

Late Victorian era. Today farming is the main activity, although the area also has some thriving foundries, light-engineering works, and collieries.

The MAIDEN WAY, the Roman road from Brough (Bravoniacum) to Hadrian's Wall, runs west of the town; and WHITLEY CASTLE, the remains of a Roman fort, can be seen to the north-west of the town. The vulnerable north and west sides of the fort were protected by no less than seven mounds and ditches. The fort doubtless defended the important supply road, but there are also traces of a further road going north-east, with bridge abutments over the South Tyne River, and one strong possibility is that this was a route to mine workings (obliterated by subsequent workings?). The direction of the road also points to a route leading to the important supply base of Corstopitum (near Corbridge), where Alston ore has been found.

Apart from the fort, there is nothing of great antiquity in Alston. The church, dedicated to St Augustine – in local legend supposed to have exorcized the demons of Cross Fell – stands on the site of former churches but dates in its present form from 1869. The shape of the town, with its odd corners, is interesting; and, like so many Cumbrian towns, Alston is designed so that the central square can be readily sealed off. This feature was possibly less for defence than for coziness and convenience: enclosure of stock is possible and organization of market days and fairs is simplified.

The area is well served with public footpaths. The Pennine Way passes through Alston, and the riverside walk to Garrigill is one of its most pleasant sections. There are several routes up to Cross Fell's summit (893m.).

Ambleside 3D4 (pop. 2,660)

Ambleside is one of the most popular holiday villages in the Lake District, mainly because it is so close to Windermere and has easy access to the central valleys. It is surrounded by fells; but not the high, dramatic ones that crowd Keswick's skyline; the Ambleside fells are softer and tree girt, with the greater peaks of the Langdales sitting far back.

Ambleside is a place of becks and rivers and before the tourist boom of the past century was a place of mills, many turning water-wheels. Horrax's bobbin mill, by Stock Ghyll and using timber from local coppice woods, was one of the area's most productive mills of its kind in the late 1830s. A corn mill stood near the town centre; the site is now occupied by a shop, but the water-wheel has been reinstated. There were also fulling mills, bark mills, cotton mills, and a paper mill. Signs of old mill races can still be seen in various parts of the town.

Stock Ghyll Force, Ambleside's waterfall, is a fine sight, particularly after heavy rain; it was much admired by the early tourists. The approach begins on a secondary road behind the Salutation Hotel, leaving the road shortly afterwards to follow the ghyll. The remains

C17 Bridge House, Ambleside

of an old mill, a four-storey structure, can be seen on the far bank: part of the building has now been converted to provide holiday flats. Several Victorian viewpoints for the ghyll, protected by iron rails, are still in evidence. A path follows the fell upwards and the top is bridged by a stone arch.

BRIDGE HOUSE, a very small seventeenth-century cottage built across the ghyll on a bridge, is the town's curiosity piece; it is to be seen close by the A591 at the northern end of the town. Local legend suggests that it was the home of a Scotsman who wished to avoid a land tax. It was probably originally built as a summer house belonging to old Ambleside Hall, but was certainly used as a permanent residence in the nineteenth century: in the 1840s it was occupied by a Mr Rigg who, in defiance of the house's proportions, brought up six children in it. Bridge House has long been a great attraction for artists (including J. M. W. Turner). It was acquired by the NT in 1926 through local subscription and is now open to the public as an information and NT recruitment centre.

The best local viewpoint is at JENKIN CRAG, which is reached through Skelghyll Wood (NT), east of Waterhead at the southern end of the town. Skelghyll Wood is of interest to geologists and botanists because of a narrow band of limestone (Coniston Limestone) that passes through the junction there of Borrowdale Volcanics and Coniston Slates. Jenkin Crag provides an extensive view of the head of Windermere as far south as Belle Isle and Bowness. On the other side of the lake is a mountain panorama stretching from the Old Man of Coniston, on the left, to Langdale Pikes and Loughrigg. Blelham Tarn, a nature reserve, and the nineteenth-century eccentricity of Wray Castle, both by the western shore of Windermere, are also clear.

Waterhead, at the southern end of Ambleside, has a pier and is served by steamers from Bowness and Lakeside. There are boat-hire services and a public launching area opposite the car park. To the west of Waterhead is a public access area and the remains of a Roman fort (NT). This is sometimes called BORRANS FORT (Borran being an old local term for a heap of stones). In Roman times it was known as Galava. There is little remaining apart from the foundations: the stones, as so often happened, were taken away over the centuries and extensively used in local building. Much of the stone used in the fort was not local and was transported long distances from sandstone quarries, probably in the southern area of Cumbria; no doubt the last part of the journey was made by lake. The fort was originally built to command the road that led from the north–south and east–west road junction at Brougham, east of Penrith, over the High Street summit road and by a road, not yet convincingly traced by archaeologists, through Ambleside to the traceable road running via Wrynose Pass, Hard Knott Pass, Hardknott fort, and through Eskdale to the port of Ravenglass. The foundations now visible belong to a fort that was built over the site of an earlier one. The dimensions are about 91m. by 137m. The River Rothay flows along the fort's western end, though the original flow was nearer than the present channel. The southern side, approaching the lake, is wet ground. On the north and east sides are traces of a defensive ditch. The main entrance was by the east gate into the Via Praetoria; on either side of this entrance, inside the fort, there would have been wooden barrack buildings. In the centre of the fort are the foundations of the stone buildings, the Principia, the administrative centre; to the north are traces of the granary building; and to the south remains of the commander's house. A road of sorts, not traceable, probably led from the south gate to a jetty on the lake. There was probably also a landing point by the river at the west gate.

According to Collingwood the original fort, a smaller one, was probably built about 79 during Agricola's successful northern campaigns. Indications are that the early fort was built of clay. The stone replacement fort was probably built c. 100, and the stronghold was occupied for about 300 years, suffering attack and burning several times. The fort held about 500 auxiliaries and a sizeable town grew up alongside it. Some of the finds from archaeological digs, including the tombstone of a Roman killed in action, are in Brockhole (qv), the NP Centre.

Ambleside is one of four towns where a rush-bearing ceremony is still held annually (the others are Grasmere, Urswick, Warcop). This pre-Elizabethan practice had a less ceremonial aspect when the floor of the church was earthen: the rushes were gathered each summer and laid over the earth, and the old rushes were burned. Rushes and flowers are normally carried through Ambleside on the first Saturday in July, and the procession is preceded by a band.

Angle Tarn   Langdale   3C4
After the lung-bursting struggle up the loose-stoned path by Rossett Gill, Angle Tarn comes as a delightful surprise to fell-walkers on their way to Esk Hause and Scafell Pikes from the head of Langdale. A typical corrie tarn, it is at a height of 580m. and is backed by the awesome crags of Hanging Knott on the northern face of Bow Fell.

Appleby   4F3   (*pop.* 1,950)
A small town on the main railway line between London and Glasgow, Appleby was the county town of Westmorland, a county that disappeared after local government reorganization in 1974. Appleby is nearer to the Pennines than to the Lake District fells and has the feel and atmosphere of a hill town, though it is only 122m. above sea-level. The town is neat and unspoiled, anciently placed in a protective loop of the River Eden with a castle on a hill protecting its open flank. In the disputed territory of the Border this positioning assured its survival.

Appleby was in Scottish hands until William Rufus advanced to Carlisle in 1092; after this date it was subject to frequent border raids.

The older part of the town, Bongate ('street of the bondsmen'), is on the east bank in the parish of St Michael, established in the eleventh century. On the west bank, in the parish of St Lawrence, the market place and the broad street of Boroughgate ('the street of the burgesses') run down from Appleby Castle to the church: there are some decent, substantial buildings of the eighteenth and nineteenth centuries in Boroughgate. At the head of Boroughgate the late-sixteenth-century MOOT HALL (with eighteenth-century windows) stands in the road centre. This building is where the burghers used to assemble for a 'mote', a meeting to transact the business of the town; there has probably been a moot hall on the site for 500 years. ST LAWRENCE'S church, like its sister on the east bank, suffered damage from border raids. The oldest fabric in the church is of the twelfth century, but the church has been burned and

ABOVE: *Church of St Lawrence, Appleby*

BELOW: *Appleby Castle: N side and tower*

rebuilt several times since; externally the style is predominantly Perpendicular, internally it is predominantly Decorated. The main portion of the tower has probably survived unscathed. An archway at the entrance to the fourteenth-century porch shows dog-tooth moulding and is of reused twelfth-century masonry. The church organ once belonged to Carlisle Cathedral and is thought to have parts dating back to the Elizabethan era; it was given to St Lawrence's by Dean Smith in 1684. The church contains the tomb of Margaret, Countess of Cumberland (d. 1616), the widow of George Clifford, the third Earl and champion to Queen Elizabeth I. Margaret's effigy is carved in alabaster. Nearby is the tomb of her daughter, Anne Clifford, Countess dowager of Pembroke, who made her mark in Cumbria by the restoration of the Clifford castles, including Appleby, Brough, and Brougham, and of churches, including St Lawrence's.

ST MICHAEL's church, Bongate, is probably older than St Lawrence's. A Saxon hogbacked gravestone, used as a lintel in a blocked doorway in the north wall, is of either tenth- or eleventh-century origin; this is an indication that a church has been on the site from that period, but the oldest fabric of the present structure is of the twelfth century. St Michael's, too, must have suffered from the border raids. Much restoration was done by Lady Anne Clifford in 1659, although there is some disagreement about its extent. Further, thorough, restoration was carried out in 1885.

APPLEBY CASTLE certainly owes much to Lady Anne Clifford's seventeenth-century restoration, undertaken in defiance of Cromwell. The large earthwork defences, of Norman motte-and-bailey form, were built by Ranulph de Meschines in the eleventh century. The Great Hall and part of the twelfth-century curtain wall still stand. A semicircular tower to the north was built in the thirteenth century. The castle is not open to the public.

Armboth Thirlmere 3C3
Armboth is still signposted from the A591 at Thirlmere although it no longer exists: it was drowned in 1894 when Manchester Corporation dammed and raised Thirlmere for its water supply. The only sign of the site of the hall is a prominent chile pine (monkey-puzzle tree), once part of the garden, now standing on the lake shore.

Armboth Fell, to the west of Thirlmere, offers a fine viewpoint but it has the reputation of being an extremely wet area: it gives botanists with an interest in mosses and bog plants a great deal of scope.

Arnside 2E1 (*pop.* 1,865)
Arnside is a village on the east bank of the Kent channel at the narrows between Milnthorpe Sands and Morecambe Bay. There was at one time a ford and a ferry there, though the speed that the tide comes in through the

narrows is notoriously fast. The narrows are now spanned by the viaduct, 159m. long, built for the Furness Railway in the latter part of the last century. The coming of the railway increased the popularity of Arnside as a holiday resort and most of the building is of late date. The village is a place of steep hills of wooded limestone, the inclined streets interconnecting with a footpath system.

There are beauty spots in the area, some with fine viewpoints. ARNSIDE KNOTT (159m.) is one of the most popular and is owned by the NT. ARNSIDE TOWER, a ruin of a defence tower to the south-east of Arnside Knott, is the remains of a house once belonging to the Stanleys.

Arnside was at one time a small fishing port and used to possess a boat-building yard.

Ashness   3C3   SE of Derwent Water

Ashness is an outstanding attraction to lovers of fine landscape and undoubtedly ranks as one of the most photographed places in Britain.

It is an area through which one passes on the road to Watendlath from Borrowdale. It is a narrow road, once almost solely the preserve of walkers but now bedevilled by traffic snarls at weekends in the season.

On leaving the Borrowdale road and climbing the hill, the road turns right over ASHNESS BRIDGE. There is a car park beyond. The view with Ashness Bridge, a beautiful stone-arch structure, in the foreground and Derwent Water and the northern fells beyond has appeared on innumerable postcards and greeting cards. It is a cliché but is still a photographer's dream: dedicated photographers feel it necessary to stand in the water for the best aspect.

A short distance beyond the bridge as the road ascends through woodland it passes close to the edge of a crag. This is Surprise View, another famous viewpoint. From this airy perch over Lodore Wood one can see the length of Derwent Water below, the western fells beyond, and, over to the north-west, the foot of Bassenthwaite Lake.

The woods offer scope to naturalists with an interest in bryophites. The whole area is in the ownership of the NT.

Askham   4E3   (pop. 390)

Askham is an ancient and pretty village 5km. south of Penrith. With the single exception of Askham Hall – fourteenth-century in parts – the oldest remaining buildings are of the seventeenth and eighteenth centuries; there is some separate modern building, rather out of sympathy with the old. Askham sits close to the River Lowther and in view of the Lowther Castle ruins (*see* Lowther).

There is evidence that the area round Askham ('the place of the ash trees') has been occupied since the Late Stone Age. To the south-west, on Askham Fell and Moor Divock, there are signs of a number of Bronze Age burials and there is a small stone circle. A track of early origin diverts from the Roman road on High Street,

Askham Hall: archway to W range

which is itself known to follow the line of an ancient British road.

The church beside the river was rebuilt in 1832 on the site of an older structure; the south transept of pre-sixteenth-century date was retained in the nineteenth-century building.

Bardsea   1D1   (pop. 1,025)

Bardsea is on the coast road between Ulverston and Barrow-in-Furness. It has the best beach in the area, with views across Morecambe Bay; well known to residents, it is less well known to holiday visitors. Bardsea is managed as a Country Park.

Barf   3C2   NW of Swan Inn

Travellers on the A66 northwards from Keswick will see, just north of a forestry plantation, an impressive eminence with a white 'figure' perched on the precipitous screes. The craggy hill is Barf; the white projection is The Bishop. The figure – field glasses will show the resemblance to a mitred bishop standing in a pulpit – is in fact a natural rock 2m. high, and by tradition is kept whitewashed by the landlord of the nearby hotel. Volunteers with a good head for heights and reasonable stamina occasionally do the whitewashing and are rewarded with ale.

The climb to the summit of Barf (366m.) is extremely rough, but the views over Bassenthwaite Lake to the great mass of Skiddaw are an awesome and beautiful surprise.

Barrow House and Barrow Cascades 3C3
4km. s of Keswick

Barrow House overlooks Derwent Water and stands by the side of the Borrowdale road on the lake's south-east side. It was built early in the nineteenth century by J. Pocklington, who also built the house on Derwent Island and other buildings in the area.

Barrow Cascades are behind the house. The waterfall is very impressive after heavy rain. It has, unfortunately, a loose and dangerous approach: access is possible only by permission of the owners.

Barrow House is now a Youth Hostel.

Barrow-in-Furness 1D2 *(pop.* 64,034)

Barrow is a frank, no-nonsense northern industrial town, a true product of the Industrial Revolution, a town showing ample sign that it has seen good times and bad. But there are differences: much of the dirt of industry is blown away by off-shore breezes; pleasant sandy beaches, which would be the envy of some popular holiday resorts, are to hand; and a close look at the town shows that in the building there was actually some sort of plan. The notion of a plan becomes immediately apparent driving down from Abbey Road, the main road, into the town: Abbey Road is good and wide, straight and tree-lined, and pleasant. It ends in Ramsden Square, a square named after the James Ramsden who worked out the scheme for Abbey Road and, indeed, for the town's whole grid-iron system of streets and buildings.

In 1835 there was just a port of Furness, exporting iron ore from a few wooden jetties; there were only a dozen or so houses. But the iron ore in the area was plentiful and of excellent quality. The developers began to move in, and among them was H. W. Schneider, a young speculator who did much to develop the local industries. By 1846 a new company, Furness Railway, had built a railway to take ore and slate from the mines and quarries into Barrow. William Wordsworth was horrified to find that the line ran very close to Furness Abbey (qv), and wrote appropriate poetical protestations. By 1857 the railway was linked to Lancaster, and Barrow began to grow to a nine-year-old plan of Ramsden's. It was reported that houses were being bought as soon as the foundations were laid.

By 1863 the export of iron ore had almost ceased – it was all being smelted at local ironworks – and the population had grown to 8,000. Only eight years later the population had reached 18,911, an increase mainly accounted for by male immigration. A naval construction works, a Ramsden enterprise, began building

ships; and when, in 1897, the company was taken over by Vickers, Sons and Maxim, the yards developed rapidly: naval vessels have remained the Barrow speciality. The premises of Vickers Limited now cover 152ha. and other industries have moved into the area.

There are four large docks, all named after landowners and developers: the Devonshire, the Ramsden, the Buccleuch, and the Cavendish.

The town has a good shopping centre, not developed too much by modern-day Ramsdens and Schneiders. The museum, in the excellent Public Library building in Ramsden Square, contains some interesting historical and archaeological exhibits.

WALNEY ISLAND, connected to the town and mainland by a bridge, was the site for Vickerstown, a settlement built on Walney to serve the growing army of workers. The name Walney suggests 'walled island', and this description has been attributed to the 'walls' of stones pushed up by storm and tide. In fact there may have been walls of early British settlements on this island. Signs of the earliest settlers of Cumbria – flint instruments of Mesolithic cultures – have been found on Walney shore; and other early settlers must have arrived by sea at various times in pre-history.

Walney Island is of interest to the naturalist. There is a gullery on the south part of the island and it is one of the few English nesting-places of the eider duck. This part of the island is a Nature Reserve in the care of the Cumbria Naturalists' Trust. A flower rarity, *Geranium lancastriense*, grows in profusion on the sand dunes.

Bassenthwaite Lake 3C2

Bassenthwaite Lake, the most northern of the Lake District waters, is 6¾km. long and around 805m. wide. It is in Skiddaw Slate country and so lacks the drama of overhanging crags and close viewpoints. The view of the lake from Skiddaw, or Dodd Wood in the east, or Thornthwaite Forest on the west, is breathtaking, if remote. The view up-lake from the lake itself is also striking if one keeps well away from the fast road (A66) that intrudes on the western shore.

Good public access to the lake is scarce. The western shore is bedevilled by the A66. The NP has provided an access point near Ouse Bridge at the lake foot, but this is in the tamer, flatter country and there is no good view up-lake. There are several rights-of-way on the eastern shore, but the public have *only* the right of passage. Another access point has been provided by permission of the landowner at Mire House. It was there, at Mire House, that Alfred Lord Tennyson stayed with his friend James Spedding and during his stay, on his walks by the lake shore, was inspired to write the description of the passing of Arthur in *Idylls of the King*. It was into Bassenthwaite on that sad, frosty night that Sir Bedivere flung Excalibur, and it was there that the black barge bore away the dying king.

The main source of water feeding Bassenthwaite Lake

is the River Derwent from Derwent Water. The land between the two lakes is flat and the field system is netted by becks and drains. It is a simple and obvious surmise that, until separated by post-glacial erosion debris, both lakes were one. Both lakes are shallow – Bassenthwaite is generally around 15½m. deep – and both lakes are inhabited by a freshwater species of whitefish, the vendace (*Coregonus albula*), not found in other lakes; there are also pike, perch, and trout.

The lake is privately owned, and the launching and hire of boats is under the control of the Bassenthwaite Sailing Club. Powered craft are not permitted.

Beacon Tarn   Blawith Fells   3C5

Beacon Tarn is a small, pretty, natural lake 1½km. west of the foot of Coniston Water and 160m. above sea-level. It is cupped in the heather-covered fells of Blawith, which are in the care of the NP. There are traces of Bronze Age settlement in the area. The tarn is approachable only on foot, by rough paths from the roadside at Blawith Common, or by a track from Water Yeat.

Beetham   4E6   (*pop.* 220)

The building of the M6 gave back to Beetham its threatened identity. No longer the queues of heavy traffic struggling through the bottleneck of Beetham Bridge on the A6. Beetham is an attractive village with an interesting old church – ST MICHAEL AND ALL ANGELS – probably dating in parts from Saxon times and certainly from the eleventh and twelfth centuries. The pillars date from the eleventh to the fourteenth centuries, the tower is a twelfth-century structure. There are panels of medieval glass, one of which incorporates a portrait of Henry IV. The north-west window depicts St Lioba, who is said to have died in 799, and St Osyth, a noble lady killed by the Danes in the seventh century. Much damage was done to the church in Cromwell's time, including the defacement of the two figures between the aisle and the chancel; it is uncertain whether or not they represent Sir Thomas Beetham and his lady. Tradition has it that the Cromwellian troops were encouraged in their sacrilegious actions by a mob of scholars and a master from Beetham School; the troops apparently even went as far as stabling their horses in the church.

An intriguing ruin can be seen by travellers on the A6. It is an old pele tower – built to protect its owner and his stock from the marauding Scots – that was subsequently extended to become a fortified farmhouse. It is now a barn.

Belle Isle   3D5

Windermere is nearly two lakes: its narrow centre is almost blocked by the lake's largest island, Belle Isle (15½ha.). This island was so named in the nineteenth century; formerly it was known as Long Holm. There has been a house on the island for many centuries, and traces of Roman occupation were found during building

activity in 1774. The manor-house of the district was built by William de Lyndsay in 1246 and abandoned in the fourteenth century. A new house was built when the island was inherited by the Philipson family. The Philipsons were Royalists and the island was besieged by Roundheads for eighty days during the absence of Colonel Huddleston Philipson (nicknamed 'Robin the Devil'); the Colonel arrived home from a Royalist victory at Carlisle to raise the siege. He later disgraced himself by riding his horse into Kendal church during worship in search of his Cromwellian enemy, Colonel Briggs.

The island passed through several ownerships until it was acquired by a Mr English, who had the notion to build the present round house. He employed as an architect John Plaw, who modelled the house on the Villa Vicenza in Rome. The building was started in 1774 and by 1781 Mr English was so tired of the constant disparagement of his house, which was alleged to be spoiling the beauty of the area (Wordsworth in *The Prelude* called it a pepper-pot), that he sold it – at great financial loss – to the heiress of Workington Hall, Isabella Curwen. Her husband, John Christian, accepting the opinion that the house was too conspicuous, planted screening trees.

The present owners, Mr and Mrs Edward Curwen, have recently opened the house and island to the public. (Details from Information Centres.)

Bewcastle (Shopford)   6E4   (*pop.* 335)

The great attraction in the village of Bewcastle, otherwise known as Shopford, is the CROSS. This magnificent column of beautifully carved sandstone, 4·5m. high, has stood there since the seventh century. The west face has four panels: the top panel is of St John the Baptist carrying the Agnus Dei; below is one of the earliest English carvings of Christ, with Christ standing on a lion and an adder; below this is a Runic inscription; and at the foot a falconer (St John the Baptist?). The east side is decorated with vine scroll. The south face contains five panels of designs and a sundial. The north side has five more decorative panels. Sadly, the top part of the cross was vandalized in the name of research: it was sent to Camden, the Elizabethan historian, and was lost. Remarkably, a cross of the same age and extraordinary quality can be found at Ruthwell over the Scottish border; Pevsner maintains that there is 'nothing as perfect as these two crosses and of comparable date in the whole of Europe'.

In about 120 the Romans built a fort at Bewcastle and called it Banna. Large enough to hold 1,000 men, it was an isolated outpost fort well north of Hadrian's Wall and linked to the wall by a road. Over the centuries since

OPPOSITE: *C15 stained glass in church of St Michael, Beetham*

ABOVE: *Bewcastle Cross: W face*

LEFT: *Bewcastle Cross: S and E faces*

the fort's abandonment the stone used in its construction has been used in the village. The Anglo-Saxons settled and put up their cross. Scandinavian settlers followed and one of them named Beuth built a castle, hence the village name; a ruined tower and sections of wall are all that remain of the castle after its destruction by Cromwell in 1641. The church has a long history, but the original structure became ruinous in the early sixteenth century. The church was rebuilt in 1792 and restored in 1901: presumably some of the stones of the old Roman fort have been used four times over.

The village, historical monuments aside, is worth a visit for its own atmosphere, unassuming and serene.

Birkhouse Moor   Glenridding   3D3
Birkhouse Moor is an outlying eastern spur of the Helvellyn range between Patterdale and Glenridding. Its ridge, offering an alternative route to the heavily-used

path from Grisedale, links up with the Striding Edge path to Helvellyn's summit. Few walkers go to the highest point of the moor (706m.): it is somewhat flattened and the best view it offers is of the east cliffs of Helvellyn. But the eastern end of the moor, clothed in trees, offers wonderful views over Ullswater. It is easily reached in a short walk from Glenridding; a left turn at a small tarn (Lanty's Tarn) ascends to the viewpoints.

Black Combe   3B6

Black Combe (600m.) is a fell at Cumbria's southwestern extremity, and, being separated from the Lake District's central fells by a large area of comparatively uninteresting moorland, is neglected by walkers. Yet its views, westwards over the sea towards the Isle of Man and Ireland, and towards the hills of Scotland and Wales, are magnificent. In 1813 Wordsworth wrote a poem in its praise: *View from the top of Black Combe*. In the same year he wrote a poem in slate pencil on the side of a stone of Black Combe in praise of Colonel Mudge, a distinguished surveyor whom Wordsworth had met on the fell.

Geologically, the fell belongs to the Skiddaw Slate Series and has the typical angular shape of a fell with a friable rock structure. From the northern and western sides the approaches offer easy walking, the path from Whicham being the most pleasant.

Black Sail   3C4

Black Sail is a mountain pass, on a pony track, between Wasdale Head and the head of Ennerdale. It curves round the western foot of Kirk Fell to its summit at 548m., between Kirk Fell and Pillar. Cumbria's most remote Youth Hostel is at the Ennerdale Head end of the pass, where the plantings of the Forestry Commission, once much criticized, begin.

Blawith   3C5   (*pop.* 95)

Blawith is a hamlet and a fell. Of the former there is nothing to see of historical interest. There are two churches: one is the ruin of a sixteenth-century building; its replacement, on the opposite side of the road, was built in 1863.

In the eighteenth century the futile attempts by the impecunious parish to raise money to restore the old church and build a steeple were the subject of an uncomplimentary verse:

> Blawith poor people
> An old church and new steeple
> As poor as hell,
> They had to sell
> A bit of fell
> To buy a bell
> Blawith poor people.

The fell is a wide expanse of bracken- and heather-covered land now under the management of the NP. On

its highest point, only 255m. high, was an ancient beacon, part of an old communication system. Below the beacon is Beacon Tarn (qv).

Blea Rigg   Langdale   3C4

Blea Rigg (Old Norse for 'Blue Ridge') is the wall of fell on the north and east side of Great Langdale between Chapel Stile and Dungeon Ghyll. It offers an exhilerating walk, giving good views over the Langdale Valley; but, because of a network of paths and a number of summits, it can prove difficult in mist. It is approached from the east at Harry Place in Langdale, or by a number of routes from Grasmere. The summit (542m.) is near its western end and is a pleasant little crag; but it is the side features of Blea Rigg that form the main interest. The southern side above the Dungeon Ghyll New Hotel is a well-known area for rock climbers. The testing climbs for the experts are on the Whitegill Crags, not easily seen from the road. Lower and to the south-east, attracting many people, Scout Crags offer more moderate climbs: the crags constitute one of the most popular training areas in the country. Tarn Crag, above Stickle Tarn on the fell's western end, is another climbing crag.

The northern side presents a craggy face, Blea Crag, stretching to Easedale Tarn; east of this is Blindtarn Moss, an area of interest to naturalists: surrounded by thickets of juniper, it is a haunt of that tiny bird the firecrest. Blindtarn is overgrown and only recognizable as a tarn after very wet weather.

Blea Tarn   3C4

There are several Blea Tarns in Cumbria, but the best known is the small tarn between Great Langdale and Little Langdale. Looking northwards across the tarn gives a perfect foreground to one of the finest views of the Langdale Pikes. Wordsworth was much moved by the sight and describes it in *The Excursion* (II 327–48).

The area is owned by the NT.

Blelham Tarn   3D5   NW of High Wray

Blelham Tarn, clearly seen from the high land on the east side of Windermere, is a natural tarn situated to the west of the secondary road between High Wray and Ambleside. It is a National Nature Reserve (access restricted) leased from the NT: interest centres on sphagnum bog developing from wet woodland. The tarn is used for research by the Windermere-based Freshwater Biological Association.

Blencathra   (Saddleback)   3C2

Blencathra is probably an old Celtic name for this bulky northern fell. Saddleback is its other common name: a fair description of its shape, particularly if it is observed as the huge and superb backcloth to the scene looking up St John's in the Vale.

Blencathra is not high in popularity with fell-walkers;

but the connoisseurs enjoy its freedom from the crowds. It is not as high as its neighbour Skiddaw, being only 868m., but is of greater interest. A narrow arête, SHARP EDGE, rivals the popular Striding Edge on Helvellyn for excitement. The fell is composed of Skiddaw Slate, usually – but not on Blencathra – a rock of uniform hardness. The grinding and plucking action of the last glaciation met resistance in some parts of the fell and left two corries containing the lonely and lovely tarns of SCALES and BOWSCALE. The steepest sides, which were undercut by the moving glaciers, are to the south and east. This interruption in the radiating glacial pattern is partly accounted for by the fact that ice pushing south-wards from Scotland met the Cumbrian ice, which was deflected east and west. The visual result is that the grim-looking steep cliffs and screes tower over the normal view from St John's and the A66 road, dwarfing the little village of Threlkeld.

The mountain is bounded by rivers. Strangely-named Glenderamackin (probably a name of Celtic origin) flows eastwards from Scales Tarn, northwards round Souther Fell, then back southwards and westwards along Blencathra's southern boundary. When it is joined by St John's Beck it becomes the River Greta. Glenderaterra, an equally strangely named beck on Blencathra's western boundary, divides the fell from Skiddaw. On the north-western and northern boundaries the River Caldew takes its water from the fell, including the flow from Bowscale Tarn, before turning northwards to join the Eden at Carlisle.

From the summit ridge five arms reach to the southern valley and each is named as a separate fell; from west to east: Blease Fell, Gategill Fell, Hall's Fell, Doddick Fell, and Scales Fell. The two outer fells fall away fairly tamely in grassy slopes. The central arms are loose and craggy, and in season are brilliant with heather bloom. To the east and north, and partly detached by the loop of the Glenderamackin, are Bowscale and Souther fells. Bowscale contains Bowscale Tarn in its northern hollow. It is a gem rarely sought out. Souther Fell is famous for its unusual haunting: a phantom army has been seen on the fell on more than one occasion, first sighting being on Midsummer Eve 1735. Observers, including quite a number of respectable, sober people, reported that the manoeuvring of the 'army' lasted as long as an hour.

The summit can be reached by a number of routes from Threlkeld or Scales. All are for well-equipped and fit walkers only. The view southwards takes in the High Street and Helvellyn ranges, and the view over the abyss into the valley holds much interest. North of the summit a cross laid out on the ground, and made of white quartz, is said to be a memorial to a walker (long past) who died nearby. There are several old mine workings at various points on the fell sides. The Blen-cathra foxhounds are lodged directly below Blencathra at Gategill. They hunt the northern area of Cumbria. All this is John Peel territory.

Boot *see* **Eskdale**

Bootle 3B6 (*pop.* 875)
Bootle is a village on the western coast road from Millom to Whitehaven (A595) and is served by the railway. The church is of early origin but is much altered: there is little of historical interest. A road from the village leads to a pleasant beach. Bootle Fell, to the east of the village, and on the north side of Black Combe, has produced evidence of Bronze Age settlement.

Bore Dale 3D3   s of Sandwick
Bore Dale is a valley lying behind Place Fell, Ullswater; the old pony-track route from Howtown to Patterdale ascends the valley to cross the pass – Boardale Hause (396m.). A ruin on the hause was once an old chapel, and a bleaker place of worship could hardly be found. The hause is a fell crossroads and it might well be imagined that walkers in mist without a compass would need comfort and guidance!

Borrowdale 3C3/C4
Borrowdale is one of the most exciting and beautiful of the Lake District dales. The first view of it is often from Friars Crag across the levels of Derwent Water and through the near-vertical tree-clad walls at the dale foot, the Jaws of Borrowdale.

Borrowdale proper begins at the foot of Derwent Water and continues through Grange-in-Borrowdale and the Jaws into the widening floor drained by the River Derwent until it reaches its head in the highest land in England. The dale's great beauty lies in the steep woodlands, mainly hardwoods – a mass of colour in autumn and spring – backed by soaring crags and high fells, and floored by a river clear to its deep, pebbled bed.

The road on the eastern side of Derwent Water goes first by Great Wood to Ashness Gate – where the Watendlath road branches through Ashness Wood – then continues to the foot of Borrowdale at Lodore Wood. The falls at Lodore flow through the wood from the source at Watendlath Tarn; they are one of the dale's most popular attractions, particularly after prolonged rain. Southey enhanced the falls' popularity in his *Poem for Children*, a tongue-twisting description of the course of the waterfall from its source to its foot.

The falls can be approached quickly through a turn-stile (coin-operated) behind the Lodore Swiss Hotel or, alternatively, by footpath through Lodore Wood (NT). A ghyllside path takes the energetic person to higher falls. After heavy rain the volume of water, and the noise, is most impressive.

The great crag on the western bank of the falls is SHEPHERD'S CRAG, one of the Lake District's most popular climbing crags; it offers climbs varying upwards in de-gree from 'difficult'. The best place to watch the climbers is from the public footpath that leaves the road under the crags for Great Bay.

GRANGE-IN-BORROWDALE is reached by an attractive stone-arched bridge. The small hamlet is on the site of a grain-store once used by the monks of Furness Abbey (hence the name). The whole of Borrowdale was in the abbey's ownership, though other nearby areas – after being the subject of unChristianlike dispute – were owned by Fountains Abbey. Looking up-valley from the bridge, the scene is dominated by Castle Crag.

Further up the valley is Quay Foot, once a profitable quarry known as Rainspot because of the fine spotted slate it produced. The waste heaps from the quarry are now covered in silver birch, largely self-seeded but with some further planting and encouragement by the owners, the NT. A secluded car park is set at a higher level than the road and is a popular place from which to walk. The focal point of interest in the area is the BOWDER STONE, just south of Quay Foot; this is a large, isolated rock, perched, apparently precariously, on a narrow base. How it got there is a subject for debate. It could have fallen from the slopes above but it is more probable that it was left in such a position by retreating ice during the last Ice Age.

On the opposite side of the river is CASTLE CRAG, an impressive tree-clad eminence, reached by crumbling quarry tracks. On the summit there are defensive ditches – and little else – of a Romano-British fort; some Roman pottery has been recovered from the site. The setting is superb. The riverside below the crag is one of the most delightful parts of Borrowdale. The valley above this point widens and the Derwent is joined by Stonethwaite Beck. After heavy rain the area sometimes floods, and is in fact the site of an older lake. Indeed, after heavy rain all of Borrowdale, fed by so many fell becks, can be one lake from Seathwaite to Derwent Water.

ROSTHWAITE VILLAGE, sitting between two rivers, is a walkers' crossroads, with a track going to Watendlath and other routes leading, via Stonethwaite, to Langdale and Grasmere. A path also leads across the Derwent and through Johnny Wood to Seatoller. Johnny Wood (NT), a typical oakwood with a luxuriant growth of ferns and liverworts, is listed as an Area of Special Scientific Interest.

SEATOLLER was at one time merely a farm but a hamlet subsequently developed for the workers in the Honister Quarries. It is at this point that the road for Honister branches from the Borrowdale road. Going still further up the dale, the shape of the valley, with its rounded lower contours, is a good example of a glacial valley; the road ends at a scattering of farm buildings – SEATHWAITE – the starting point for the high fell-walks. Up on the fellside, to the north-west, can be seen the waste heaps of the once highly profitable Plumbago Mines. Plumbago, or in local jargon 'wad', is otherwise known as black lead. It was used as a medicine, as a dye, in foundries for mouldings (particularly for musket and cannon balls), and of course for pencils. It was the black lead from these mines that started the pencil manufacture in Keswick, an industry that still exists (but now uses imported lead). In the eighteenth century the mineral was so valuable that an armed guard was based on Seathwaite and on at least one occasion the guards had to thwart an armed robbery.

Seathwaite is also well known, although it might prefer otherwise, as the wettest area in England. The average rainfall is 333cm. At the very head of the valley, at Sprinkling Tarn, south of Seathwaite Fell, it is thought that the average might be as much as 470cm. This is a dramatic contrast to the fall in Keswick, only a few km. north; there the average is around 145cm. The number of rainy *days* in Seathwaite does not vastly exceed that in places away from the influence of the high fells: it simply rains harder in Seathwaite. In August 1966, after continuous and heavy rain, there was much destruction from flooding at the head of Borrowdale. Stockley Bridge, a stone pack-horse bridge above Seathwaite, was badly damaged and had to be restored. The valley floor was covered in large boulders and rock debris. Paths and tracks were washed away and road surfaces torn up. It was some years before the debris was cleared and the scars began to heal.

The pack-horse road from Seathwaite via STY HEAD PASS to the coast must once have taken a great deal of traffic. It is now very rough and wet but still one of the main routes for fell-walkers making for Great Gable, the Scafells, or Wast Water. An alternative to the direct route up Sty Head from Seathwaite is to take a footpath westwards through the farm buildings, crossing the ghyll by a footbridge, then taking a path on the ghyll-side to climb past Taylor Gill Force to the Sty Head track. The force is at a point where the ghyll drops from the heights down a cliff below the scree-filled gullies of Base Brown; it is a thrilling spectacle but a head for heights is a prerequisite for enjoyment.

An alternative route up the valley head branches southwards from Stockley Bridge to reach, via Grain Gill, the high fells under Great End, the northernmost peak of the Scafells.

The fells walling Borrowdale from head to foot are as follows: at the head are Great End and, lower, Allen Crags, Green Gable, and Seathwaite Fell; on either side of Seathwaite are Grey Knotts (west) and Glaramara (east); on the west side from Seatoller to Derwent Water are Dale Head, Eel Crags, Maiden Moor, and Black Crag; on the east side are Great Crag and Grange Fell.

A substantial portion of Borrowdale, including the popular areas of Bowder Stone and Castle Crag, is in the ownership of the NT.

Bouth 3D6

Bouth is a small village that grew out of the woodland industries. To the north of the village is HAY BRIDGE NATURE RESERVE, a wild-deer sanctuary; this grew from the plans of a local resident, and advisor on deer to the

Forestry Commission, Mr H. Fooks, and was developed by his widow. Access is by permission only: this should be obtained by prior application to the warden.

Bow Fell 3C4

Bow Fell, seen by travellers as they turn for Hard Knott, appears as a huge pyramid at the dale head above Eskdale. From this perspective it looks like the mountain it is. The walker's view of it from Lang Strath, below its northern side, is equally impressive. The fell really belongs to Langdale – it is its 'top wall' – but Langdale winds and from some points the mountain hides its true lights. By any direction, the climb to its 902m. summit is enjoyed every season by a large number – one could almost say droves – of walkers.

The most usual approach is from Stool End Farm at the head of Langdale, and up a sloping buttress of fell known as The Band. Many people regard this as a long, dull slog, and prefer the approach from Stool End that runs to the left of The Band, through Oxendale and by the dark ravines of Hell Gill, to the shoulder of Bow Fell at Three Tarns.

Overlooking Langdale are the climbers' crags; a path leaving the direct route from The Band to the summit leads to them. The first crag is Flat Crag, separated from Cambridge Crag, the next, by The Slab. At the far, north, end is the great Bow Fell Buttress.

The summit of Bow Fell, a mass of shattered rock, is very rugged and the whole of the eastern and northern faces are extremely craggy. The view from the summit is extensive and takes in Cross Fell in the Pennines. Walkers bound for Esk Hause from Rossett Gill have a view of the northern face of Bow Fell across the water of Angle Tarn.

A path from the summit ridge running northwards, then westwards, crosses Ore Gap. The path is red at that point from a rich deposit of iron ore. The presence of the mineral led to the strongly-held belief that compass readings could be seriously affected on Bow Fell. Some research, mainly by the Brathay Exploration Group, has shown that compasses are only affected if a reading is taken in certain places with the instrument lying on the ground.

Bowness *see* **Windermere**

Bowland Bridge *see* **Winster Valley**

Brandreth 3C4 N of Great Gable

Brandreth is a fell crossed by the popular fell-walkers' route from Honister Hause to Great Gable; its summit stands at 714m. The fell commands a superb view over Ennerdale and Buttermere and takes in nearly all of the main Lake District summits.

Brant Fell Bowness-on-Windermere 3D5

'Brant', in the local jargon, means steep. Brant Fell

(192m.) is a viewpoint at Bowness-on-Windermere and is approached from Brantfell Road. It has fine views of the lake.

Brantwood 3C5

Brantwood, the home of John Ruskin for twenty-nine years, overlooks Coniston Water from the lake's eastern shore. The house was a century old when Ruskin bought it in 1871 for £1,500, but his alterations and extensions considerably modified the original. At the height of his fame, as artist, author, prophet, first Slade Professor of Fine Art at Oxford, Brantwood was his much-loved retreat and he became an ardent advocate of the preservation of the Lake District. He was buried in Coniston churchyard in 1900. Brantwood, which still contains many of his drawings, paintings, and personal possessions, is open to the public every day, except Saturday, in the summer, and by appointment out of season. For Ruskin enthusiasts a visit is essential. Others may feel unrewarded.
(*See also* Coniston.)

Brathay, River 3D4

The Brathay rises at the summit of Wrynose Pass (393m.) and flows eastwards down waterfalls into Little Langdale, through Langdale Tarn, and over Colwith Force, before turning north to enter Elter Water, where it is fed from Langdale Beck. From Elter Water it drops over Skelwith Falls and turns eastwards to run into Windermere with the River Rothay. During heavy rain on the Langdale Fells the Brathay rises very rapidly and flows swiftly, but soon falls to normal when the rain ceases. When the river is in flood the rapids at Clappersgate near Ambleside are popular with canoeists.

The river was the county boundary between Lancashire and Westmorland until the creation of the new county of Cumbria in 1974.

BRATHAY HALL and OLD BRATHAY CLAPPERSGATE were established in the seventeenth century as family seats, but they have now been much altered and their new rôle is as centres for outdoor pursuits and field studies for young people.

Brigflatts *see* **Dent**

Brockhole 3D4 NW of Windermere

About halfway between Windermere and Ambleside, and between the road (A591) and the lake, is the NP visitor centre, Brockhole. Formerly a large country house built by Henry Gaddum, a Manchester businessman, and later a convalescent home for Merseyside women, it was acquired by the NP and opened in 1969.

The house has been adapted to present permanent displays, exhibitions, demonstrations, lecture programmes, slide shows, and films. There are special facilities for schools (which must book in advance) and refreshments are available. Beautiful gardens descend to green fields and to the lake shore: a jetty on the shore gives visitors access from the lake.

One of the main statutory duties of a NP is to help the public enjoy the amenities: the object of Brockhole is to explain what the countryside of the Lake District NP has to offer. Subjects covered include: geology, hill farming, the area's literary associations, archaeology, mountain walking, natural history, and ornithology. A number of special courses are run from time to time and these are being further developed. There is a one-day course intended to teach map reading, and there is another short course entitled 'People in the Park'. Sheep-shearing demonstrations and other similar events are occasionally arranged.

Brockhole, open daily from about mid March to November (the car-park charge is calculated per head rather than per vehicle), is liable to get crowded on wet days during the high season; but to enjoy the whole complex – including gardens and lake shore – a fine-day visit is recommended.

An early Brockhole visit is useful for those who wish to enjoy the NP to the full.

Brothers Parting   Grisedale Tarn   3D4

In 1805 William Wordsworth accompanied his brother John, who was returning to the command of his ship, the *Earl of Abergavenny*, along the Patterdale side of Grisedale Tarn. They bade farewell and William returned to Grasmere never to see his brother again: John's ship was lost in a storm off the coast of Dorset. To commemorate the sad farewell Wordsworth carved some lines in a rock near the place of their parting; time has made these illegible. An engraved plate now marks the spot.

Brothers Water   3D4

Brothers Water is a small lake near Hartsop at the foot of Kirkstone Pass. It is completely natural, although its straight-line shores misleadingly suggest the contrary. It was probably once a much bigger lake and may have joined with Ullswater; but following the last glaciation, and before the fell slopes were stabilized by plant growth, massive deposits of alluvium were washed down from the heights into the area now separating the two lakes.

The lake contains perch and trout and possibly the schelly, a freshwater whitefish also in Ullswater.

Brough (Brough-under-Stainmore)   4G3   (*pop.* 575)

The natural way from Carlisle to York is southwards via the Eden Valley to Appleby and Brough, then by Stainmore over the Pennines to the Yorkshire plain. This was the route that must have been taken by the prehistoric settlers and traders from the east. The Romans probably built their road along the line of an existing British road; the modern A66 still follows it. Brough stands strategically on this natural crossroads between south and east.

The Romans chose the brow of a steep escarpment to build a fort to command this important gateway and called it Verterae; they occupied it for 300 years. Little remains: the Brough Stone, now in the Fitzwilliam Museum, Cambridge, a memorial to a sixteen-year-old Roman soldier, is a single, sad reminder.

The imposing ruins of the Norman castle, built on the site of the Roman fort and using the fort's stones, dominate the landscape. BROUGH CASTLE is in the care of the Department of the Environment and is open to the public. The great keep is on the western end and the walled bailey extends eastwards: the foundations of the keep and sizeable portions of the bailey walls are of the original eleventh-century structure. On the north side of the gatehouse some coarse herring-bone masonry can be clearly seen.

The castle was probably built shortly after 1092, the date of William Rufus's acquisition of north Westmorland and part of Cumberland: it was a frontier castle, for north-west Cumberland was still part of Scotland. In 1174 the castle was breached and taken by William the Lion of Scotland. There is evidence that the castle was repaired in the early thirteenth century when it was granted by King John to Robert de Vipont, ancestor of the Cliffords. During the Scottish wars Brough Castle was repeatedly under attack, but although Robert the Bruce's forces, after their victory at Bannockburn, burned the town of Brough in 1314 and again in 1319, the castle was undamaged; and throughout the fourteenth century there was further strengthening of the defences.

The ninth Lord Clifford, who held Brough Castle during the Wars of the Roses, was a Lancastrian and because of his persecution of the Yorkists was nicknamed 'Bloody Clifford' and 'The Butcher'. Shakespeare places him as an outspoken supporter of Henry VI (*Henry VI Part III*). He was killed in action, reputedly by an arrow in his throat, in 1461, and the castle was taken by Warwick the Kingmaker.

The Tudors restored the castle to the Cliffords and Henry, the son of the ninth Lord Clifford, came back to Brough.

The castle was accidentally set on fire in 1521, and remained a ruin until, in 1659, Anne Clifford, Countess dowager of Pembroke, Dorset, and Montgomery, and restorer of so many Clifford castles and village churches, began the work of repair. Much extra work was done, including the rebuilding, on existing fourteenth-century base courses, of the Clifford Tower in the south-east corner. In 1666 there was another fire and the castle's life came to an end: by the end of the century masonry was being removed for building material elsewhere and the remains were allowed to become ruinous. In 1923 the castle was handed over by the owner, Lord Hothfield, to the Commissioners of H.M. Works for conservation.

ST MICHAEL's church stands in the half of Brough known as Church Brough (the other half is known as

Brough Castle

Market Brough). The original church was built in the mid twelfth century, but, like most other buildings of that age, was much damaged by raiding Scots. The church was under royal patronage from the reign of Richard Coeur de Lion to that of Edward III; it then came under the patronage of Queen's College, Oxford.

The sloping floor of St Michael's nave, to allow worshippers at the rear of the church a greater degree of participation, is a medieval feature. There is a typical Norman main doorway arch. The roof of the nave is Tudor, the Norman original no doubt being destroyed by the Scots. The stone pulpit's age is debatable: although dated 1624, it is thought to be a fifteenth-century work.

The church tower is a sixteenth-century addition and its bells, given to the church by John Brunskill, a yeoman of Stainmore, were the subject of a poem by Southey. Brunskill, with two priests, also founded a chantry in Market Brough: one of the priests taught grammar and the other taught singing; the chantry included a hospital with two beds for travellers. Following reports of miracles, the chantry became a place of pilgrimage.

The charter giving Brough a market and fair day two days before St Matthew's Day (21 September) was obtained by Lord Clifford in 1330. The charter is now

almost forgotten: the present fair is celebrated mainly by gypsy families, gypsies having followed the east–west trade route crossing through Brough for centuries.

Brougham   4E2   (*pop.* 270)

Brougham was once strategically placed at an important cross-roads where the north–south route from England to Scotland met the east–west road from Northumberland and Yorkshire to Cumberland. The modern road system (M6) misses the village only for the need to by-pass Penrith.

The Roman roads, probably based on earlier British roads, went northwards to Old Penrith and Carlisle (Luguvalium), southwards, via Low Borrow Bridge, to Lancashire and Chester, eastwards, via Catterick, to York, and westwards over the Lakeland fells, via High Street and Ambleside (Galava), to Ravenglass (Glannaventa), the port on the Cumbrian coast. The Romans built a fort at Brougham and there is evidence of a large, thriving village. Remains of the fort (Brocavum) can be seen in a field to the south of Brougham Castle. BROCAVUM was probably built, or rebuilt, in the second century and was occupied until the late fourth century. Its size suggests an occupation of up to a thousand troops of auxiliaries, and inscriptions indicate that both infantry

BROUGHAM

ABOVE: *Brougham Castle: the keep,* c. *1175, from the SE*

BELOW: *St Wilfrid's Chapel, SW of Brougham Castle. The C15 Flemish triptych was removed to the V & A Museum in 1968 for restoration*

Brougham Castle: chapel, c. *1300, in the SE corner of the keep*

and cavalry used it, doubtless to patrol the road system.

After the death of David I of Scotland, Henry II brought the area – Brougham had previously been under Scots tutelage – into English hands. Gospatric, son of Orm, was granted land and built a keep. Lordship passed to the Vipont family in the late twelfth century and to the Cliffords, through marriage, a century later; it remained with that family until the death of Lady Anne Clifford, last of the line, in 1676.

The original CASTLE would have consisted of the keep, with outer wooden buildings, and a stockade and ditch. Accommodation quarters, with protective stone curtain-walls, were progressively added from about the early thirteenth century. In later building programmes the keep was heightened, a south-west tower built, and the external defences improved, the keep being brought into the inner defences with the building of inner and outer gates.

The castle remains are substantial enough to stir the imagination. Entrance is by the outer gatehouse, which carries the inscription 'thys made Roger' (Roger was the fifth Lord Clifford). In the gate-hall beyond, an inscription records the repair of the structure in 1651 by Lady Anne Clifford. Passing through a small courtyard the inner gatehouse and the keep are reached; much of the

keep is well preserved and reveals some interesting details. Beyond this is the Great Chamber, now completely ruined, but further remains of buildings to the south, including hall, kitchen, chapel, and lodgings, can be seen. The south-west tower, the Tower of League, was built in the late thirteenth century by Robert Clifford and still stands to its top, third, floor. The moat and banks are likewise well preserved.

The chapel of St Wilfrid's, easily overlooked, is south-west of the castle. The chapel perhaps dates from the fourteenth century but certainly fell into disrepair until the seventeenth century, when it was taken in hand by Lady Anne Clifford. In the 1840s Lord Brougham and Vaux was responsible for some unfortunate alterations; he also introduced a miscellany of woodwork, belonging mainly to the sixteenth and seventeenth centuries.

A few km. north-east of the castle is the church of ST NINIAN. A Saxon church on this site was replaced by a Norman one, which in turn was heavily restored by Lady Anne Clifford in 1660. It is a fine example of Gothic Survival.

Broughton-in-Furness   3C6   (pop. 1,035)

There is nothing of any historical moment in Broughton but it does have an unusual character all its own, perhaps because it was built largely in the eighteenth century when the vernacular architecture was still traditional and 'untainted'. The MARKET SQUARE can hardly have changed over the last two centuries. A plaque on the market hall records that the square was designed in 1766; the clock, of the same date, still chimes out the hours. An obelisk is a memorial to John Gilpin, the donor of the land for the market. Stone slabs for the market stalls are still in evidence, but, alas, the Wednesday market has been lost to the larger attractions of other towns. Broughton, though, is still a place to stop and shop: it is a small, friendly community with the old traditions of hospitality.

Nearby BROUGHTON TOWER (not open to the public) was – from before the Norman Conquest – the seat of the Broughton family. The present nineteenth-century building is on the site of an ancient defensive tower. One of the better known of the Broughtons is Sir Thomas, although his tale is one of ignomony. When Lambert Simnel, having been crowned King of England in Dublin, landed in Furness in 1487 with 2,000 Flemish and Irish mercenaries Sir Thomas unwisely leant his support to the pretender's cause. After Simnel's defeat at Stokefield, near Newark, Henry VII punished all such supporters: Sir Thomas's possessions were seized and Broughton Tower was taken over by the Stanleys (and later sold to the Sawreys).

Sylvan, in his guide of 1847, remarks on the mild-air's contribution to the longevity of the inhabitants and points out that a tombstone in the churchyard records the death of Mrs Anne Walton at the age of 104 (d. 1791) and of Mr T. Walton at 101 (d. 1748).

Burgh-by-Sands   5C5   (pop. 830)

Burgh (pronounced 'bruff') is where Edward I, weary and ill and facing another campaign against the Scots, died at the age of sixty-eight. A monument of 1803, replacing one of 1685, supposedly marks the spot on which his tent was pitched.

There are many old cottages in the area. The CHURCH was built in 1181 – although little of this period remains – with stones taken from Hadrian's Wall. It is another of the few fortified churches in the Border lands; there parishioners could seek sanctuary during raids. The mid-fourteenth-century walls of the tower are 2m. thick and entrance has to be made through the church. The tower has only narrow windows, and, indeed, the church, disinclined to provide targets for raiders, lacked glass until the nineteenth century.

Horse racing was a regular feature at Burgh until 1900.

Burnmoor (Eskdale Fell)   3B4

Between Boot in Eskdale and Wasdale is a hump of heather-covered fell. This is Eskdale Fell, more commonly known as Burnmoor: a wild place in winter, it is delightful walking country in summer. A pony track from Boot village goes by Burnmoor Tarn, a tarn almost as large as Devoke Water, to Wasdale Head. There is evidence that in pre-Roman times the area was covered in oak wood and there are signs of Bronze Age settlement; some good examples of cairns are to be seen, particularly to the south of the tarn.

Before consecrated ground was available at Wasdale Head it was necessary to take corpses by pony over the Burnmoor track to the church of St Catherine at Boot. Funeral processions had to endure some hardship in bad weather and there are stories of ponies taking fright and bolting with their burdens. Perhaps inevitably there is an old tale that one such escape was never found and, so the tale goes, a ghostly pony carrying a coffin has ever since haunted the moor.

Burton-in-Kendal   2F1   (pop. 1,050)

Burton was a staging post in stagecoach days, a place where horses could be changed and refreshment taken. Now the motorway (M6) passes close by and, since there is a service area at this point, it would appear that the tradition, though with modern modifications, continues.

Burton is an attractive place of long standing: it is mentioned in the Domesday Book. Few of the buildings are very old but those with projecting storeys show the continuation of a building technique long past the period of its general usage. As in so many of the old villages, street and yard names are evocative: Neddy Hill, Tanpits Lane, Cocking Yard, Boon Walk.

Burton was once noted for its prosperous corn market, established in 1661, but this declined when communications to the larger towns improved in the nineteenth century. The market-place contains a cross of the eighteenth century; the recesses in the steps were for leg-irons. The old Norman church was very thoroughly restored in 1844 and 1872.

Buttermere 3B3

In the early days of tourism it was considered fashionable to rave about Buttermere. Buttermere was considered to be the quintessence of natural beauty, to show perfect harmony of form, and to be a refuge of peace and quiet. The still waters of the lake contrasted with the raging white becks pitching down the crag sides. The level mere and the soft lines of trees were equally matched with the wild craggy outlines of the fells behind. Hardly anything has changed; and though it is no longer fashionable to rave about the place, one may still be permitted to gasp a little at this gem of the English countryside.

The secondary road between Buttermere village and Honister Pass is on the north-eastern side of the lake. On the opposite side of the lake is a wall of high crags containing great hollow coves; there are three peaks: from left to right, High Crag (745m.), High Stile (805m.), and Red Pike (756m.). Dominating the scene at the head of the dale is HONISTER CRAG, its summit Fleetwith Pike (648m.).

Most of the land and the lake itself is owned by the NT, though the wooded shore at Hassness, between the road and the lake, is owned by the NP, the large house being let to the Ramblers' Association as a hostel. It is possible, given good footwear, to stroll by footpaths all round the lake, although care is needed to keep to the paths on the farmland at each end.

At its head Buttermere is fed by Warnscale Beck and by Gatescarthdale Beck. Gatescarthdale Beck, which runs alongside the road over Honister, is polluted by slate dust from the Honister Quarries. But rather than these sources, it is the becks falling from the High Stile ridge that contribute to the drama of Buttermere; these becks, notably Sour Milk Gill, which pours over the crags from Bleaberry Tarn, look particularly impressive after rain.

Buttermere varies in colour from green to blue to blue-grey, depending on the weather and the time of year. In squally weather wind currents whip up the lake into moving spirals of spray.

Buttermere village (*pop.* 255) is small; it has two good hotels and a very small church. In the early nineteenth century Buttermere was linked with a story containing all the ingredients of that period's melodrama (indeed, the story was produced on stage in a few of London's minor theatres). The story centred around the activities of a man falsely calling himself the Hon. Augustus Hope. He deceived a local girl, Mary Robinson (subsequently known as the 'Beauty of Buttermere'), into marrying him, but his falsity was soon discovered: he was arrested and hanged in Carlisle for forgeries against the Post Office. Authentic melodrama might require that the

girl should have been ruined; but in fact she married again, had a large family, and was buried in Caldbeck churchyard. An entertaining account of the whole episode is given by De Quincey in *Recollections of the Lakes and the Lake Poets.*

Caldbeck 3C1 (*pop.* 635)

Caldbeck is famous for its association with JOHN PEEL, the huntsman, who was born in 1776 and was the eldest of thirteen children. At the age of twenty-two he eloped with the eighteen-year-old daughter of a prosperous farmer from Uldale; although they went through a wedding ceremony at Gretna Green, they were later remarried in Caldbeck church. It was at this time that John Peel started hunting his own pack of hounds. The song 'D'ye ken John Peel' was written by his friend John Woodcott Graves, but the tune Graves used was different to the one that later became popular; the 'popular' tune was composed by Mr William Metcalfe, the organist at Carlisle Cathedral. Peel died at the age of seventy-eight and his pack of hounds was disbanded. His grave can be seen in the churchyard, to the left as the church door is approached.

The CHURCH is the only building of note in the village. Built on the site of St Mungo's Well, the evidence suggests that there was a religious building there as early as the sixth century. The Norman stone church dates from 1118 but there is little of the original structure identifiable.

Calder Abbey, Calder Bridge 3B4

Calder Bridge is a small village on the west-coast road. The ruins of Calder Abbey, a short distance from the village, stand by the banks of the River Calder. The ruins are very picturesque, quiet, and solitary, the walls too unsafe to allow free public access.

The abbey was founded for the order of Savigny, later united with the Cistercians, in 1134. A west doorway (the oldest surviving detail) remains with five high bays of the north aisle; the tower, now standing at 19½m., is half its original height. There are still the north- and south-transept arches; and part of the chancel survives.

The abbey suffered from the Scottish raids and its existence was at times a precarious one. In 1138 raiders drove the twelve monks away. They walked to Furness Abbey but, meeting with an oddly uncharitable reception, left, eventually finding their way to Byland in Yorkshire; there they founded another abbey. Calder Abbey was repossessed by Furness Abbey monks. It was dissolved in 1536.

Calder Hall 3A4

Calder Hall, with its two pairs of cooling towers and its reactor buildings, and WINDSCALE, with its high concrete towers and large spherical reactor, dominate the western landscape from many viewpoints, and in particular from the western fells. It is hardly possible to look at these

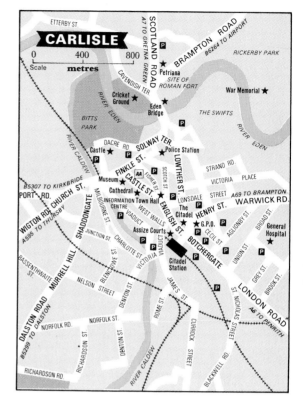

Calder Abbey from the NW

developments objectively: if they are a cruel intrusion into some magnificent scenery, they are also an inspiring and bold piece of design and something of a symbol (variously interpreted). Windscale, a major producer of plutonium, was opened by the United Kingdom Atomic Energy Authority in 1951. Calder Hall was the world's first full-scale nuclear power station: it opened in 1956. In 1958 there was a serious leak of radioactive material into the atmosphere, and worrying, if minor, incidents have occurred since. The large sphere is the Advanced Gas-cooled Reactor, put into operation in 1963.

Calder, River   3B4/A4
The Calder rises on Caw Fell, the bleak heights south of Ennerdale Water, and flows into the sea near Calder Hall. It contains salmon, sea trout, and brown trout. A point of interest on the river is MONK'S BRIDGE, east of the junction of the minor road with the Ennerdale road, $5\frac{1}{2}$km. from Calder Bridge: this pack-horse bridge is possibly the oldest bridge of its kind in Cumbria and was probably built by the Calder Abbey monks. The bridge is also variously referred to as High Wath, Matty Benn's Bridge, or Hannah Benn's Bridge. It was built without parapets to allow passage for horses' panniers.

Carlisle   5D5   (*pop.* 71,582)
Carlisle, a busy market and an industrial centre, is Cumbria's cathedral city. Its history is long and troubled: few other English cities can have endured so much strife and contention. Carlisle is still obviously a border town – Scottish accents and names are much in evidence and the Scottish border is only 15km. away – but there is little evidence in the modern city of the kind of pressures that once compelled the city's defenders to tear down the walls of the cathedral to make hasty re-pairs to the castle. There were many occasions in Car-lisle's history when 'border' effectively meant 'frontier'.

Carlisle acquired the status of a town and administra-tive centre during the Roman occupation, mainly be-cause of its strategic position and its easily-defended site (the River Eden is on one side and the Caldew and Petterill tributaries are on two other sides). The Roman town of Luguvalium was laid out on a typical Roman grid pattern and later towns, including the present one, have been built above it. Some of the Roman finds from excavations in the city are on view in the Tullie House Museum, along with other Roman objects from the sur-rounding area. The Roman fort at Stanwix, on the northern outskirts of the present city, protected the

Carlisle Castle

Roman town and was part of the defence system of Hadrian's Wall; all the stones from the fort have long since gone.

William the Conqueror's subjugation of England did not touch Carlisle, still held by Dolfin, a descendant of Saxon kings. But in 1092 William Rufus advanced 'with a great army', drove out Dolfin, and built a castle (probably of wood). He then drafted people into the city – Normans and Flemings and Saxon peasants from Kent, Essex, and Middlesex – to set up the town's industries and commerce and to till the land.

Henry I, William's successor, recognized the importance of Carlisle: in 1122 he founded a priory and in 1133 sent his confessor Aethulwulf to be the first bishop of the new see.

On Henry's death, Stephen took the throne, but the succession was a disputed one: in the North Stephen was opposed by David, King of the Scots, who supported the rival claimant Matilda. David sent his troops across the Border and took Carlisle and all the northern area of what is now Cumbria into Scotland; he died in Carlisle Castle in 1153. His successor, Malcolm, was forced to surrender the city to Henry II and the Border was again pushed back.

Malcolm's successor, William the Lion, demanded Northumberland's return to Scotland and also made two attempts to capture Carlisle Castle, on the second occasion unsuccessfully laying siege for three months with a force of 80,000 men. He eventually abandoned the attack and was defeated by Henry's forces at Alnwick.

During John's reign, Alexander II of Scotland took the castle at the second attempt and the land was again a Scottish territory; but in 1292 Edward I retook the city and tried to come to a final reckoning with Scotland. It was during this period that Carlisle Castle became a royal palace and was substantially improved. Two parliaments were held there, in 1300 and 1307.

Edward II was not able to contain the Scots as effectively as his father, and Robert the Bruce carried out crippling raids across the Border. After sacking Lanercost Priory in 1311 Bruce entered Carlisle, but was unable to take the castle. After Bruce's success at Bannockburn in 1314 he made another intensive attack on the castle but found its defences, under the command of Andrew D'Harcla, impregnable. He abandoned the attempt and instead contented himself with plundering raids all over Cumbria as far south as Furness Abbey. Andrew

D'Harcla was made Earl of Carlisle, but – such is the political life – became a Court scapegoat for mismanagement and was arrested by the Sheriff of Cumberland; the Earl was subsequently executed.

The Scottish raids continued and during the reign of Richard II Carlisle was twice besieged: the castle withstood all assaults but on one of the occasions the city was taken. Inevitably the castle fabric suffered damage from these attacks and during Edward IV's reign Richard of Gloucester was sent to take responsibility for the repair of the Border stronghold. Extensive repairs and alterations were put in hand under Richard's direction and, apparently suitably impressed, the Scots gave it a wide berth in ensuing troubles.

Under Elizabeth I a policy of reconciliation with the Border Scots was encouraged, but at the same time the Queen prudently ordered extensive repairs to Carlisle Castle. In 1568 Mary Queen of Scots, out of favour and defeated in her own country, fled to Cumbria and lodged in the castle. The green sward below the southern castle wall, where Mary took her exercise, has since been known as Lady's Walk. Although she was allowed the freedom to attend services at the cathedral and to hunt, she fell under increasing suspicion and was held virtually as a prisoner for two months before being sent to Bolton Castle.

For the next seventy years there was no serious conflict in the area beyond isolated incidents of castle-raiding and family feuding; although even such small-scale disturbances no doubt had a serious effect on the area's economy.

In 1644 the Civil War brought more strife to the city. Sir Thomas Glenham, Commander in Chief of the King's forces in the North, fled to Carlisle after York's surrender. General Lesley, a Scot, laid siege for Parliament with 4,000 troops but the castle held out, the inhabitants eventually being reduced to a diet of rats, dogs, and linseed meal; only when the Royalists heard of the defeat at Naseby did they lose hope and capitulate. The Parliamentarian forces – Presbyterian Scots – then repaired the castle, tearing down the abbey buildings and the canons' residences for stone: when this supply was discovered to be insufficient they even began removing stone from the cathedral. Six bays of the nave were destroyed in this way. Sir Phillip Musgrave took the castle for the King three years later but was forced to surrender it in the same year to Cromwell's troops, fresh from their success at Preston. The castle was quickly garrisoned by the Parliamentarians with 800 infantry and 1,200 cavalry and was used as a base for forays into Scotland. Then, for almost 100 years, Carlisle was left in peace.

In 1745 Charles Stuart's men under the Duke of Perth advanced on the city to find that the castle was both poorly garrisoned and poorly organized. The 700 hastily gathered, weary Cumbrians, with insufficient arms, surrendered after a week. On the day after the surrender

Carlisle Castle: carvings done by prisoners on a cell wall in the keep

the Prince proclaimed his father King of England at Carlisle Cross and, leaving a very small garrison in the castle, advanced south. Before the end of the same year Charles was back with a shattered and retreating army. Falling back across the Border, Charles left only 400 of his supporters to make a stand in Carlisle. The Duke of Cumberland ('Butcher Cumberland') took the city and castle without difficulty and pushed across the Border in pursuit of the remnants of Charles's army. After Culloden, Carlisle became a place of misery for many captured Jacobites. Both the castle and the cathedral were filled with prisoners, many of whom died in appalling conditions. Some of the prisoners were hanged at Harraby on the south-east side of the city, others were transported. Following the gruesome aftermath of the Jacobite defeat, Carlisle was left in comparative peace.

The castle, in the care of the Department of the Environment, is open to the public. Over the centuries it has been battered and repaired many times. The stonework contains Roman material from the settlement of Luguvalium (some still bearing the Roman masons'

Carlisle Castle: remains of C14 gatehouse

bewilderment to visitors from the quiet countryside of Cumbria and the Scottish Borderlands.

The city's industries are diverse, which has perhaps buffered the trade recession that has hit so many northern cities. Engineering firms make mine and quarry machinery, cranes, and safety equipment. Food factories make biscuits and confectionery and mill flour; a dried-milk plant processes twenty million gallons of Cumbrian milk per annum. Textile manufacturers produce fabrics of all kinds.

The history of Carlisle from the Roman occupation has very often been conditioned by the city's strategic and well-favoured position. It is a position that assures Carlisle's future.

Carlisle Cathedral 5D5

One of the most obvious features of Carlisle Cathedral is its small size: among English cathedrals only Oxford is smaller. Carlisle Cathedral was not always so small; but troubled times – and in particular a serious fire in 1292 and partial demolition by the Parliamentarians during the Civil War – combined with friable stone to leave the present truncated structure.

Although as early as *c.* 1102 a site for the foundation of a religious establishment was provided by Henry I, building probably did not begin until Ranulph de Meschines had left Carlisle. Henry introduced Augustinian Canons and, in 1133, made the town the see of a bishop: the priory accordingly became Carlisle Cathedral and was the only Augustinian house in England to achieve such status.

The early years were hard: the see was poor, vacant for some of the time, and not unaffected by the turbulence of secular politics. But the cathedral had been built. Of the early building little remains; what there is can be seen in the south transept and the nave (now the Border Regiment Chapel). The depressed Norman arches are a structural abberation; they perhaps serve to remind that medieval building on this scale fell down almost as often as it stayed up. The Norman cathedral is externally quite distinct: built of dark-grey stone, probably taken from Hadrian's Wall or from the remains of Luguvalium, it contrasts strongly with the red sandstone used in later building.

A decision to extend the Norman cathedral was taken in the early thirteenth century and building had probably begun by 1225: the new plan allowed for a seven-bay choir and the addition of a short aisleless chancel.

The fire of 1292, already alluded to, greatly damaged the fabric of the cathedral. The rebuilding that followed gave Carlisle most of its Decorated features, including the magnificent east window, the largest example of Flowing Decorated in England (15m. high and 8m. across). There is little original glass but the tracery – said to have been struck from 263 different centres – is imposing and delightful.

By the end of the fourteenth century the cathedral was

marks), old grey sandstone removed from Hadrian's Wall, and stone from the abbey and cathedral. The earliest portion of the castle, the keep (*c.* 1150), is in excellent repair, although – even for a keep – is bleak and depressing. The carvings done by prisoners in the wall of a cell on the east side of the second floor are of interest: only the most unreflecting can fail to be moved. A military exhibition occupies part of the castle buildings.

If the castle took some punishment, the city of course took even more. Little remains of the city wall: much of the material that had survived the troubles and battles of earlier centuries was destroyed by the developers and 'improvers' of the nineteenth century.

Carlisle is the 'capital' of Cumbria, housing most of the County Council's administrative offices, the region's local BBC radio station, and the studios of a commercial television company. It is still an important main-line railway centre and has its own city airfield; but neither the opening of the M6 motorway nor a (confusing) one-way system have solved its traffic problem. Carlisle remains what it has perhaps always been: a source of

LEFT: *Carlisle Cathedral: choir and E window*   ABOVE: *Carlisle Cathedral: the Salkeld Screen*

largely in the form that it displays today (but the Norman nave was still at its full extent). In points of detail, though, there was much of importance still to be added; and many of the additions were inspired by Bishop William Strickland. The tower as we now see it is largely the work of his time – it is admittedly a rather sad, squat affair, but it was then surmounted by a spire – the rebuilding of the north transept is also Strickland's responsibility, together with the Perpendicular strainer arch, and the forty-six well-preserved stalls with large and vigorously-worked misericords are from the same period. The paintings on the back of the choir stalls, restored in 1936, are of the late fifteenth century; they represent stories from the life of St Augustine, and St Cuthbert, and St Anthony, and also the twelve Apostles: the level of artistic achievement is well below that of similar work done on the Continent.

The Reformation in some ways marked the nadir of the cathedral's fortunes (although in terms of damage to the building, the next century was little short of catastrophic) and the Renaissance Salkeld Screen is a physical – not unpretty – embodiment of the new order: secular motifs, such as the Tudor rose and the Tudor beasts, seem to have virtually ousted the conventional religious symbols and devices.

The Civil War siege of 1644–5 was the event that directly led to the partial demolition of the cathedral by Parliamentary forces, though we may suspect that a combination of neglect and sheer age had perhaps reduced some of the fabric to a dangerous condition. Charles I himself, in 1639, warned of the 'ruines into which it [the cathedral] is now lyke to fall'. At any event, six bays of the nave were pulled down and the chapter house was demolished. (The upper part of the fratry subsequently became the chapter house.)

The cathedral was more lucky with its Victorian

TOP: *There is a delightful variety of misericords – of which this is one – in Carlisle Cathedral. Not by any means the highest expression of their art form, they are nevertheless full of life.*

BOTTOM: *Carlisle Cathedral, chancel: capital representing the month of July; early-C14. The other months of the year are similarly symbolized*

restorers (principally Ewan Christian and G. E. Street): they had occasional lapses of taste (eg the removal of the single Perpendicular windows from each choir aisle), but generally the handling was sensitive. The semi-circular chancel ceiling of oak was restored by Owen Jones in the 1850s; the present decoration – stars on a blue background – is his, but he did also replace many of the coats of arms of local families that were originally on the medieval roof.

Carrock Fell   3D2

On the eastern end of the Caldbeck Fells, above the Caldew, is Carrock Fell. It is not conspicuous for its height (662m.) but it is attractive in every other way. It is one of the most remarkable fells in Cumbria.

Geologically, the fell is extraordinarily complex, and it would reward years of study. The material of which the fell is composed is volcanic, and twenty-three minerals have been identified. At the Carrock Mines (closed) tungsten was found in quantity together with wolfram and scheelite. The rocks include gabbro, granophyre, and felsite.

The FORT on the summit is an archaeological puzzle. The date must be pre-Roman and there have been suggestions that it was a stronghold of the Brigantes. But for a fort of its age it was a major one: the dimensions are 244m. by 112m.; the walls must have been massive. Various theories have been expressed about the gaps in the walls; Collingwood's suggestion is that the Romans, having taken the fort, methodically rendered it useless by throwing down large sections. Heavy masonry suggests gateways in the south, east, and west. It is pleasant to climb up and speculate.

Cartmel   3D6

The village of Cartmel, due west of Grange-over-Sands, is an extraordinary delight: it contains seventeenth-, eighteenth-, and nineteenth-century buildings clustered around secluded yards, a village square complete with village pump, and a Norman priory church of exceptional beauty and interest. The village is a magnet for artists (there are a number of galleries). The whole form of the settlement suggests a quiet coziness, although, alas, the atmosphere of the village is often rather spoilt by the intrusion of parked cars.

The church dominates all and it has an endearing touch of eccentricity – a tower set diagonally on another tower – architecturally an aberration but an aberration that has stood defiant over the centuries. There is a legend that the choice of the present site was dictated supernaturally to the monks, who were told to build between two rivers, one flowing north, the other south.

CARTMEL PRIORY was founded by William Marshall, Baron of Cartmel and Earl of Pembroke, in *c*. 1188 for Canons Regular of St Augustine. With it William Marshall endowed all the Cartmel land, which extended northwards to the east side of Windermere, and some

C15 stalls, Cartmel Priory. The stall backs are the gift of George Preston of Holker Hall (1620s)

lands in Ireland. Now nothing can be seen of the priory except the church and a gatehouse (NT). The destruction at the Dissolution was thorough, the Earls of Derby and Sussex acting as Henry VIII's Commissioners. The lands were confiscated, all metals were stripped from the buildings, including the lead from the church roof, and the summary destruction of the church was only prevented by documentary evidence that the founder ordained that an altar and a priest be provided for the people. The Commissioners appealed for guidance and it was stated that as the laws were directed towards the dissolution of monasteries, not parish churches, so a portion of the church, the south aisle, could be preserved for the parish. The rest of the church was in a bad state and open to the weather until, in 1620, a benefactor, George Preston of Holker, with help from parishioners, began restoration. The church was roofed, and the very fine Renaissance screens and stall canopies were presented by the benefactor. Further necessary restoration

Cartmel Priory: one of the beautifully carved misericords

was carried out in 1859 by the seventh Duke of Devonshire.

Because it was largely built in a transitory period and has been altered since, the church contains a variety of architectural styles. The great east window dates from the middle of the fifteenth century: the surviving medieval glass, including the Virgin and Child, and John the Baptist, was cleaned and reset in 1964. Some other glass from Cartmel, removed at the Dissolution, can be seen in a window at St Martin's church, Bowness-on-Windermere. In the middle of the fifteenth century work on the tower and nave was done, but the fact that the nave is short and is built with irregular stones suggests that funds were short.

Dog-tooth moulding can be seen above the north door. In the north transept can be seen the church's only Early English window. The arch into the Piper Choir is oddly formed, of Gothic shape but bearing Norman chevron moulding. Only in the Piper Choir is the original roof intact.

To some people, especially children, the best feature of the church is the beautifully carved oak MISERICORDS, which fortunately survived the years of ruin that spoiled the bench heads. The carver, or carvers, betray a monkish sense of humour: there is a mermaid with two tails, an ape doctor, and a number of grotesque faces, as well as carvings of The Trinity, Alexander's Flight, Pelican in Piety, Elephant and Castle, a Unicorn, and some intricate foliage decoration.

Of the tombs, the oldest intact is that of the first Lord Harrington (d. 1347) and his wife. There is also an effigy of an unknown priest. Some of the tablets in the floor are of interest. One is in memory both of a young man who was drowned on the sands (probably when crossing to or from Lancaster) and of his mother who, not long afterwards, was drowned on the same spot. Amongst early documents owned by the church is a first edition of Spenser's *Faerie Queene*; this was stolen in the 1930s but brought back after the thief had tried, unsuccessfully, to sell it in America.

The atmosphere of the church is very moving and one has to be indifferent indeed not to feel some consciousness of the centuries of continuous worship.

Cartmel caters for the secular too. Appropriately sited at the opposite end of the village centre to the church is a RACE-COURSE.

Castlerigg Stone Circle (Keswick Stone Circle)   3C3
E of Keswick

The Castlerigg Stone Circle is reached by taking the Penrith road from Keswick, and then taking the first branch road, a narrow one, to the right. The early guide-books referred to the remains as 'The Druids' Circle', and there was a ridiculous legend invented to go with it, repeated by several authors, telling of a maiden about to be sacrificed by fire but saved by a miraculous deluge of waters gushing from the ring of fells. In fact stone circles of this kind pre-date the coming of the Druids by many centuries: they are generally Late Neolithic or Early Bronze Age, somewhere between 3,000 and 4,000 years old. One can only guess at their purpose: there is no evidence to support the contention that the sites were used for human sacrifice. The circles were probably places of worship; it is argued convincingly that they may also have been 'calendars' to guide the early farmers in sowing and harvesting.

The Castlerigg circle is differently placed in relation to the other stone circles in the county. The others generally occur round the high land, and on the fringes: the Cumbrian coast, the Cumbrian plain, and the Eden Valley. Keswick's circle is in the fell centre and its setting adds very much to the drama. There is a strong possibility that the site was chosen for the setting. If so, this is

Castlerigg Stone Circle

unusual; it could hardly be said of most of the others. It is calculated that the view from the natural amphitheatre in which the circle is set takes in all the high peaks on a circumference of about 160km. On a clear day one can hardly be unmoved by the effect; even if the weather is poor it is still strangely evocative. Keats wrote of it:

> a dismal cirque
> Of Druid stones, upon a forlorn moor,
> When the chill rain begins at shut of eve,
> In dull November, and their chancel vault,
> The Heaven itself, is blinded throughout night.

(*Hyperion* II 34–8.)

The Castlerigg circle is slightly oval. There remain forty-eight stones, some of them quite bulky, and on the east side is an unexplained, and unusual, oblong 'chamber' within the circle. The size of the circle is roughly 30m. by 33m.

Cat Bells   3C3   E of Stair

The oddly-named fell has an odd shape: that of a camel-hump. To strollers from Keswick it is one of the most familiar views from Derwent Water's east shore, and to many holidaymakers it is irresistible, it looks so green and pleasant and easy: it is, after all, only 452m. high. But, of all the fells in Cumbria, Cat Bells has the reputation of collecting among the highest number of minor accidents, simply because it attracts people who are not used to walking, or have the wrong footwear. In certain conditions the grass can be as slippery as ice. And the fell is full of old mine shafts and mine levels, not all of which can be guaranteed as filled in and protected. Miraculously, no one in recent years has met a sticky end. All that said, Cat Bells offers some of the most beautiful views in Cumbria.

Ascent is usually made from Hawse End, at the fell's northern tip. Newlands Valley is on its western side, with Little Town, familiar to readers of Beatrix Potter, below the southern end of the fell. Mrs Tiggy Winkle's house is in the Cat Bells hillside above the hamlet.

Causey Pike   3C3

Seen from Derwent Water's east shore is a very prominent fell in the middle-distance, with an odd knob poking up to the left of its summit. This is Causey Pike, a great pile of Skiddaw Slate. This type of rock, given to angular shapes, invariably suggests a greater height than the true measurement. Causey is only 620m. high. It looks formidable.

Causey Pike belongs to Newlands Valley, from which the fell's eastern spur, Rowling End, offers the best line of ascent; but the summit ridge is rough.

Chapel Stile *see* **Great Langdale**

Claife Heights   3D5   W of Windermere

Claife Heights is a heavily wooded eminence on the west side of Windermere, north of the ferry. The mixed hard-

wood and softwood plantings, which overlook the lake and look so attractive in spring and autumn, are in the care of the NT. Beyond the NT land is an extensive area planted mainly with spruce and larch by the Forestry Commission. The woodland has a population of roe deer and red deer and is the haunt of the red squirrel.

Claife Heights is served with a network of footpaths and bridle paths. The views from the top overlooking Windermere are very beautiful. On the western slopes are several tarns: a bridle track passes near Wise Een Tarn and Moss Eccles Tarn. There are fine views over Wise Een Tarn towards the Langdales. The Heights can be approached from Near and Far Sawrey, from the ferry, or from the road on the lake shore between the ferry and Wray Castle.

The Crier of Claife was a ghost who, tradition has it, haunted the Heights of Claife. The phantom was exorcized by a priest who put the spirit to rest, it is said, in a quarry. The quarry in question is known as Crier of Claife Quarry.

Cockermouth 3B2 (*pop.* 6,363)

The town of Cockermouth has a fine, wide, tree-lined street, at the far end of which is a Georgian house that has made Cockermouth famous. The fame derives not from any architectural merits of the building but from its associations, for it was here, in 1770, that William Wordsworth was born. The house is now in the ownership of the NT and two rooms are open to the public between Easter and the end of September, except Fridays and Sundays.

The CASTLE, on the east side of the town, has been in existence since the twelfth century. The original structure was built by Waltheof, son of Gospatric, Earl of Dunbar, in 1134; little of it remains. Some of the stones for the castle were obtained from the Roman fort at Papcastle (Derventio). Much of the structure seen today dates from the fourteenth century although some of the lower courses of masonry date from the mid thirteenth century. The castle has had a troubled history. It was greatly harassed by the Scottish raids and particularly by Robert the Bruce. During the Wars of the Roses it was a disputed strongpoint: it was held by Lancastrian forces until the battle of Towton Moor, after which it passed to the Yorkists. In the Civil War the castle was held for Parliament under Major Bird and held out for two months against an attack led by Sir William Huddleston; relief finally came from Parliamentary forces sent from Lancashire. After the Civil War the castle was allowed to fall into ruin until some restoration was done during the last century by General Wyndham. The castle is open to the public when Lord Egremont, the present owner, is not in residence.

LEFT: *Castlerigg Stone Circle: the chamber stones. Helvellyn is in the distant background*

Cockermouth Castle: the outer gatehouse, essentially c. *1360–70*

JOHN DALTON, propounder of the atomic theory, was born of Quaker stock in the nearby village of Eaglesfield on 6 September 1766. He showed an early genius and was appointed a schoolmaster at Pardshaw Hall at the age of thirteen. He afterwards left there for a private school in Kendal. He published papers on his atomic theory in 1802, 1803, and 1804.

FLETCHER CHRISTIAN, born in 1764 at Moorland Close, Cockermouth, was altogether a more infamous native of the town: he was the leader of the mutiny on the *Bounty*.

Colwith Falls   3D4   s of Elter Water

The River Brathay, flowing from Little Langdale Tarn, drops down a series of falls at Colwith before turning north into Elter Water. The falls were at one time a great tourist attraction, and they are certainly attractive after heavy rain. But the approach to the falls is now difficult and even hazardous, and the land is not open to the public. The land on the south side of the river is in the ownership of the NT, but the approach this way is also difficult and wet.

Conishead Priory   1D1

Conishead Priory is by the side of the short road between Ulverston and Barrow. The first building, erected in the twelfth century as a hospital for the relief of the poor and for the care of lepers, was later converted into an Augustinian priory. The priory owned land in Great Langdale at Baysbrown.

The priory changed hands several times after the Dissolution; and in 1821 a Colonel Bradyl demolished the building and built himself a country seat. Typical of the time, the building was ornamented with battlements, mouldings, and ostentatious decoration. It was designed by Phillip Wyatt. The owner sold out some time later and since then the priory has been used as a rest and convalescent home for Durham miners. It is not open to the public.

Coniston   3C5   (*pop.* 1,060)

The grey village of Coniston has almost as dramatic a setting as the town of Keswick. Behind it crowd the wild and rough craggy summits characteristic of the Borrowdale Volcanics, but it sits on a floor of slates and shales looking across the expanse of Coniston Water to the heavily-wooded, rounded hills of the eastern shores. Its geology was the reason for its growth: rock weaknesses at junctions are often exploited by surfacing volcanic magma, exposing important minerals. Coniston became a mining village in the eighteenth century and extracted great wealth from its fell side. As the mines became uneconomic another geological bonus was at hand. The 'slate', a form of intensely compressed volcanic dust, found on the edge of the Borrowdale Volcanics, cleaves easily and is almost metallic in hardness. The rock takes a high polish and is much favoured for facing buildings; it is exported all over the world.

The COPPER MINES were probably in operation from Norman times, but much more actively from the sixteenth century, when it was recorded that German miners from Keswick were used; the ore was carried by pack-horse on what must have been a very laborious journey to the Keswick smelters. Later the mines at the head of Church Beck (still called Coppermines Valley) were more efficiently exploited and were worked until the end of the 1914–18 war. The railway to the village, originally planned to carry the slate and ore, was linked to the Furness Railway at a junction near Broughton; it was opened in 1859. The railway is, alas, no more. Since the end of the railway the village has declined in popularity in comparison with other towns and villages. DOW CRAG on Old Man of Coniston, once the mecca of enthusiastic rock climbers, has lost much of its popularity to other more easily accessible crags in Langdale and Borrowdale.

CONISTON HALL is the oldest building in Coniston and is by the lake shore south of the village. With its tall cylindrical chimneys, typical of its time, it looks rather like a steamer ready to launch off into the lake. It was the home of the Flemings, the largest local landowners, and was built in the sixteenth century: it is cruck-framed and has some unusual architectural features for its age, notably the large windows. In more recent years it has been altered and used as a barn and store for the farm, but now, in the care of the NT, it is in process of restoration; the aim is to return it to its seventeenth-century condition.

Coniston is noted for two completely opposite people: John Ruskin and Donald Campbell.

JOHN RUSKIN, who lived at Brantwood (qv) on the east side of Coniston Water for twenty-five years, died in

CONISTON WATER

1900. For his quarter century of residence he was the object of a local awe that has lasted until today. A monument of local stone, designed by a local artist, W. Collingwood, and consisting of a large decorated cross of Coniston stone cut from the quarry at Tilberthwaite, marks his grave in the churchyard. An explanation of the intricate design can be read in the local Ruskin Museum.

The second notable character was a very frequent visitor rather than a resident. DONALD CAMPBELL was killed on the lake in 1967 (*see* Coniston Water). His memorial is in the form of a slate seat on a green in the village centre.

The RUSKIN MUSEUM was built to honour Coniston's most notable resident. It contains some of his studies and pictures, and many letters, manuscripts, and photographs. There are also a collection of geological specimens, an assortment of local Neolithic objects taken from burial mounds in the locality, and some fine pictures by W. Collingwood. Placed oddly and incongruously in the museum is a panel of pictures of Donald Campbell during his fatal attempt at the water speed record.

Coniston Old Man range *see* **Old Man of Coniston range**

Coniston Water 3C5
Before the coming of the motor car, Coniston Water was one of the most popular lakes because of good rail access by the Furness Railway. The journey from the main line at Broughton-in-Furness was particularly beautiful. The railway line is now closed. At one time the Furness Railway also operated a steamer service on the lake. This no longer exists, although the remains of the boat, the *Gondola*, can be seen at the southern end of the lake. There has been some discussion about the possibility of restoration.

The lake lies between the Borrowdale Volcanics to its west and the Silurian rocks to its east. The views from the lake change in accordance with the different geology: dramatic and craggy on one side and rounded and heavily afforested on the other. The lake is fed by a number of fast-flowing becks near the lake head, most of the waters coming from the Old Man of Coniston range. The lake, 56m. deep at its deepest point, is about 8½km. long, and 804m. wide. It has only three small islands. Peel Island, in the southern reaches, is the Wild Cat Island in the popular children's book *Swallows and Amazons*. The islands are in the care of the NT.

Most of the lake shores of Coniston are available to the public. The shore south of Coniston village at Coniston Hall Park and Water Park is in the ownership of the NT. South of Hoathwaite, Torver Back Common, which fronts onto the lake for a considerable distance, is in the

RIGHT: *John Ruskin's tombstone, by W. Collingwood*

ownership of the NP. After the common the A5084 comes close to the lake shore; it finally leaves by the popular picnic area of Old Brown Howe, also owned by the NP.

The east shore, north of Water Park, is largely in the ownership of the NT and the Forestry Commission. The road on this side of the lake is very narrow and on busy days in the holiday season becomes congested.

There have been human settlements in the area around Coniston Water since the Bronze Age, and there was considerable settlement during the Norse period. Coniston Water was originally known as Thurston's Mere, the mere of the Lord Thurston. After the Norman Conquest the land at the head of the lake and the whole of the land to the east came into the ownership of Furness Abbey, and from that time the woodlands and the minerals of the area were exploited. Coniston Water was used as a highway and it is, to this day, in law still a public highway. Ore from the mines at the head of the lake was carried down in barges to the foot of the lake, then transported by road the short distance to the quay at Greenodd.

One of the most important industries of southern Lakeland, particularly round the lower reaches of Coniston and Windermere, was the production of charcoal. This industry made huge demands on the southern woodlands. The charcoal was so vital to the smelting of metals that it was sometimes more economical to bring the ore to the charcoal-producing woodlands; iron from the Furness mines would often be brought up the lake and smelted in small bloomeries. Traces of these bloomeries can be found in many places on the lake shore, where masses of clinker are mixed with the lake-shore pebbles. It is not known how long these bloomeries were in action but they were certainly operative from the fifteenth to the seventeenth century, and there are doubtless more ancient bloomeries in the area. At one time the whole of the fells around the lake were covered in forest, but the woodlands were continuously plundered for the manufacture of charcoal. There is no natural forest left: the hardwoods on the lake shore have, for the most part, been planted from the nineteenth century onwards, and on the east side the huge block of conifer forest spreading over from Grizedale was planted by the Forestry Commission.

Coniston Water holds trout, char, pike, and perch. Boating activity is concentrated at the head of the lake, near the village, where there are boats for hire. Coniston Yacht Club has its headquarters at Coniston Hall.

The lake, a quieter expanse of water than Windermere, has been used on several occasions for attempts at the world's water speed record. The last attempt was in 1967; in this attempt Donald Campbell was killed when his boat somersaulted at an estimated speed of 515km.p.h. This occurred in the upper reaches of the lake over very deep water and Donald Campbell's body and most of the wreckage have never been recovered.

Corby Castle 6E5

Corby Castle sits across the river from Wetheral, southeast of Carlisle. It originated with a thirteenth-century (?) pele tower erected by the Salkeld family; only a fragment of the tower now remains. In 1611 the Salkelds sold out to Lord William Howard, third son of the Duke of Norfolk, and he built a house onto the tower. In 1809 Peter Nicholson, a well-known architect, was commissioned by Henry Howard to modernize the house, and the present mansion is the result.

The grounds (open to the public on Thursdays) were laid out by Thomas Howard (d. 1740).

The Gondola, *photograph of 1890*

The derelict Gondola

Crinkle Crags 3C4

Looking across to the Langdale Valley from the eastern viewpoints, a serrated ridge of rock appears as a great wall in the head of the dale on its western side. The ridge is the aptly-named Crinkle Crags. For well-equipped walkers in clear weather it is one of the best ridge walks in the country. Seen from the Langdale Valley there are five 'crinkles', one to the left and four grouped together. The highest point (858m.) is the left one of the group, though its true summit is hidden.

The crags can be approached from Langdale or from Wrynose; the less direct and more gradual way is via Red Tarn, but that way is very rough and scrambly. Walkers on the fell frequently lose themselves in poor visibility as the ridge walk nowhere follows a straight line.

Crosby Garrett 4F4 (*pop.* 105)

Crosby Garrett is a hamlet with some old houses, and with a part-Anglo-Saxon church high on a hill. The builders must have had a sound reason for putting it there, but local legend has it that the Devil saw the stones ready to build the church at the bottom of the hill, popped them in his apron, and carried them to the top to make the true way as difficult as possible. The church has some interesting carvings, and the builders have gone to the trouble to make a hagioscope, a hole in the wall, to allow the congregation in the north aisle to see the altar.

Crosby Ravensworth 4E3 (*pop.* 535)

Crosby Ravensworth is a neat and attractive village east of Shap. The original fabric of the church of ST LAWRENCE probably dates from the twelfth century, but much alteration and restoration has been undertaken over the centuries, particularly following damage from Scottish raids. There still remains quite a fine Early English doorway. Restoration work was done by Robert Smirke in 1811 when he took time off from his labours at Lowther Castle (*see* Lowther). Further restoration was put in hand between 1865 and 1880. A memorial by

Crummock Water

David Dunbar (1792–1866), representing Faith, Hope, and Charity, is to George Gibson, the instigator of the 1811 restoration work.

South-west of the village are the remains of a large settlement, one of the most important in the north of England. (There are no less than seven others in the area.) The settlement, EWE CLOSE, is a complicated system of enclosure walls and hut circles measuring about 213m. by 167m. In the main, and more regularly-shaped, enclosure is a large hut base (chief's hut or assembly hall?) 15m. in diameter. The suggestion that the settlement is pre-Roman carries conviction: the Roman road from Lancaster to Carlisle, which passes 18m. to the west of the settlement, seems to make a deliberate detour to visit the site.

Cross Fell   4F2

In 1747 a geographer described Cross Fell as 'a mountain that is generally ten months bury'd in snow, and eleven in clouds'. Cross Fell is the highest point in the Pennines (893m.), but the description is libellous.

When volcanic magna breaks through into the earth's crust it sometimes forces its way horizontally along the bedding plane of sedimentary rocks. In subsequent erosions this table rock protects the softer rock below while all around may crumble away. The result is a steep-faced hill with a large summit plateau. Such is Cross Fell, the volcanic rock being part of the Whin Sill, which also supports Hadrian's Wall to the north-east. Every aspect of Cross Fell appears austere; but there is evidence to indicate that at one time this now treeless fell had forest growing to within 150m. of its summit.

Cross Fell has long been well known for the HELM WIND, a violent wind generated by strong north-easterlies scouring over the peculiar configuration of the mountain mass; the air stream behaves rather like a torrent of water pouring over a weir. While air further west might be calm, a furious wind can be damaging the roofs of houses below the western escarpment.

Crummock Water   3B3

Crummock Water is separated from Buttermere by an 800m. strip of low-level land. This was formed from deposits of eroded material laid down after the Ice Age, before the land was stabilized by vegetation. Because the whole of the area around the lake is of the Skiddaw Slate Series, Crummock Water lacks the dramatic, craggy background of Buttermere. The lake is about 4km. long and 1km. wide. It is in the ownership of the NT.

The lake's narrowest point is at the upper reach where the rock is hardest. On the east side is Hawes Point and above this is a hill known as Rannerdale Knotts: it is a scramble on rough ground to reach the hill's summit but it affords an excellent view of the lake.

The secondary road on the east side runs close to the lake and, as the land is owned by the NT, there is access

on foot at other points. There are no facilities for boat launching.

The lake contains pike, perch, trout, and char.

Dacre   3D3   (pop. 965)

The village of Dacre is found off a by-road between the A592 at the foot of Ullswater and the A66. The CHURCH is one of the most interesting in the area. It almost certainly stands on the site of a Saxon monastery mentioned by the Venerable Bede in his *History*. Virtually all that remains of the Saxon structure are traces of foundations and an old drain. The present church dates from Norman times, although of course it carries subsequent additions and modifications. The round piers are of the mid thirteenth century. The octagonal piers show some reconstruction around 1400. The Norman west tower was

Dacre Castle: battlemented approach to the W turret

The four bears of St Andrew's, Dacre. LEFT *to* RIGHT, TOP *to*
BOTTOM: *Sleeping bear; bear attacked by cat; bear tries to
shake off cat; bear eats cat*

rebuilt in 1810. A windowsill in the late-twelfth-century chancel has a piece of cross-shaft with a carving showing a winged creature, probably dating from about 800. On the south side of the chancel is a stone with a carving, traditionally said to represent the 'Peace of Dacre' signed in 926 between Athelstan of England and Constantine of Scotland. In the churchyard are four mysterious stones of unknown origin. It is suggested that they may originally have come from Dacre Castle. They represent four bears; anti-clockwise from the north-west, the first bear is asleep with his head on a pillar, the second bear is attacked by a cat, the third bear tries to shake the cat off, and the fourth bear eats the cat.

The NORMAN CASTLE of Dacre is approached by a public footpath opposite the little green in the village centre. It is open to the public only by written appointment and only in the summer months. The castle is on the site of an earlier structure, but the present building was erected in the early fourteenth century; its fortunes varied with those of the Dacre family. Leonard Dacre unwisely led a rebellion against Elizabeth I and was defeated close by the River Gelt in 1569 by forces under Lord Hunsdon, Elizabeth's cousin. The castle was restored under the ownership of the Earl of Sussex in 1675 and there was further restoration in 1789.

Dalemain 3D2

Dalemain is the large Georgian-fronted house visible from the Ullswater–Penrith road (A592). It has been the ancestral home of the Hasells since 1665. Much of the land around Ullswater, including Martindale Forest with its herd of red deer, is in the ownership of the Dalemain Estates. A herd of fallow deer is kept in the grounds of the house itself.

Plans to open the house and grounds to the public are currently being discussed.

Dalton-in-Furness 1D1 (pop. 11,235)

Dalton was once the principal town in Furness. For four centuries the monks of Furness Abbey held their courts in Dalton and it was an important market town.

The CASTLE was built by the Abbot of Furness as a refuge from Scots raiders. The tower had a ground floor with two rooms, and three floors above. Repairs to floors and roof were ordered by Henry VIII; and with unconscious symbolism stone from the Furness Abbey walls was used. The castle served as a prison until the eighteenth century, and courts were regularly held there until the twentieth century. There was some restoration work done in 1856. The building is now owned by the NT and houses a small exhibition; admission is gained on local application.

The decline of Dalton came, it is said, when the town was stricken by the plague, alleged to have been brought in from Walney in a bale of ribbons. It is recorded that when the disaster came many left their homes and camped in the fields. Some prosperity returned when

mining developed. During its operation Park Mine produced 7,000,000 tons of iron ore. The town was also noted for its maltmaking industry.

GEORGE ROMNEY, the great portrait painter, was born in Dalton in 1734. He died in Kendal in 1802 and is buried in Dalton churchyard. His stone is marked simply 'Pictor Celeberrimus'.

Most people now look on Dalton as a shopping street on the way to Barrow. The old part of the town with the castle is at the end of the street beyond the Barrow turning.

Dent 4F6 (pop. 590)

'Dent Town' is a village at the head of a small dale south of Sedbergh. It is sought out as a typical dales' village with typical cobbled streets, but fortunately it has not been vulgarized by tourism, and should be able to rely on the protection afforded by being in the Yorkshire Dales National Park. One of its greatest sons was ADAM SEDGWICK (1785–1873), the pioneer geologist. He was educated at Dent and Sedbergh (where else?) and Trinity College, Cambridge, and was appointed Woodwardian Professor of Geology, a post that he transformed from a mere sinecure and held until shortly before his death. A memorial of Shap Granite stands by the church.

Wool made Dent. Southey referred to 'the terrible knitters of Dent'; everyone knitted, young and old.

Dent stone, because it did not contain iron pyrites likely to raise dangerous sparks, was valued for mill stones used in gunpowder works.

The church has portions dating from the early thirteenth century and seventeenth-century pews.

Higher up-valley, south of the River Dee, is WHERNSIDE MANOR, built by a Liverpool merchant, a Mr Sill, in the late eighteenth century. Mr Sill was a slavetrader and it is said his manor-house, then called West House, was provided with an ample retinue of black servants. It is now an Outdoor Pursuits Centre catering for potholers.

At the foot of the valley is BRIGFLATTS, where there is a Quaker Meeting House dating from the seventeenth century. George Fox, founder of the Quakers, was strongly supported by the dalesmen of these parts. In his journal he wrote (1677): 'The first day following I had a meeting at Brigflatts, to which most of the Friends from the several meetings round, with a great concourse of other people, came; it was thought there were five or six hundred people. A very good meeting it was, wherein truth was largely declared, to the comforting and refreshing of the faithful, and the drawing near them that were afar off'.

Derwent, River 3C4/C3/C2/B2/A2

There are several Derwents in Britain. The word is probably of Celtic origin, meaning 'white water' or 'clear water'. The description is apt for the Lake

Taken on Friars Crag, looking across Derwent Water towards Borrowdale

District's best-known river, which has its sources in the highest land in England, and flows for some 53km., through Derwent Water and Bassenthwaite Lake, westwards through Cockermouth, where it is joined by the River Cocker, and then into the sea at Workington. The river is fished for salmon, sea trout, trout, pike, perch, and herling.

Derwent Water   3C3

A short walk from Keswick brings one to the boat landings at Derwent Water and, a short distance further on, to FRIARS CRAG, one of the finest viewpoints in Britain. The view along the levels of the lake to the rugged backcloth of the Borrowdale Fells, together with the framework of broad-leaved woodlands, offers a complete harmony of form. Few people would have appreciated that better than John Ruskin, first Slade Professor of Art at Oxford. His memorial is by the crag and on it Ruskin is quoted as saying that a visit here was the first event he remembered in his life.

Derwent Water is about 4·8km. long and about 1·8km. wide. It is a shallow lake, reaching a depth of 22m.: for this reason it is one of the first lakes to freeze after a period of hard frost, offering some wonderful skating. Derwent Water is fed from scores of sources. The main body of water comes from the head of Borrowdale – Sty Head Tarn, Sprinkling Tarn, Langstrath, and Honister – and down through the River Derwent. Water from the Watendlath Fells flows down into the lake through Watendlath Tarn and over the falls of Lodore.

The lake has four islands: Derwent Isle, by Friars Crag, Lord's Island, south of Friars Crag, Rampsholme Island, and, in the centre of the lake, St Herbert's Island. The lake, the islands, and much of the lake shore are in the care of the NT.

St Herbert's Island is reputed to have been the hermitage of St Herbert, the disciple and friend of St Cuthbert of Holy Island. It is said that they were so attached to each other that, in accordance with the prayer of St Herbert, they died on the same day. The island became a place of pilgrimage and Friars Crag is said to have got its name from the tradition that it was there that friars would wait to embark to visit the Saint, or wait to receive the Saint's blessing.

On Derwent Isle an eccentric named Joseph Pocklington chose to build a number of odd buildings in the 1770s, including a church, a fort, a battery, and a 'Druid's circle'. From the island he organized regattas on the lake, installing himself on the island as 'Governor'. Part of the attraction of a regatta was a mock sea-battle.

It is possible to walk round the lake for almost its entirety. One is helped in this by a scheduled motor-boat service that has a number of pick-up points round the lake. It is possible to walk south along the shore by Calf Close Bay and Great Wood to a landing stage at Ashness Gate. A well-made footpath (sometimes flooded after heavy rain) also leaves the roadside by Shepherd's Crag to follow the lake shore round to Great Bay and through Manesty Woods to Brandlehow Bay. At Brandlehow there is an old mine level and the ore was once taken from here, by water, to Keswick. The path continues northwards through the beautifully wooded Brandlehow Park to Otterbield Bay. Extensive views over the lake can also be admired from a secondary road on the west side of the lake between Grange and Hawse End; but it is a narrow road and is best avoided at busy holiday weekends. At a point on this road, in Manesty Park, is Brackenburn. This was the home of SIR HUGH WALPOLE (1884–1941), the best-selling novelist, the author of *Rogue Herries* (1930). Sir Hugh Walpole bought Brackenburn in 1924 when he was forty and spent the last eighteen years of his life there. 'The Herries Chronicle' made him famous and his books from that time were set in the Cumbrian landscape around Derwent Water. The house is not open to the public.

Boats can be hired at the boat landings by Friars Crag, where permission can also be obtained for launching light boats: the NT does not allow the launching of motor-boats over its land. Sailing is not popular on Derwent Water because of its tricky and treacherous cross-winds; nearby Bassenthwaite is preferable, and the Bassenthwaite Sailing Club offers all facilities.

To many regular visitors to the Lake District, Derwent Water was a first love. The lake probably has a more faithful following than any other.

Devoke Water 3B5

Devoke Water is as large as Rydal Water or Elter Water, but is reckoned to be not a lake but a tarn. When is a lake not a lake? A walk to Devoke Water will furnish the answer. It lies to the west of the minor road over Birker Fell between Ulpha and Eskdale Green and is only approachable on foot. Its setting is in wild moorland and the visual contrast between this large tarn and Rydal Water is obviously extreme. Dr T. T. Macan of the Freshwater Biological Association has suggested that a tarn can be biologically distinguished from a lake by its emergent vegetation; in a lake, to take one example, the characteristic plant is the common reed, whereas in tarns the common emergent plant is the bottle sedge. Evidence indicates that at one time Devoke Water was

a 'lake': analysis of sediment has shown that Devoke Water was once surrounded by forest. The clearance of the forest came about 1000 BC; at that time the whole area around Devoke Water was settled by Bronze Age people: the characteristic cairns of Bronze Age origin can be found all around the tarn. In that period the soil was obviously very productive, but centuries of leaching have reduced the land to heather moor.

Devoke Water has its attractions for those who seek peace and solitude, but its atmosphere is rather too austere for some.

Dove Cottage (Wordsworth's Cottage) 3D4

Everyone who knows of Wordsworth knows of Dove Cottage, for it was while he was living in this cottage that Wordsworth wrote some of his finest poetry. The cottage, on the by-road near Grasmere, still stands; it is preserved largely as it was, owned by an imaginative trust, staffed by enthusiastic guides, and open to all.

The cottage was originally a small inn known as The Dove and Olive Branch. William, who had long hoped to live in Grasmere, took the cottage at a rent of £8 per annum in December 1799. The existence there – an existence shared with his sister Dorothy – was frugal, eked out with the produce from the small vegetable garden. The compensations, though, were obviously great: there was an uninterrupted view to the lake, some delectable walking country, and no shortage of visiting friends. During his seven and a half years' residence Wordsworth wrote: *The Prelude, Intimations of Immortality, Miscellaneous Sonnets, Lyrical Ballads*, and a number of other poems, including some of the 'Lucy' poems (the chief of these were written in Germany), *Ode to Duty, To the Cuckoo, The Rainbow, I wandered lonely as a cloud*, and *The Solitary Reaper*.

Dorothy's *Journals* give detailed descriptions of the life at Grasmere.

The discharge of a long-standing debt to the Wordsworth family by the successor to the Earl of Lonsdale – the Earl had incurred the debt – relieved the financial situation sufficiently to enable William to marry Mary Hutchinson, a childhood friend, in 1802. He brought her to Dove Cottage where over the years she bore him three children: John, Dorothy (Dora), and Thomas. Mary's sister also came to live at the cottage and, predictably, there were frequent staying visitors. Samuel Taylor Coleridge was a regular caller, as were Thomas De Quincey, friends from various parts of the county, and Sir Walter Scott and his wife.

When Mary was expecting a fourth child the Wordsworths were forced to look for larger accommodation. Dorothy wrote: 'We are crammed into our little nest edge-full'. In May 1808 they moved into Allan Bank in the village of Grasmere.

On the departure of the Wordsworths the cottage was taken by De Quincey. He held the tenancy for twenty-eight years, although he lived there only for twenty-two years: during that time he wrote the two works for which he is best known: *Confessions of an English Opium-Eater* and *Recollections of the Lakes and the Lake Poets* (the latter work published originally as magazine articles between 1834 and 1840 and republished as *Recollections* in 1862). In 1818 he married a local girl, Peggy Simpson; she must have despaired at the quantity of books De Quincey managed to pack into the small cottage!

A converted barn near Dove Cottage now serves as a MUSEUM. It contains a reconstructed farm kitchen, furnished in the style of the early nineteenth century. On the upper floor Wordsworth enthusiasts can gaze with due reverence at a display of early notes and MSS, including those for Dorothy's *Journals*. There are also some of Coleridge's MSS for *Christobel* and *Dejection*.

Duddon Sands *see* Dunnerdale

Dufton 4F3 (*pop.* 205)
Dufton is a village of neat cottages around a green and is within striking distance of the high Pennines and the Pennine Way. The village shares its thirteenth-century church with the next hamlet of Knock.

Dufton Pike (418m.) is to the north of the village. High Cup is to the east. Dufton Pike is one of the few real 'peaks' in the Pennine chain. The area is of great interest to naturalists and geologists. Although the fell is of limestone, a volcanic intrusion, lying laterally along a bedding plane, has capped and protected the vulnerable, normally easily-eroded, limestone. High Cup is a shattered cliff with a notch, High Cup Nick, in the escarpment.

Dunmail Raise 3C4
The A591 between Ambleside and Keswick goes over the pass of Dunmail Raise (238m.), a geological fault between high fells of Borrowdale Volcanics: Steel Fell to the west, Seat Sandal to the east. Between the carriageways is a large cairn that once marked the boundary between the old counties of Cumberland and Westmorland. It also marks the spot of a great battle between the Norse king, Dunmail (Duvenald) of Cumbria, and the Anglo-Saxon king, Edmund of Northumbria, in 945. Edmund's victory meant that the north-western area of Cumbria passed over to the Scots: Edmund presented it to Malcolm on the condition that the Scots king lent his support when required.

There are several old theories about the raising of the cairn. One suggests that it marks the grave of Dunmail. But there is evidence to suggest that he died in Rome some years later. Another theory claims that it was raised by Edmund to celebrate the victory. It is also possible that it was raised by Malcolm to mark the boundary between England and Scotland. More alluring, though maybe less probable, is the theory that it was a battle 'scoreboard'. Before joining battle, it is suggested, each man in one of the armies picked up a stone and dropped it in one spot to make a pile. At the end of the battle each survivor picked up his stone and threw it away: the remaining cairn recorded the deaths and became a memorial. If the latter theory is true the battlefield must have been a bloodbath, or the entire army fled the field!

Another story tells that Dunmail fled eastwards by Raise Beck and Grisedale Tarn, flinging his crown jewels into the tarn to lighten his load and speed his escape.

Dunnerdale 3C5
The River Duddon rises at Wrynose Pass, flows westwards to Cockley Beck, and then south-westwards through one of the loveliest dales in Cumbria. From Cockley Beck the old Roman road to Hardknott fort runs straight to Black Hall before turning northwards to climb Wrynose Pass. South of Black Hall are the Forestry Commission's plantings; much criticized when planting began in 1936, the woods seem to be more acceptable now that they have matured. A car park has been provided by the Forestry Commission below Hinning House and a little south of this is the famous little packhorse bridge known as BIRKS BRIDGE. The river at this point has cut and polished its way through a narrow gorge to produce a unique scene, one that is much photographed and painted. South of the Forestry Commission plantings, the narrow road takes a turn south-eastwards and is joined by a lane from the north-east, the Walna Scar road, which crosses the side of the Old Man of Coniston to Coniston. It was once, in the days of horse traffic, a much-used public road; it is now purely the province of walkers. South of the junction a number of becks join together with Tarn Beck, and one could be excused for thinking that this was the River Duddon. In fact, the river is some distance to the west.

The tiny hamlet of SEATHWAITE has a small church and once had one of the Lake District's most famous parsons. The original chapel, in spite of John Ruskin's protests, fell prey to those terrible vandals, the nineteenth-century 'improvers'. 'WONDERFUL WALKER', the parson made famous by Wordsworth's reference in *The Excursion*, was born in Dunnerdale in 1709, the twelfth son of Nicholas Walker. As he was considered unfit to follow the life of a farmer, he was encouraged to study. After studying at Ulpha in Dunnerdale, he became a teacher at Gosforth, and later at Buttermere. He then took Orders, went back to his birthplace, and was appointed to the living of Seathwaite with a stipend of five pounds per annum; he was then twenty-seven and had married. He remained curate in charge of this little church for no less than sixty-six years and died at the age of ninety-two, in the same year as his wife. Although he was poor, he was the soul of thrift and even had enough put by for charitable work. He worked every day in the fields as a farm labourer, spun his own wool, and his wife made their clothes. He taught the local children in his church for eight hours every day, wrote letters for his parishioners, and administered to the sick. The couple raised and educated a family, and when 'Wonderful Walker' died he left a sum of £2,000 in his will.

After Seathwaite, the road and river turn west, and on the river's north bank is the exciting wall of WALLOW-BARROW CRAG, a climbing area; the valley then begins to open up between wooded crags. The road crosses the river and reaches the hamlet of ULPHA. 'Ulpha' is an interesting name and is of Norse origin. There are two theories to explain its significance: one suggests that it was the 'hay' or park of Ulf, the other that it means 'wolf hill', from the old Scandinavian *ulf-hauga*. The hamlet contains a row of almshouses, a pub, on a steep hair-pin bend at the junction with Birker road, a school, which has been modernized to an unfortunate design, and a small church of no great antiquity but built four-square of rough stone on high ground in a delectable setting. The church is thought to have begun life in the sixteenth century, though there may have been an earlier chapel sited elsewhere.

The road divides at Ulpha: one road crosses the river to take the more direct route to Duddon Bridge and Broughton (qv), while the westerly route meanders through narrow ways, away from the river and by old farms and farm tracks, and is strictly for travellers not in a hurry. It passes an old water-driven mill that once made wooden bobbins for the Lancashire cotton mills, climbs a fierce hill, then travels through tortuous bends, giving tantalizing glimpses of an old ruin on a hill to the east. The ruin is FRITH HALL, a hunting lodge of the Huddleston family in the seventeenth century, and later an inn catering largely for the travellers on the pack-pony trail that went this way. There are local suggestions of a smuggling trade, and its history is somewhat mysterious. It is said that there was a violent death at the inn and marriages of the Gretna Green type were reputedly celebrated there. Later, more prosaically, it became a farm.

South of Frith Hall is a hill with the name of 'Penn'. This is Celtic for 'hill', and one can wonder why the odd Celtic names survive in an area almost solely Norse. The road by Penn crosses Logan Beck and it has been suggested that 'Logan' is also Celtic, from *lagan*: a small hollow.

The dale road then descends through woodland and DUDDON HALL is to the east. This Georgian hall is better seen from the higher road on the east of the valley. It cannot be approached, and is not open to the public. The hall replaces a building known as Wha House or Whoyes, which was in the possession of the Cowper family, a family whose presence in the area was recorded as early as the thirteenth century. A 'Cowper' of the eighteenth century, by which time the family were known as 'Cooper', became the local man of fame. Myles Cooper was born in 1736, educated at Carlisle and Oxford, and later became president of Columbia University; in that rôle he expanded the college, saw the Medical School's beginning, and was a promoter of New York Hospital. George Washington met Dr Cooper several times, corresponded with him, and invited him to Mount Vernon. Duddon Hall has changed hands several times since and is said locally to be haunted.

South of the hall is Duddon Bridge. Here in the woods to the west was an early-nineteenth-century blast furnace. The choice of site might seem odd. But the materials were all to hand: woodlands to supply the charcoal, water power for the bellows, iron ore from the various mines in the area, even limestone from the band of Coniston Limestone in the vicinity, or from Furness over Duddon Sands.

Several tracks crossed DUDDON SANDS, sands into which the Duddon flows below Duddon Bridge. Cockles from the Duddon Sands were once said to be the finest to be obtained and were available in large quantities. Salmon were also once very plentiful and were salted down by the local people. It is now a lonely stretch of muddy sand with the distant signs of Millom's industry at its end; any few human venturers are likely to be birdwatchers.

Easedale and **Easedale Tarn**   3C4   w of Grasmere
In their early days at Grasmere, William and Dorothy Wordsworth called Easedale 'the black quarter' because it seemed to them that the bad weather came from that direction. The dale hangs over Grasmere, spilling down its rocky steps a skein of white water (Sour Milk Gill). The way up Easedale starts from a lane going north-east from Grasmere. The road for Easedale Tarn is to the left, by a slate bridge: the path has been so heavily used over the many years and the gulleys and drains have suffered such neglect that at times it is like walking in a trench. The path follows waterfalls nearly all the way to the tarn, a gem in a wild setting. There is a good view of Helm Crag to the east with the rock formation known as The Old Lady Playing the Organ prominent.

On the approach to the tarn there was once a refreshment hut. But by the 1960s vandals had wrecked the building. National Park Voluntary Wardens dismantled the hut and converted it into a cairn and windbreak.

The way beyond the tarn goes by a notoriously wet route to Codale Tarn and Langdale. CODALE TARN, in a cove above a cove, is an even wilder prospect than Easedale Tarn. South of Easedale Tarn is the ridge of Blea Rigg (qv). North of it is another long fell, Tarn Crag; the north face of this fell, broken by fierce crags, including a fine climbing crag known as DEER BIELD CRAG, towers over the valley of Far Easedale. This valley contains the old pony track from Grasmere to Borrowdale via, high on a valley rim, Greenup Edge (608m.).

Eden   River Valley   4G5/G4/F3/E2/E1, 5D5, 6E6
The River Eden rises above Mallerstang Common on Black Fell Moss, 688m. above sea-level at the south-east of the county, and flows north-westwards for 105km. to Carlisle and the Solway. It flows through a vastly different kind of country to that found in the rest of Cumbria:

the area has only half the rainfall of the county's centre and west and is rich, green agricultural land suited to cultivation and stock rearing, for which purposes it has been profitably used since the first Neolithic settlement.

In its early history the valley suffered for its success; and also because its setting between the Lake District fells and the steep, wild Pennines made it the only obvious route from Carlisle and the Borders to York and the east. It was a highway for robbers from Scotland and open to pillaging from hungry English armies marching north. The Romans, and later the Normans, fortified the route at the strategic centres of Brough, Appleby, Brougham, Penrith, and Carlisle, and in later centuries the wealthy built defensive towers against the Scottish raiders; even some of the farmers built fortified farmhouses.

The villages are largely red sandstone, of better lasting quality than the stone of west Cumbria. In some places the roofs are slated with sandstone or millstone, giving the buildings a heavy, sturdy look.

From Brough, the western edge of the Pennines goes north-westwards in a straight line to Castle Carrock, east of Carlisle. Between Brough and Melmerby the Pennine fell-tops are all above 600m., rising to the highest point of the Pennines at Cross Fell (893m.) (qv). West of the Eden Valley rise the Shap Fells (*see* Shap), bounded on their eastern side by the main north–south highway.

The Eden is a clean river and provides good fishing for trout, grayling, and salmon.

Edenhall   4E2

There is little to Edenhall, north-east of Penrith, other than a handsome church and a good story. (Edenhall itself, by Smirke, has been demolished.) The former has a lovely setting, is dedicated to St Cuthbert, and the present building dates from the fourteenth century, although there are Norman portions remaining. The story concerns the 'Luck of Edenhall', a thirteenth-century Surian glass goblet that was probably brought home from the Crusades by one of the Musgrave family; it is now in the V & A Museum. One day a butler, it is said, saw it on the lawn of the hall with fairies dancing around it. When he seized it he was warned:

Whene'r this cup shall break or fall
Farewell the luck of Edenhall.

The hall was demolished in 1934 (though the cup apparently survives). Longfellow translated a poem by Johann Uhland that used the legend:

As the goblet ringing flies apart
Suddenly cracks the vaulted hall;
And through the rift the wild flames start
The guests in dust are scattered all
With the breaking luck of Edenhall!

Egremont   3A4   (*pop.* 7,255)

Egremont, like some other Cumbrian villages, has a wide main street, a feature that sometimes deludes the unfamiliar traveller into believing that it has a large town to match. The place has seen bad days but latterly has gained a fresh lease of life as new industries have developed. The United Kingdom Atomic Energy Authority plant at Calder Hall is a main provider. Traditionally, though, iron ore of good quality has been Egremont's strength. The industry dates back for centuries: the earliest extant record shows that a gift of an Egremont iron mine was made to Holme Cultram Abbey by the third Earl of Albermarle (d. 1179).

On a hill south of the town is the ruin of the NORMAN CASTLE of Egremont. Unlike many of the older buildings, which are of the local limestone, the castle is built of sandstone blocks, most probably brought from St Bees (qv). It is presumed to have been built by William de Meschines in 1135. The best part of the ruin is the gatehouse, where typical Norman herring-bone work can be seen, and the domical rib vaulting of the roof is of interest. The front wall of the Great Hall still stands with doorway and windows; it dates from the first half of the thirteenth century. There are also remnants of the massive defensive walls, the domestic buildings, and the postern gate.

Like other castles in the area, it was built as a defence against the raiding Scots, and must have suffered and endured several serious attacks. The improbable legend associated with the place concerns the 'Horn of Egremont': this horn, supposed to have been hung above the castle gate, could only be blown by the true Lord of Egremont. Sir Eustace de Lucy, the true lord, went on Crusade with his brother Hubert. Hubert hired assassins to drown Sir Eustace in the Jordan and promptly returned to claim the estate; but of course he dared not blow the horn. One day as Hubert was feasting, the true Lord of Egremont returned, unscathed by the assassins. He blew the horn and Hubert took off by a side gate. It is said that Hubert returned filled with remorse and that Sir Eustace was forgiving.

There is free access to the castle ruins.

Egremont's church, ST MARY, was restored in 1880–1, principally by T. Lewis Banks. Four original lancet windows and some carved stonework of the thirteenth century, medieval sedilia, and font are among the remains from the original structure. There is also a beautifully carved reredos.

Elter Water   3D4

Elter Water is a derivative from Old Norse meaning 'swan lake'. It is a strangely elusive lake, half-hidden by reeds. In winter it is sometimes visited by the shy whooper swans, natives of Scandinavia.

Elter Water is at the confluence of Langdale Beck, from Great Langdale, and the Brathay, flowing from Wrynose through Little Langdale. With a length of only 800m., it is one of the smallest of the Lakes, though it has a very irregular shape. The lake is privately owned with

Elter Water in winter, with the Langdale Pikes in the background

private banks, although the NT own a good deal of the eastern and northern banks and it is possible to admire the views across the lake from NT land.

The village of Elterwater is small; it has a pub, one or two shops, a Youth Hostel, and a small central green spoiled by parked cars. On the north side of the village is a wooded caravan site, the site of a gunpowder mill that was in full production from 1824 until the close of the First World War. The local industry is now provided by a large quarry producing hard slate.

ELTERWATER COMMON, a large common to the east of the village, is managed for the lord of the manor by the NT. It is popular for picnic parties and as a car park for walkers.

Ennerdale 3B3/B4

Ennerdale is one of the more remote and less accessible dales, and is sought out for that reason by seekers of peace and solitude. Unfortunately these people are on the increase and what is sought is not guaranteed at busy summer weekends and bank holidays, particularly since the Forestry Commission, owners of most of the valley, have publicized a number of walking trails.

Ennerdale Water is a beautiful lake and it is hardly noticeable that its level has been raised by a dam to provide water for the industrial west-coast areas. Rumours of a further raising have been current for some time and they have led to the demolition of the Anglers' Hotel, a famous hostelry that stood at the lake foot. The head of the lake sits in a bed of granophyre, a hard volcanic rock that breaks into blocks; its foot is in the more friable Skiddaw Slates, rocks that allowed the glacier responsible for carving the valley to splay out. The water is exceptionally pure, with a maximum depth of 45m. Because of its purity it does not support a great deal of life, but there are brown trout and char, and salmon run through the lake.

The head of the dale is spectacular. Above and beyond the dull conifer plantations rise the heads of Steeple (819m.) and PILLAR (892m.), the latter much used by

On Ennerdale Fell looking towards Pillar Mountain

climbers. The best viewpoint of lake and fells is from BOWNESS POINT (NP access land) above the north shore. On a warm sunny day this is one of the finest picnic areas in the Lake District. Beyond Bowness Point the road is closed to vehicles, but offers a very easy and pleasant walk along the lake shore until the farm buildings at Gillerthwaite; after this point the path belongs to the dedicated walker and climber. Black Sail Youth Hostel, the most isolated hostel in Cumbria, is right at the dale head.

It is possible to walk all round the lake, though the path on the southern shore is rough and skirts a rugged cliff called Angling (Angler's) Crag.

Eskdale 3B5/C5, C4

Eskdale, with its head among England's highest land and its foot in the sea, is one of the most interesting dales in Cumbria. ESK HAUSE (759m.) at the dale top is the highest pass (by footpath only) in the Lake District. It is one of the 'crossroads' of the fells and is well trodden by

walkers on their way to Scafell Pikes, Langdale, Borrowdale, and Wasdale.

The path from the hause falls steeply and roughly, together with the beginnings of the River Esk, to Great Moss, a wet upper valley underneath the great eastern crags of the Scafells. The floor is littered by detached fragments of rock, some of them huge, and a group is aptly named Samson's Stones. A beck flowing almost from the summit of the Scafells falls to the floor down a steep wall in Cam Spout, a waterfall. The valley is awesome and dwarfing. Lower down the dale the way is crossed by a dyke – now frequently used as a footpath to get by the boggy ground – that is the remains of a wall put there by the monks of Furness Abbey, under licence from the Lord of Millom, to enclose an extensive grazing area for sheep; the monks were required to build the wall low enough to allow deer and fawns to cross it. Deer have long deserted this wet desert, once a well-wooded area. All Upper Eskdale was managed by Furness Abbey.

Following the River Esk further, the dale drops down a step to a lower valley, the river falling steeply and beautifully at Throstle Garth; the river is then joined by Lingcove Beck. The contours soften and another green valley floor is reached under the eye of Hard Knott (qv) and a Roman fort: the fort's position suggests that the track from Esk Hause was used by the British. Just by the farm of Brotherilkeld (a farm originally owned by the Furness Abbey monks) the track joins the road from Hard Knott Pass, and it is only from there down-valley that Eskdale is known to the greater number of tourists, though it is little more than half of the total length of 21km.

The tourist's Eskdale is less dramatic than the head of the valley, but it is extremely beautiful. The dry-stone walls and the old buildings are made of the warm, pink Eskdale Granite. The fells, capped with rocks and broken by cliffs, are bright green in spring, russet brown in autumn. The River Esk, falling down steps of pink and grey stone, curls around broadleaved trees. The scene is idyllic.

After the well-known Woolpack Inn, the village of BOOT is encountered. A walk past the village pub leads to an old stone bridge over Whillan Beck and an old water mill. This mill has recently been put into working order by the County Council and it is intended to open it to the public. The mill building includes a loft where the grain was dried over tiles before grinding. The wheel is 'overshot'.

Just below the village of Boot is a focal point for one of Eskdale's main attractions – the narrow-gauge railway – for here is Dalegarth station, the terminus of the 10km. run from Ravenglass. The railway used to serve the mines and, later, the quarry, taking ore and slate to the mainline railway. It is now a pleasure railway running scale steam models of the railway engines of the past. The company is dignified with the title of the Ravenglass and Eskdale Railway; but everyone knows it as 'La'al Ratty'.

A lane from Boot leads down to the river and the small, hidden church of ST CATHERINE. No church could have a more delightful setting, with the murmuring of the river sounding like a congregation at perpetual prayer. There was a chapel here, maintained by the monks of Furness, in the fourteenth century. The present barn-like structure is not old but fits perfectly into the scene. The churchyard should be searched for the headstone of Tommy Dobson, the huntsman: it is carved with fox and hounds.

Below Dalegarth station a track goes riverwards from opposite the old school. This leads over the deep-pooled river and past DALEGARTH HALL (not open to the public), home of the Stanleys. The hall has the traditional cylindrical chimneys of the old south-Cumbrian houses. A path beyond leads to STANLEY GILL (NP Access Land), a ravine in a geological fault, through which a waterfall descends in three drops. Unfortunately the falls are in a very narrow ravine and are approachable only by well-shod climbers and scramblers: ordinary walkers have to be content with a view of the lower falls from a bridge. But the approach to the falls by a granite path and bridges, through the green ravine overhung by a great variety of trees and rhododendrons and covered with mosses, ferns, and liverworts, is a delight. The ghyll in spate, falling and swirling through rock pools, is fascinating.

The road forks at an inn below Dalegarth. The right-hand road leads down to Eskdale Green, on the way passing another station of the narrow-gauge railway. At Eskdale Green are the Eskdale Green Outward Bound School, a shop and a post office, some old buildings, one of which was a smithy, and little else except a homely atmosphere. The railway loops to the far end of the village stopping at Irton Road Station, just short of Bower House, a small hotel. The railway then leaves Eskdale to take the next valley, from the foot of Miterdale to Ravenglass. To follow the Esk one must take the southward road east of Eskdale Green, turning right again before the kennels of the Eskdale foxhounds. This route leads down a very narrow road, meandering as wildly as the river, to a junction with the A595. The little that is left of Eskdale can then be followed on foot, or by a wide southerly road detour, to Newbiggin, where the dale finishes in sand dunes.

Eskdale Fell *see* **Burnmoor**

Esthwaite Water   3D5
To the west of Windermere by the roadside between the ferry and Hawkshead is the small lake of Esthwaite, much loved by Wordsworth. The lake is mentioned in *The Prelude*:

<blockquote>
My morning walks
Were early; – oft before the hours of school
I travelled round our little lake, five miles
Of pleasant wandering. Happy time!
</blockquote>

(II 329–32.)

Esthwaite Water is set in green fields and bounded by woods and reeds. On the approach from the ferry there is a classic view over the lake to the Pikes of Langdale in the distance: the area has all the charm of Grasmere or Rydal without the pressure of passing traffic or crowds of tourists. The lake is fed by a number of becks that join Black Beck flowing through Hawkshead and is drained by Cunsey Beck into Windermere. The lake is 2½km. long by 600m. wide and is 24m. deep. Being small, low-lying, and in an area that is intensively farmed, the water is nutrient-rich and supports a rich flora and fauna. There are trout, pike, perch, rudd, and roach. The great crested grebe frequents the lake.

Above the lake head is a detached portion of the lake known as PRIEST POT – which is surrounded by typical fen conditions on a base of accumulated silt. The area, of scientific interest, has been studied over a number of years. The 1½ha. site is a National Nature Reserve.

Though a section of the lake shore at the Hawkshead end is in the ownership of the NT, and a small area of the south-west bank is a NP Access Area, both the lake and most of the land about are in private ownership and permits to fish and launch rowing-boats must be obtained from Esthwaite Estates. The area is owned by the Sandys family, whose seat, now at Graythwaite Hall, was once Esthwaite Hall. This sixteenth-century building can be seen from the roadside by the south-west shore.

Finsthwaite 3D6

The village of Finsthwaite sits across a by-road near Lakeside at the foot of Windermere. There is nothing remarkable about the village itself except a grave in the churchyard. Who was the mysterious 'Clementina Johannes Sobiesky Douglass, of Waterside', who died in May 1771? It has been suggested that she was a Polish princess, but one strong suggestion is that she was Prince Charles Edward Stuart's daughter by his mistress Clementina Walkenshaw, God-daughter of his mother, Clementina Sobiesky. If this were true it would amply account for the secrecy surrounding her identity.

Nearby is FINSTHWAITE HEIGHTS, capped by a tower erected 'To honour the officers, seamen, and marines of the Royal Navy, whose matchless conduct and irresistible valour decisively defeated the fleets of France, Spain and Holland, and promoted and protected liberty and commerce, 1799'. The walk through the woods to the tower is most pleasant.

Below the village is a building that was one of the last operative bobbin mills. There were a large number of

these mills at one time, built wherever water power and wood were plentiful. Restoration work is in hand on the Finsthwaite mill and it is hoped to open it to the public in due course.

A small lane off the road down to the Hawkshead road leads into a wood with a car park and public access to HIGH DAM. A steep footpath leads to two small lakes, both of which were dammed to keep a head of water for the mill. The setting, among hardwood and conifer trees, is superb. The area was bought by the NP for the public in preference to it going to commercial forestry. It has been described as a 'miniature Tarn Hows', though it lacks the long views.

Firbank 4E5

North-west of Sedburgh is Firbank Fell. In 1652 George Fox, founder of the Society of Friends (Quakers), addressed a crowd of over a thousand people – most of whom had been at Sedbergh fair – on this fell. A memorial tablet marks the spot. Asked why he preached on a 'mountain' and not in the church he replied: 'the steeple-house, and the ground wherein it stands, is no more holy than this mountain'. It is unlikely that the natural amphitheatre has changed much since Fox's time.

Furness Abbey 1D1

The visitor to Furness Abbey is invariably impressed by the height of the remains: the transepts and the choir stand within a stone or two of their original height. The great east window, 154m. high and 75m. wide, was no

Furness Abbey: interior of chapter house, looking E

doubt designed to uplift the soul as it uplifts the eye; its effect has not diminished over the centuries. The window, probably of the fifteenth century, was glazed by Sir John Petty, the York glass-painter. The western tower is also near its original height; but most of the nave has gone except for part of its early-twelfth-century south wall, reckoned to be the oldest remaining fabric in the abbey.

Building activity at Furness began in 1127 under the Savigny Order after Stephen, then Count of Boulogne, had transferred the abbey from Tulketh, near Preston. The Savigny monks and lay brothers probably spent the first twenty years erecting temporary buildings and making a start on the church. Because of the narrowness of the site, orientation had to be out of the usual, and the church is set roughly north-east to south-west. The building work probably accelerated when the Savigny Order was merged with the Cistercians in 1147; after this date the church transepts were enlarged and the ten-bay nave was built. In the nave only the bases of the pillars remain. The seven western bays were divided from the rest by a stone screen – the base of which survives – because the western end of the church was for use by the lay brothers.

The north transept is well preserved, but the windows are late, fifteenth-century, additions. The eastern end of the church, the presbytery, has in its south wall, and still in good condition, the sedilia, the stone elaborately carved and little damaged, though insensitively protected by an ugly iron fence. The piscina is alongside the four seats and is also unusually elaborate. The south transept, like the north, was remodelled in the fifteenth century. The crossing belongs to the twelfth century, as did a low belfry tower built above it (a usual feature in Cistercian abbeys of the period). As at Fountains Abbey, an attempt was made – in the fifteenth century – to rebuild the tower to a greater height. The consequences were the same as at Fountains: the foundations could not support the extra weight, in spite of reinforced piers, and the tower probably fell. The western belfry tower, c. 1500, is the consequence. Unusually, because of the tightness of the site, the tower had to be inset into the end of the nave and not built outside.

The chapter house, south of the south transept, is entered through a beautifully vaulted vestibule. This portion of the abbey is thought to date from the second quarter of the thirteenth century. Only portions of the slender columns remain, but the beauty of the arched windows, with green leaves behind and the sky visible through what was once the upper floor, makes a profound impression. The parlour, where the brothers were

BELOW: *Furness Abbey: looking W along the nave aisle and showing the W tower*

OPPOSITE: *Furness Abbey: the arches to the chapter house*

Furness Abbey: one of the architectural fragments

allowed conversation, is south of the chapter house and next to the slype. Viewed from the cloister square, the chapter house, parlour, and slype, with two book cupboards, are seen to have entrances through five decorated arches. The weathering of the sandstone adds to the beauty of the arches and the whole scene produces one of the abbey's most memorable effects.

South of these arches are the long ruins of the dorter undercroft, with twelve bays, a total length of 57m., the largest undercroft in England. Above was the monks' dormitory: its great size testifies to the abbey's importance. The buildings – probably of the mid twelfth century – occupied by the lay brothers were at the opposite side of the cloister: little remains. Even less remains of the buildings that were to the south of the cloister: the frater and, against the dorter undercroft, the warming house.

The great infirmary, about 38m. long, probably built in the early fourteenth century, was south of the other buildings. The chapel at its eastern end still stands and has its original vaulted roof; an unusual feature of the chapel is the triangular-headed windows. The chapel, used as a small museum, is kept locked: the key can be obtained from the keeper. On the west side of the chapel was the buttery, and a passage led from this to the octagonal kitchen, the foundations of which remain. The interesting channelling of the watercourses in this area can be admired; the beck was obviously carefully used to give the abbey its planned drainage.

North-east of the kitchen, and hard against the sandstone cliff, are the remains of the abbot's house; originally the infirmary, it was converted to a house after the completion of the great infirmary. The upper storey apparently projected over piers and, at the rear, was fixed into the solid rock.

A guest house occupied the space between the abbot's house and the dorter undercroft. The whole of the abbey site, amounting to about 9ha., was walled and traces of walling survive. The Department of the Environment, which has care of the site, fights a losing battle with the Barrow children, who use it less reverently than they might. Visitors seeking an atmosphere of peace and quiet in which to enjoy these unique ruins should go during school hours.

Garburn Pass   3D4   w of Kentmere
The old road from Kentmere to Troutbeck and Windermere is now a ruin, fit only for walking. The top of the pass is at 449m. as it crosses the flank of Yoke.

Gatescarth Pass   4E4   SE of Haweswater
Before Manchester Corporation submerged the hamlet of Mardale in the enlargement of Haweswater (qv), the route over Gatesgarth Pass and down Longsleddale was the quickest way from the hamlet to Kendal market. It was once possible to do the journey with carts, but the road over the 579m. summit has been long neglected and can now only be walked. It is quite a pleasant path.

Glaramara   3C4
Travelling up Borrowdale to the head one sees a great hump of fell that, until Borrowdale curves west, appears to block the valley. This fell, usually known as the Tongue of Borrowdale, is Glaramara. It is often used by fellwalkers as an interesting route, via Allen Crags, to Esk Hause.

Glaramara is really only a summit ridge on what is a complex mass of fell between Borrowdale and Lang Strath. The fells are named on some maps as Rosthwaite Fell on the eastern side and Thornythwaite Fell on the west; but Glaramara is the highest point and guidebooks for over a century have referred to the whole fell as Glaramara. No doubt it is the surviving Celtic name that attracts.

The fell has some interesting features. Viewed from Mountain View, east of Seatoller, the deep gash of a gill can be seen left of the summit: this is the ravine of COMB GILL. There are natural caves in the ghyll's depths that offer excellent wet-weather exercise for rock climbers. Dove Nest Crag on the eastern side is a jumble of rocks, an indulgence for climbers. Above is a gap in the ridge called Comb Door, with the small peak of Comb Head to the right. A lesser peak (550m.) on the east of Comb Gill has the odd name of Bessyboot. Just south of it is a tarn known as Tarn at Leaves.

There appear to be two summits on Glaramara: the true one (780m.) is on the north-east. On a fine day the views are very extensive indeed.

The fell is rough and is strictly for well-shod fellwalkers. The only reasonable approach is from Seatoller in the north, walking up the ridge from Thornythwaite. The descents west or east to Upper Borrowdale or Lang Strath are very steep.

GOSFORTH

Glenridding *see* **Ullswater**

Gosforth   3B4   *(pop.* 1,075)
Gosforth is famed for its Viking cross; and historians who
gaze upon the cross's slender beauty – it stands intact,
4m. high, in the churchyard – must chew their nails
nervously and wonder why it is not safe in some museum.
The carvings on the sandstone cross show a mixture of
Christian and Norse themes; evil being overcome by
good is the essence of each. One of the panels shows the
crucifixion with a soldier piercing Christ's side with a
spear; another tells the story of the struggle of the gods
against Fenris Wolf, the offspring of evil Loki and
Angrboda the giantess: Loki is bound in chains; Vidar
slays the monster, the double-headed Fenris Wolf; and a
hart tramples on a serpent. The base of the cross is carved
to represent a tree bole, Yggdrasil, the mythological ash
tree that supported the Norse universe. Inside the church
are a fragment of another Norse cross and two hogback
tombs.

　　Also in the churchyard is a cork tree, reputed to be the
northernmost specimen; it was planted in 1833.

　　Gosforth, the gateway to Wasdale, is an interesting,
friendly village given some fresh life by the developments
at Windscale ar d an influx of new residents.

Grange-in-Borrowdale *see* **Borrowdale**

Grange-over-Sands   3D6   *(pop.* 3,474)
Until recently Grange and the whole of the Cartmel
Peninsula were part of Lancashire. For this is 'Lonsdale
North of the Sands', and, before the days of turnpike
roads, the main highway came across the sands of the
bay, now known as MORECAMBE BAY, to Kents Bank, now
part of Grange-over-Sands. The road across the sands
is still in law a highway, and every year the official guide
(once appointed by the monks of Cartmel, now appointed by the Duchy of Lancaster) arranges group
walks across the sands; the journey has of course to be
done at low tide with a full knowledge of the position of
the channels – which tend to move – the quicksands, and
the river depth. Over the ages the sands have claimed
many victims and some of their memorials can be seen in
Cartmel church. It is said that at one time some 'gentle-
men' at Kents Bank would watch the sands and, seeing
a traveller who had scorned the guide and missed the
tide, would cast lots to decide who was to have his coat,
his bags, or his saddle.

　　The road-builders took some commerce and trade
away from the Cartmel Peninsula, but the coming of the
railway in the last century 'made' Grange-over-Sands:
it rapidly became an important holiday resort. Grange,
an attractive, grey town, has expanded in recent years.
Gifted with some of the highest average temperature

RIGHT: *Gosforth Cross: E side*

*Looking over Grasmere from the S with Helm Crag (The Lion
and the Lamb) left of centre. The gap in the hills is Dunmail
Raise, with the slopes of Helvellyn on the right*

figures in the north of England, it is a place where many
retired people choose to live (though the hills are somewhat severe on the aged). Were the sands of Morecambe
Bay not so muddy, it is possible that Grange would have
become another Blackpool. But that was not to be, and
rather than the dedicated tourist, it is another type of
person who walks the traffic-free promenade – the birdwatchers, for instance, admiring the great variety of
waders, ducks, geese, and gulls that visit the bay.

The countryside around Grange is a sort of naturalists'
paradise, with an immense variety of habitats: on
Silurian Slates, limestone, peat moss, and salt marsh.
This is perhaps one reason why the Nature Conservancy
Council has a headquarters and research station at
MERLEWOOD, east of the town.

Above the town is an area of limestone pavement. This
is HAMPS FELL. On the summit a 'hospice' was built by a
'former pastor of Cartmel parish for the shelter and
entertainment of wanderers over the fell'. Though it is
sad that the direction indicator at the hospice, naming
all the points of interest, has fallen into disrepair, the summit is a superb viewpoint, which should not be missed.

Grasmere   3D4   (pop. 990)

Grasmere is the combination of lake, small dale, and village that is generally thought to be the quintessence of

Lakeland landscape. Wordsworth thought so, and made
the village his home.

Grasmere, for all the tourists, has remained unspoilt
thanks to the NP, the NT (which owns a good deal of the
area and manages the lake), and the restraint of the inhabitants. The only regrettable features are the dearth
of village shops in favour of tourist gift shops, and the
commercialization of the sports field; that commercialization packs the most prominent area in the valley with
caravan rallies at the height of the holiday season.

The delightful lake is almost completely surrounded
by public access land owned by the NT or the NP. It
must be approached on foot: the only vehicles in sight
are those rushing by on the A591, which comes in regret-
tably close on the eastern bank. The walks by the lake are
a delight. The best view, from LOUGHRIGG TERRACE, a
well-made path some 6om. above the lake on its south-
eastern side, shows the lake in the foreground, the village behind, and the craggy backcloth of Helm Crag.

Most of the village buildings are nineteenth- or
early-twentieth-century. The old buildings have to be
sought out, and some of them have been altered and
improved; but Wordsworth would recognize many. THE
SWAN HOTEL, where Sir Walter Scott on his visits to the
Wordsworth household would repair for a dram (Dove
Cottage being uncontaminated by the stuff), still stands,

and some of the village-centre houses also survive. ST OSWALD'S church, where Wordsworth and his family worshipped, has remained unchanged since the description of it in *The Excursion*:

> With pillars crowded, and the roof upheld
> By naked rafters intricately crossed,
> Like leafless underboughs, in some thick wood,
> All withered by the depth of shade above.

(V 146–9.)

The oldest visible part of the present church dates from the thirteenth century. The numerous alterations over the many generations make it something of an architectural curiosity.

Until the nineteenth century the floor of the church was earthen, and at intervals the rushes that were strewn on the floor were cleared and replaced. This gave rise to a traditional ceremony that is still followed on the Saturday nearest to St Oswald's Day. Village children, dressed in their best, carry rushes and flowers, in a procession preceded by a band, to the church (cf. Ambleside). In past generations the church 'paid' for the rushes with ale, and no doubt in those days it was an adult ceremony.

Another famous Grasmere tradition is SPORTS DAY. The Grasmere sports are by far the most popular in an area that has probably had sports meets since the Viking settlement. As well as the normal activities of sports days – the running, throwing, cycling events – there are other, more unique, contests: Cumberland and Westmorland Wrestling, for example. The wrestlers, in tights and embroidered pants (prizes are offered for the best dressed), grasp each other at the shoulder and attempt to throw one another off balance. The sport apparently has an ancient origin. There is also the guides' race, a muscle-straining, lung-bursting, almost perpendicular fell race, demanding seemingly impossible stamina for the climb, and unnatural agility for the breakneck descent. At the end of the day there are the hound trails: some time before this takes place a 'trail' is laid with a rag soaked in aniseed and paraffin. The hounds are unleashed to vanish over the fell and the excitement is intense as the fastest hounds reappear. At the finishing line the hound owners shout, whistle, and wave to spur their hounds home, and the finish is usually a very close issue.

Dove Cottage (qv) is at Town End, east of the village, and this is where the Wordsworth family lived until they outgrew the place. In 1808 they moved to Allan Bank, to the west of the village; the house is now owned by the NT but is not open to the public. Wordsworth did not like Allan Bank, calling it a 'temple of abomination', and three years later they moved to the Parsonage. They were at the Parsonage for two years, and while there lost two children: Catherine (3) and Thomas (6). Wordsworth then secured a post as distributor of stamps for Westmorland, with a salary of £300, and the family

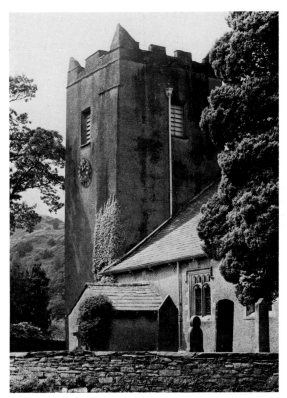

Grasmere: St Oswald's church. The thick encrustation of pebble-dash makes impossible a dating of the exterior

were able to move out of the village to the more accommodating Rydal Mount.

Dove Cottage and Rydal Mount are both open to the public.

The graves of the Wordsworths are in St Oswald's churchyard. William and his wife Mary are buried under a simple stone by the riverside. Dora Quillinan, their daughter, is in the next grave. Hartley Coleridge, son of Samuel Taylor Coleridge, is buried to the north.

Many good walks start from the village. Helvellyn can be climbed north of the village, beyond the Travellers' Rest inn, by a track via Tongue Gill to Grisedale Tarn. The Fairfield range can be reached by a path leaving the lane behind the Swan Hotel and going via Greenhead Gill and Heron Pike. The nearby fells of Loughrigg, Helm Crag (The Lion and the Lamb), and Silver How all offer beautiful viewpoints.

For strollers there is the Rydal and Grasmere round of footpaths and the path to Alcock Tarn.

Great Gable 3C4

After Helvellyn and Scafell Pikes (qqv), Great Gable follows closely in popularity. It instantly seizes the imagination. Viewed from Wasdale Head, its name describes it well. It is like the huge gable-end of a monstrous dale church. The best view of all is probably that from LINGMELL CRAG, its southern neighbour; from there the full extent of its rough, steep side, 777m. to the valley floor of Wasdale, can be appreciated. If it is gable-shaped from Wasdale Head and Lingmell, viewed from the east or the west it is a huge, ugly stump, thrusting above the shoulders of its lesser neighbours. From the north it is seen as a great arc of cliff.

Great Gable is 899m. high and belongs, if it belongs to any dale at all, to Wasdale, though it is set back well above the head of the dale. It is separated by suitable

Napes Needle, Great Gable

gulfs from its neighbours, the Scafells, which sit at a respectable distance to its south. There are three main approaches to the summit. From Styhead it is a direct assault up 410m. of rough, sometimes loose, path. An easier approach is to take a car to the top of Honister Pass from Borrowdale, take the quarry road to Drum House, then walk by Gillercomb Head, Green Gable, and Windy Gap, a walk of just over two hours with a climb of 594m. From Wasdale Head the best ascent is by Gable Beck, then, by a track called Gavel Neese, directly upwards, leaving Gavel Neese by another track going northwards, at about the 450m. contour, for Beck Head; from Beck Head there is a direct path up to the summit; the distance of the walk is 3½km. with an ascent of 823m.

The fell has a lot of interest. Rock climbers contour westwards round from Styhead on the GIRDLE TRAVERSE, not a path for inexperienced walkers, nor a reasonable route to the summit, unless one wishes to scramble up sliding scree-shoots, aptly named Hell Gates. But the path does pass some of the most exciting rock-climbs in the country. The first crag is Kern Knotts, then the rough path crosses Great Hell Gate to Great Napes, a large wall of rock. This is the location of most of the climbs, often with names given to them by the first climbers: Tophet Bastion, Needle Ridge and Gully, Eagle's Nest Ridge and Gully, Arrowhead Ridge and Gully, Sphinx Ridge, and, low on the crag and near the centre, NAPES NEEDLE, a spire of naked rock first climbed in 1886 by the legendary father of climbers, Walter Parry Haskett-Smith. (He climbed it again fifty years later at the age of 74!) The Needle does not always look impressive from the path, but a scramble up the gully behind brings one to a ledge called the Dress Circle, which is the usual viewpoint. The top of the Needle is a large, separate block of stone: it has not yet threatened to slip off its perch in spite of the number of climbers it has had to endure. Beyond Great Napes is another scree-run, Little Hell Gate, followed by White Napes, another rock wall; the Girdle path then circles to Beck Head.

From Beck Head a path, Moses Trod, contours round under the north-facing crags of Gable to Drum House above Honister Quarries. 'Moses' was a local folk figure, a Cumbrian rogue who is said to have made illicit whisky near Honister and smuggled it to Wasdale. Doubtless there were a number of hidden worms in the remote fells in earlier years, but the excise men would have been hard-pressed to find them.

The summit of Great Gable is a great mass of stone blocks and detritus. On the topmost point is a bronze-tablet war memorial, which also records the gift of the fell to the NT by the Fell and Rock Climbing Club. Every Remembrance Sunday scores of walkers, sometimes over a hundred, congregate here to observe a moment's respectful silence.

RIGHT: *Sphinx Rock, Great Gable*

Great Gable seen from the track up to Scafell Pike

South-west of the summit is a superb view over Wasdale; the viewpoint is marked with a large cairn, Westmorland Cairn. On a clear day the top of Gable offers very wide views of the fells, stretching to the Pennines, the Isle of Man, and the Scottish hills.

Great Langdale 3C4

With Borrowdale, Langdale rates as the valley most popular with visitors to the Lake District. It is essentially a walkers' and a climbers' valley and in recent years the question of its increasing use by motorists has become an embarrassment to the Planning Department of the NP and to the Highway Authority. The valley is served by a narrow winding road between dry-stone walls; the only outlet at the head is to Little Langdale (qv) by a very steep, even narrower, road with hairpin bends.

The dale is walled by some of the most distinctively-shaped and impressive crags of the Lake District. LANGDALE PIKES, seen across Windermere from Brockhole or Low Wood, or, at less distance, across Esthwaite, Elter Water, or Loughrigg Tarn, form one of the most familiar scenes in the Lake District. Right at the head of the dale is Bow Fell (902m.), a classically-shaped mountain; and southwards from it is the long serrated

edge of Crinkle Crags, followed by the cairned cone of Pike o'Blisco (702m.).

The small village of CHAPEL STILE is at the dale foot. The grey stone and slate buildings were built mainly to house quarrymen and the employees of a gunpowder works near Elterwater village. The rest of the buildings in Langdale are mainly farms: there is no great lord's hall in this valley. The one church, HOLY TRINITY, dates only from 1857; an earlier chapel on the site was a century older. The curate of this chapel, in this poor place, recorded Clarke in 1787, 'is obliged to sell ale to support himself and his family'. Harriet Martineau wrote in her guide of 1858 that 'A few years since, the pulpit of the old chapel fell, with the clergyman, Mr Frazer, in it, just after he had begun his sermon from the text "Behold I come quickly"'. The pulpit fell on an elderly dame who escaped wonderfully. She refused the clergyman's sympathy with the words "If I'd been kilt, I'd been reet sarrat [rightly served], for you threatened ye'd be comin doon sune"'.

Travelling up-valley from Chapel Stile, a row of recently-built cottages are the only blot. In an area subject to delicate NP planning, the failures scream; the successes are invisible.

Chapel Stile, near Great Langdale

Most of the farms of the valley are in the ownership of the NT. Much of the credit for this must lie with the historian George Trevelyan who began the acquisitions by buying Stool End and Wall End farms and the Dungeon Ghyll Old Hotel and presenting them to the Trust in 1928. He added further farms in 1944, and his daughter and his old college (Trinity, Cambridge) contributed to further purchases in 1963. The ownership of the valley head by the NT has removed the untidyness of a hutted camp, and a number of small, unscreened, and insanitary camp sites have been gathered into one screened unit with facilities.

The flat floor of the valley upwards from Chapel Stile continues for 7km. and, for much of its length, was probably once the bed of a shallow lake. Much work has been done by the River Authority in flood prevention, but, even so, after prolonged rain the valley takes on the appearance of a shallow lake, as in 1967 when 74cm. of rain fell in 29 days. The annual average for the valley is 274cm., but right at the valley head in the high fells it is estimated to be 380cm., probably twice the average figure for Windermere.

The long walls of the valley are, at first, BLEA RIGG on the north side and LINGMOOR on the south. The former is well walked, the latter, with no easy ascent possible except from Elter Water or the next valley of Little Langdale, is a quiet fell for the more discerning. The first notable centre of activity is by the Dungeon Ghyll New Hotel (where there are two car parks). Rock climbs are accessible from here: Scout Crags, used mainly as a training ground, and White Gill are just to the east. Above the hotel the waterfalls of STICKLE GILL (Mill Gill) attract the casual strollers, and on either side of the ghyll are two of the most heavily-used paths on the fells. Volunteer work parties have been assisting the NT to repair erosion damage.

Many people mistakenly assume that Stickle Gill is the famous DUNGEON GHYLL, a major tourist attraction in the nineteenth century. Dungeon Ghyll in fact falls through a deep ravine just to the east; two hotels were built upon its reputation as a spectacle.

The worn paths up Stickle Gill end at STICKLE TARN. This was dammed last century to provide a controllable head of water for the valley mills. When the dam fell into disrepair the tarn became a small pond surrounded by bog and the dam was therefore restored by the NP in 1959.

Behind the tarn is the great hogback hump of PAVEY ARK (697m.). The scene brings a gasp of excitement to the strugglers who at last breast the dam: the contrast between flat water and rugged cliff is strangely moving. Across Pavey's cliff, diagonally from the foot of it on the right to the top left, is a groove called JACK'S RAKE. This is the most exciting scramble in Cumbria for well-equipped walkers; it needs no great skill but a very good head for heights: the way is distinctly 'airy'.

On the left of Pavey Ark is a rough pass leading over a saddle. This is one of the ways up the Langdale Pikes, which look oddly tame from their sides facing the fells.

The easternmost and highest of the Langdale Pikes is HARRISON STICKLE (732m.), isolated from the other pikes by the ravine of Dungeon Ghyll, by the side of which is one of the routes to the summit. South-west of this pike is Thorn Crag (640m.), below which is the famous climbing crag, Gimmer Crag. Westwards is the second distinct volcanic boss of PIKE O'STICKLE or Stickle Pike (708m.): this is the most impressive of the Pikes. Its steep front to the valley is avoided by climbers, most ascents being from the rear. Just east of the pike a long runnel of scree goes to the valley floor: this used to be a good 'scree-run' line of descent, but erosion has exposed smooth rock and it has become an accident black-spot. At the top of the scree is the site of a 3,000-year-old Neolithic stone-axe factory discovered in 1947. The rock is a hard volcanic tuff that flakes when struck: ideal raw material. It has so far been established that axes were roughed out at this site and taken to the coast for

TOP: *Looking eastwards down Langdale, from the track up Bow Fell*

BOTTOM: *Pavey Ark (697m.) in the Langdale Pikes. Stickle Tarn is just to be seen in the foreground*

finishing. Rejected rough-outs are less easy to find here than they once were. A small, man-made cave in the crag face is near the axe-factory working area: the purpose of the cave is a matter for conjecture; possibly it was used as shelter for the axe-makers.

Below the Pikes is the Dungeon Ghyll Old Hotel. This is another starting point for the fells, and is the nearest access to another climbing area, RAVEN CRAG, directly above the hotel. So popular is the Raven Crag area that in recent years erosion around the crag foot has accelerated alarmingly and the NT with the help of volunteer work parties is attempting to stabilize the scree. A small outbuilding at the hotel serves as the dalehead headquarters of the Langdale/Ambleside rescue team.

Up-dale from the hotel is MICKLEDEN, the 2km.-long valley floor. At its head is a series of moraines, debris piles left by the melting ice after the last glaciation. Two main walking routes leave here. To the north, the old pack-pony trail to Borrowdale climbs over Stake Pass (in the days of its commercial use it was probably marked by stakes). Westwards, a notoriously loose and rough track, the general route to Angle Tarn, Esk Hause, and Scafell Pikes, climbs steeply by the side of Rossett Gill. It is an unpleasant path, yet, strangely, an old pony track, zig-zagging more gently to the same goal south of the path, receives much less use. At the foot of Mickleden, by the farm of Stool End, another well-pounded path goes westwards along a finger of fell, The Band. This is the route to Bow Fell, or to Three Tarns and the Crinkle Crag ridge, or south-westwards into Eskdale. South-west from Stool End, another path goes upwards into a small feeder dale, Oxendale. This is the way to Pike o'Blisco or, by Red Tarn, to the summit of Wrynose Pass.

In spite of its popularity, green Langdale has avoided complete ruin under the pressure of tourism. The credit for this must go to the owners – the NT – the planning policy of the NP, and the remarkable ability of the dale farmers not only to survive, but to keep up a traditional way of life.

Great Mell Fell   3D3
Travellers between Keswick and Penrith can see across the comparatively level floors to the south, between Troutbeck and Penruddock, two surprisingly symmetrical conical fells. These are Great Mell Fell and Little Mell Fell. Geologically, their position is interesting: composed of conglomerates formed of stony accumulations of debris, a material that does not vary in hardness, glaciation and subsequent erosions have treated all the surfaces equally: hence the symmetry.

Great Salkeld   4E2
Great Salkeld is one of the most attractive villages in Cumbria: it is neat, clean, and airy, with red-sandstone buildings set among greens. It is almost too good to be true: a chocolate-box picture. But it is more than a pretty face. The village is kept as it is by hard-working inhabitants.

An unusual feature in the village is the fortified tower of the church of ST CUTHBERT's. This was built onto the Norman nave in the late fourteenth century as a safe retreat for the villagers during the Border troubles. It is entered by a massive and protected door in the church's west wall. The doorway to the church itself is a fine example of Norman work.

The church of St Cuthbert, Great Salkeld: E capital of the Norman S door

The village of Little Salkeld is across the River Eden and can only be approached from Great Salkeld by the bridges at Lazonby, to the north, or Langwathby, to the south. There is little to note in this village apart from an old watermill that an enterprising gentleman has put into working order and opened to the public. It is possible both to see corn being ground and to buy the resulting flour. Just north of the village lies the remarkable stone circle called Long Meg and Her Daughters (qv).

Grisedale Pike   3C3
Looking westwards from Keswick a shapely and distant mountain bites into the sky behind the nearer peak of Causey Pike. This is Grisedale Pike, a bulky fell planted on its northern and eastern flanks by Forestry Commission conifers. Close to its head is the barrier of Force Crag, from which drops Low Force. Nearby are the buildings of an old mine, Force Crag Mine. The scene is rugged and impressive. At the head of Coledale Valley, on the southern side of Grisedale Pike, is Eel Crag. Going upwards to Coledale Hause another, higher, valley and another rock barrier, over which flows High

Force, are encountered; and there are other mine buildings. The most recent products from the mines are barytes. (The mines are dangerous places to explore.)

WHINLATTER PASS (a secondary motor road) is to the north of the fell, but forest obscures most of the views from this pass.

The best routes for the ascent of Grisedale Pike are either direct from Braithwaite or from Coledale Hause. The summit (790m.) gives excellent views between east and south, from Derwent Water to Scafell Pikes.

Grizedale   3D5
Not all that long ago the Forestry Commission were not very happy, to say the least, at the prospect of the general public wandering freely about their plantations, there being, for one thing, the question of fire risk. Times have changed and the Commission are beginning to welcome, and indeed invite, people into their forests: Grizedale Forest, a large forest between Esthwaite and Coniston, was one of the first to open its gates willingly. There has always been woodland in the area of the Lake District known as High Furness, south of Coniston and Windermere. For 700 years the woods provided one of the area's main industries. The herds of wild red deer, and the roe, have descended from stocks that were here prior to human settlement.

In 1937 the Commission took over the Grizedale Hall estate for reafforestation. During the war the HALL itself became a German officers' prison camp. Franz von Werra, the German Air Force pilot who eventually escaped to Canada, made a clever but unsuccessful attempt at escape from Grizedale by dropping undetected over a wall near Satterthwaite while on exercise.

To the dismay of many people the hall was demolished after the war, leaving only the outbuildings. Below the hall site a well-screened camp site, managed by the Camping Club of Great Britain, has been provided. Nature-trail leaflets can be obtained from a shop in a nearby building.

Across the road from the hall site, stables and other outbuildings have been converted. One of these buildings is a wild-life museum containing mounted subjects displayed against their natural backgrounds; a room in the museum is devoted to deer. In another building is an exhibition explaining the purpose of forestry and the mechanics and products of the industry. And a large barn has been converted into a theatre: The Theatre in the Forest. This not only presents regular films and lectures on natural history, but has a programme of concerts given by well-known national and international artists. The extremely popular Grizedale Piano Festival is an annual summer event. Not far away, on the Hawkshead road, a farm has been converted to a restaurant to serve visitors to the theatre and forest.

The Commission has a number of 'high seats', screened viewing shelters on high platforms, where visitors can observe deer and other wild life. A charge is

made for this service. Nature trails are explained by leaflet and are also waymarked, but it is very easy to get lost in the forest, even with a large-scale map: extraction roads, constantly added to and extended, cause much confusion and sometimes obscure rights-of-way, and landmarks are occasionally hidden by trees. A compass is necessary for free wanderers.

The forest can hardly be missed, but Grizedale itself is found by taking the first road west from Hawkshead, following the Newby Bridge road. Approaching from the south, it is just north of the village of Satterthwaite.

Gummers How   3D6   E of Lakeside
The fell of Gummers How is only 321m. high but is strategically placed for views over southern Windermere; it is approached so closely by a high-level road that its summit can be reached in about fifteen minutes, though the last section is steep and rough.

The high-level road (signposted Kendal) begins near Fell Foot and turns upwards, rising steeply, from the Newby Bridge–Bowness-on-Windermere road. Near the brow of the hill are one or two lay-bys. A public footpath leaves the higher lay-by going northwards to the summit.

It is necessary to walk about the heathery summit for the best views.

There is no right of access to the summit other than on the public path.

Hadrian's Wall   6F4/E4/E5, 5D5/C5
Anyone who wishes to explore Hadrian's Wall should first see the displays and exhibits at Carlisle Museum.

The construction of a wall was ordered by the Emperor Hadrian in 122; it stretched between the Solway and the Tyne, taking advantage of the north-facing cliffs on the Whin Sill, a natural barrier. Its intention was in part to define the new frontier after the retreat from Scotland, but it was also designed to frustrate attempts at collusion between northerners and Brigantians – a catalyst for trouble in the past.

The wall was 80 Roman miles long (117·5km.) and a further defence system extended down the Cumbrian coast. Nowhere in Cumbria is the wall as impressive as it is through Northumberland. The Cumbrian part of it from Gilsland westwards was at first built of turf because of a shortage of building material, but before 163 this sector was rebuilt in stone. Much of the stone has of course been robbed over the centuries, the wall being regarded as a useful quarry wherever there was a natural shortage of stone.

On the north side of the wall was a ditch about 8m. wide and 3m. deep. Between the wall and the ditch was a berm, a narrow open space. Set into the wall at intervals of one Roman mile were the MILECASTLES, and between these were two TURRETS, evenly spaced. The size of the milecastles varied between 15m. and 20m. in breadth and 20m. and 23m. in length; they were of two-storey construction with gateways north and south, and

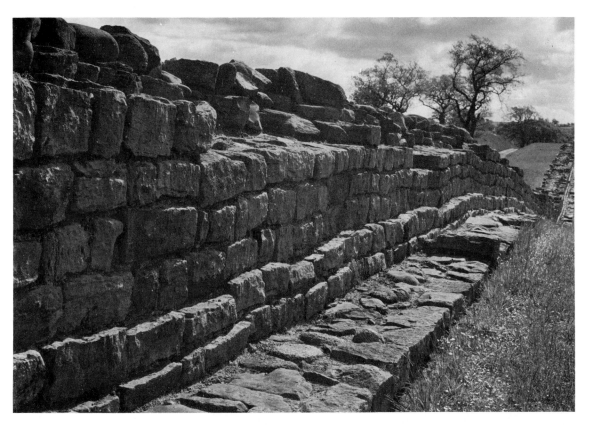

TOP: *Hadrian's Wall, Gilsland*   BOTTOM: *Hadrian's Wall: Camboglanna (the fort at Bird-oswald): inside E gateway*

could house about fifty men. The turrets, also two-storey, were about 6m. square.

South of the wall ran the MILITARY WAY, a road about 6m. wide, and between this and the wall was the VALLUM, a formidable ditch normally 7m. wide and as much as 3m. deep. Along the wall were a number of FORTS, some astride it, some behind it, and these varied in size according to the strength of the garrison each was intended to accommodate. Some were designed to take 500 infantry, but at Stanwix, Carlisle, the fort enclosed 3·7ha. and was intended to hold a cavalry regiment of 1,000 men and horses. In Cumbria, in addition to Stanwix, there were wall forts at Birdoswald, Castlesteads, Burgh-by-Sands, Drumburgh, and Bowness. If the coastal defences are considered to be part of Hadrian's defence system, we should also count four further forts at Beckfoot, Maryport, Barrow Walls, and Moresby. Milecastles and watch towers were also constructed along the coast, at least to Maryport.

From east to west the remains in Cumbria are as follows: at Gilsland, lengths of wall in what was the vicarage garden and foundations of two turrets, 48a and 48b; a well-preserved milecastle, 48, is to the west of the railway station. There is a bridge abutment on the Irving bank in farm fields, where the wall arched across the river. It climbed from the river to milecastle 49 and from this point there is a good length remaining as far as the fort at Birdoswald, Camboglanna (Crooked Valley), where there is much to see and admire. (A farm occupies part of this site.)

From Birdoswald the wall has been uncovered and preserved and can be walked; to the south of it can be seen signs of the original turf wall, which took a different line to milecastle 51. At the fourth turret on from here, 52a, it is possible for the initiated to identify a turf-wall turret that was later incorporated into the stone wall on the same line. There is little to see for the next 13 Roman miles. Then at Castlesteads, just south of the wall, a bluff on the east bank of the Cam Beck can be seen: this was the site of Vxellodunum. At Stanwix, Carlisle, where the large fort of Petriana stood, only small sections of wall are visible. The fort is covered by buildings, including the church and the churchyard. The wall crosses the Eden south-west of Petriana and follows a devious course with the river's west bank before turning westwards at Beaumont, turret 70a, to Aballava, a fort now beneath part of the village of Burgh-by-Sands. The church at Burgh is built largely from stone filched from the fort by the Norman builders.

After Burgh-by-Sands the wall goes westwards over the marshes, and just north-east of Drumburgh traces of milecastle 76 can be seen. A short distance to the west of this was the fort of Congavata: its stone has long since disappeared. The wall then takes a zig-zag course to Port Carlisle and to Bowness-on-Solway. At Bowness was the fort of Maia, covering 3ha; there was probably also a small port. No doubt the fort was necessary at this point because of a ford across the Solway. The stones from Maia have been robbed for the village's buildings: in the wall of a barn near the King's Arms Hotel, for instance, is a small Roman altar dedicated to Jupiter.

Was Bowness the end of the wall? It has been thought so. Shortage of stone, it was assumed, made further building impossible. It has been suggested that from this point on to Maryport the milecastles, which can be seen on aerial photographs, and the turrets served as watch and patrol points. But some archaeologists have remained uneasy with this conclusion. In the drought of 1975 Professor Barri Jones of Manchester University studied parch-marks at Biglands, west of Bowness, from the air and identified them as parallel ditches 46m. apart. Further west still at Cardurnock (a name that means 'fort in a pebbly place') the Professor traced a kilometre stretch of parallel ditches 30m. apart. At Biglands excavations made into the silt of the ditches showed that the northern ditch had been cut at least twice: pottery fragments suggest a possible dating of around 124, when Hadrian's Wall was still being constructed and strengthened. An excavation near Cardurnock showed that the forward ditch had been reinforced by a palisade of stakes pointing forward at 70°–80° on the outer lip and that both ditches had been recut. The suggestion is made, therefore, that milecastles and turrets were built between defensive ditches; the recutting showed that the Romans were put to some difficulty with the unstable sand and gravel subsoils. If nothing else, the findings show that there is still room for research into the type of Roman defence system on the Cumbrian coast.

South of Silloth there was a fort at Beckfoot; characteristically the stones have been stolen. Excavations point to building in Hadrian's time and occupation well into the fourth century. Maryport's fort (Alauna) stands on a hill north of the Ellen and probably had connexions with a port. There was also a village. In excavations, pits round Alauna's parade-ground revealed a fine selection of altars. On the outskirts of Workington, under fields overlooking the River Derwent, is the site of Gabrosentum: this also seems to be of Hadrianic period, with reconstruction in the fourth century. At Moresby, north of Whitehaven, was Tunnocelum, another fort of the Hadrianic period; the church of St Bridget is inside the fort area. This might logically seem the southern end of the defence system but there are perhaps other discoveries to be made. The Romans would certainly have had to keep a keen watch and patrol on the coast and St Bees Head would have been a key watch-point. The next fort southwards was Glannaventa, at Ravenglass, 27km. as the crow flies, and probably built solely to protect an important port.

Hard Knott   3C4

Hard Knott is a crag-peaked fell at the foot of Upper Eskdale. Between this fell and Harter Fell is Hard Knott

Hardknott Roman fort: aerial photograph from the SW

Pass, a pass containing one of the most awkward roads in England. The road is narrow with hairpin bends and has gradients of up to 1 in 3. Although the surface has been improved (to the regret of some people) the road is still testing to vehicles and drivers: despite this, or perhaps because of this, the road is frequently jammed at weekends and holiday periods, sometimes for hours. The pass offers a direct link between Eskdale and Upper Dunnerdale and a further link, via Wrynose, another fierce pass, to Langdale and Ambleside.

HARDKNOTT FORT is passed by motorists on the Hard Knott Pass, many of whom are blissfully unaware of the fort's existence. Dramatically set on a shelf on the Eskdale side of the pass, it is one of the most exciting Roman forts in Britain. The walls, some portions restored by the Department of the Environment, stand quite high.

Hardknott fort: the gap in the fells is the summit of the pass

Standing in the fort's centre one is surrounded by high fells. The north gate opens on to a cliff edge. Mediobogdum, as the fort was called, was built in the early second century to command a road from Ambleside over the passes to the Roman port and fort at Ravenglass (Glannaventa). Traces of the road can still be seen; following it is a strenuous excursion. The Roman road probably followed a route taken by Britons: there was certainly traffic from Langdale long before the Roman invasion. The fort also commands a view of Upper Eskdale and a surprise attack on the post would have been difficult.

Although at the time of building the fort would have been surrounded by trees, a sense of wild isolation must have been felt by the occupying garrisons. With typical Roman thoroughness a PARADE-GROUND, covering an area larger than the fort itself, was dug into the fellside above the fort: that, in some ways, is the most remarkable feature of Mediobogdum. A tribunal, or review platform, is on the north side, approached by a ramp. The labour involved in levelling the rocky site must have been immense.

The fort was built (or rebuilt?) during the reign of Hadrian in the early second century: an inscription found near the east gate testifies to this. The inscription, cut in good Lakeland Green Slate, which must have been transported from Langdale, reads: 'For the Emperor Caesar Trajan Hadrian Augustus, son of the divine Trajan, Conqueror of Parthia, grandson of the divine Nerva, Pontifex Maximus, thrice Consul, the Fourth Cohort of Dalmatians'. Archaeologists assume that the fort was abandoned during the reign of Antoninus Pius (138–61), when the northern frontier was pushed northwards, but was re-occupied upon the abandonment of the Antonine Wall. An inscription mentioning Sextus Calpurnius Agricola suggests this, and pottery finds have supplied further evidence. The fort was probably finally abandoned in the late second century or early third century.

The foundations of the stone buildings can still be seen: the headquarters building is in the centre, the commander's house to the west, and the all-important granary to the east. All the other buildings would have been of wood. The bath-house is outside the fort.

The views from the fort are exceptional: on a clear day the Isle of Man is visible; the view from the north gate takes in the Scafell range and gives an eagle's-eye view of Eskdale; the view up the pass dwarfs the foreground but the whole aspect is affected by the mood of the changing conditions – cloud, shadow, drifting mist, or humid haze – the view of the fort from the parade-ground is likewise awesome. Indeed, the sight of this large area of completely flat ground among such mountainous surroundings is in itself a striking and imposing novelty.

Harrop Tarn 3C4 NW of Steel End
Harrop Tarn, on the south-west side of Thirlmere, hides its light under a thick bushel of conifer plantations. It is worth a visit.

Before Manchester Corporation destroyed the hamlet of Wythburn (nicknamed The City) by raising the level of Thirlmere, an important fell track linked the settlement with Borrowdale and Keswick. The track, long neglected, is now the territory of the fell-walker: the Borrowdale stretch has the reputation of being the wettest fell-walk in Cumbria, although as far as Harrop Tarn the track is not too formidable. The path is signposted at the southern end of the minor road on the west side of Thirlmere, and the tarn is reached in a short walk, but with a climb of about 100m. The plantings about the tarn, once said to be haunted by a headless ghost, have enhanced rather than detracted from its appearance.

Harter Fell   Eskdale   3C5

Harter Fell, Eskdale, stands between Eskdale and the head of Dunnerdale, towering over Hardknott Roman fort (*see* Hard Knott) across the pass. It is not high (649m.) but has an impressive appearance viewed from the road up Eskdale: it has broadleaf woodlands on the lower slopes, masses of heather above, and an imposing array of crags on the crown. Its Dunnerdale side, though, has been planted by the Forestry Commission to 450m. The afforestation scheme raised a great deal of concern and anger when it began in the early 'thirties, but time heals all: the forest is now accepted. If its clear-felling were proposed perhaps preservation societies would raise even louder protests than those heard some forty years ago.

From the lay-by at the Eskdale foot of Hard Knott Pass there is a good ascent of the fell: the summit is a short scramble up naked rock. The view of the Scafells is one of the best; and the view towards the sea down the wooded dales of Dunnerdale and Eskdale is elating.

Harter Fell   Kentmere   4E4   E of Nan Bield

Nan Bield Pass takes the walker from Kentmere to Haweswater, and, to the east, Gatescarth Pass joins Longsleddale to Haweswater. Both passes cross the flanks of Harter Fell (774m.), the highest and northern-most point in the ridge between Kentmere and Longs-leddale. The fell finishes abruptly in steep crags above Mardale and the deep valley holding Small Water. Routes to the summit from all three valleys are good and the views northwards from the summit down over Haweswater are excellent. It is a fell to avoid in bad weather.

Hartsop   3D4

Travelling southwards from Ullswater towards Kirk-stone, and before reaching Brothers Water, a large conical hump of fell is neared: it seems to block the valley. This is Hartsop Dodd (615m.), lying to the south-east of Brothers Water. As the valley is turned, its sister mountain, High Hartsop Dodd, occupies the opposite side of the Kirkstone road; it is not greater in height: 'High' refers to its position in the dale. Hartsop Dodd is in fact not a fell in its own right but the end of a spur from Caudale Moor.

The HAMLET of Hartsop is up a narrow lane on the Kirkstone-road bend. It contains some seventeenth-century farm buildings. A path beyond the lane is the route to Hayeswater.

Hartsop possibly gets its name from the deer that ran here when the whole area as far north as Greystoke was a hunting forest in the days of William Rufus. In winter, deer from the Martindale herd can sometimes be seen on Hartsop and Caudale Moor. Much of the property in the area is owned by the NT, including Brothers Water (qv).

Haweswater   4E3

In the middle of the last century the green valley that contained Haweswater sent, by railway, 3,000 pounds of butter to Manchester market every week. At the valley head was the hamlet of MARDALE. Harriet Martineau in her *Guide to the English Lakes* (1855) wrote: 'The inn at Mardale Green is full a mile from the water; and sweet is the passage to it. . . . The path winds through the levels, round the bases of the knolls, past the ruins of the old church, and among snug little farms'. But the picturesque was not for Manchester and she needed something more than butter: she needed water, and Thirlmere was not enough to supply her needs. The Haweswater reservoir scheme was launched and the construction of a dam was begun in 1929. The water level was raised by 29m. and Mardale and the dairy farms had to go. The loss of the inn, The Dun Bull, was particularly mourned; and to make amends the Corporation built another one, the Haweswater Hotel, half-way down the lake on the side of their new road. Some architect in the Corporation's offices was probably proud of his design. Indeed the hotel would have looked fine in a Manchester suburb. But, hospitable though it is, it does not belong to Cumbria.

The modern Haweswater, even with some inevitable conifer planting, the bleached shoreline caused by level fluctuations, and the concrete dam itself, is not without its attractions. It is off the beaten track, and the wild crags at the dale head, the High Street range, loud with falling water, give the upper reaches a dramatic effect; and ornithologists have been delighted to see that golden eagles have returned to hunt the quiet valleys.

Haweswater is fed by many becks. From the head, in hanging valleys high on High Street, becks cascade from two mountain tarns: Blea Water (which reaches an astounding depth of 63m.) and Small Water. From the craggy heights of the western bank flow Riggindale Beck, Randale Beck, and Whelter Beck, and, from Bampton Common at the northern end, Measand Beck. From Mardale and Swindale Common, numerous small becks flow in from the east side. Haweswater is also fed by underground pipes from Ullswater. No one would know: Manchester Corporation latterly learned to be more sensitive.

The water authority that took over the responsibilities from the old Manchester Corporation is at present considering allowing public access to the lake, raising the dam still higher, making drastic alterations to the Haweswater Hotel.

During droughts walls and ruins of the drowned village of Mardale can sometimes be seen.

Hawkshead: this corner, through an old archway, is known as 'Grandy Nook'

Hawkshead 3D5 (*pop.* 680)

Hawkshead became an important wool town in Norman times, and, as a measure of its success, it once had seven inns. It later became just a village, somewhat off the beaten track; and it is now on every Lakeland visitor's itinerary. Indeed, it is sometimes difficult to appreciate the attractive squares and cobbled streets overhung by seventeenth-century timber-framed buildings for the sheer volume of visitors.

Hawkshead was the much-loved village of Wordsworth. He went to the grammar school there, and lodged with a 'kind and motherly Dame', Ann Tyson. When he went to Cambridge he spent his holidays here, and he has much to say about the area in *The Prelude*:

Thence with speed
Up the familiar hill I took my way
Towards that sweet Valley where I had been reared.
(IV 17–19.)

The 'familiar hill' was the hill from the Windermere ferry, for this has always been a main approach to Hawkshead.

There is an old cottage in the village, in Vicarage Lane, known locally as Ann Tyson's cottage. If Wordsworth did stay there it was only for a short period, for the Tysons left the village centre and moved to Green End Cottage, Colthouse, a hamlet separated from the village by a beck and a couple of fields. This is where the young scholar lodged and the descriptions in *The Prelude* remove all doubt.

Wordsworth described Hawkshead's 'snow-white' church upon her hill as a throned lady 'sending out a gracious look all over her domain'. The setting of the church is perfect, and the view from the churchyard quite beautiful. Dedicated, like so many hill churches, to ST MICHAEL AND ALL ANGELS, the present building dates from the fifteenth century – with Elizabethan improvements – but there are signs that there was an earlier structure on which the present rather massive tower is built. First record of a chapel here was made in the early thirteenth century, when its revenues were assigned to the Abbot of Furness. The present church is built of local undressed stone plastered smooth. Unusually, the nave and chancel are separated from the aisles by arcades. There are some decorations and painted texts dating from 1680.

There are two squares in the village with a communicating passage, several seventeenth-century buildings, and a fascinating mixup of narrow streets – some cobbled – and yards. Several of the buildings are in the care of the NT, the gift of the late Mrs W. Heelis (Beatrix Potter).

The GRAMMAR SCHOOL (open at reasonable times on enquiry locally) is largely as William Wordsworth knew it, with original desks and benches; William's name is carved on a desk among the initials and names of other inattentive pupils. The school was founded and endowed by Edwin Sandys (1516?–88), Archbishop of York from 1576; Sandys was the son of a local family and was born at Esthwaite Hall.

On the north side of the village near the Coniston-road junction is HAWKSHEAD COURTHOUSE (NT); the present building dates in part from the thirteenth century but is mainly of the fifteenth century. All the land between Windermere and Coniston belonged to Furness Abbey, and the monks held the manor of Hawkshead for 300 years. The Manor House has gone and the courthouse is the only remnant of the monks' manorial buildings. It has now been made into an attractive folk museum.

About Hawkshead is a scattering of small settlements. Colthouse, where Wordsworth lodged, has changed very little since his day. It is by the Wray junction from the ferry road. Green End Cottage is not open to the public. The seventeenth-century Quaker Meeting House, where Wordsworth occasionally worshipped on 'very hot or very wet Sundays' when it was too inclement to go to Hawkshead church, remains little changed and is still used.

There are old stories attached to most villages. One curious and unanswered question in Hawkshead's history is: why were the Vicar of Urswick, William Sawrey, and his chaplain so much hated in 1548? The Vicar was lodging in what is now the Old Courthouse and it is recorded that he was besieged for two days by a 'tumult or insurrection', when men assembled armed 'with swords, bucklers, staves, bills, clubs, daggers, and other weapons'. Being unable to get at the Vicar, they demanded that he should come out 'for they would have one of his arms or legs before going away'. They were eventually dispersed by neighbours.

Hay Bridge Nature Reserve *see* **Bouth**

Helm Crag (The Lion and the Lamb)   3C4
NW of Grasmere
Above Grasmere, north-west of the village, a steep fell crowned with large rocks dominates the scene. This is Helm Crag. In earlier days tourists liked to exercise their imagination in suggesting 'explanations' for the odd shapes against the skyline. From the Dunmail Raise road, at the foot of the hill, the most prominent rock on the south-east side of the crag looks very like a lion couchant, with a lamb lying between its paws. Hence the popular name for the crag: The Lion and the Lamb. The most prominent rock viewed from the top of Dunmail Raise was described by early guide-books as a howitzer or mortar. Wordsworth wrote of 'the ancient woman sitting on Helm Crag'; his imagination, for once, seems less fertile compared with that of his contemporaries. From the Easedale-path side of the crag, or from the Tongue Gill ascent to Grisedale Tarn, on the eastern side, there is a prominent rock formation known colloquially as The Old Woman Playing the Organ. (Early guides leading walking parties used to say 'listen and you will hear the music', and there would usually follow a moment's anticipatory silence before the hoax was discovered.)

The crag is usually climbed by a path leaving the Far Easedale track. It is exhaustingly steep, and tricky on descent. The best views from the summit, a shattered mass of large rocks, are over Grasmere.

Helvellyn   3D3
Helvellyn is the most popular mountain in the Lake District, mainly because it is very accessible and central. The highest point is at 950m., and the whole range from Grisedale Tarn in the south to Threlkeld Common in the north is about 14½km. long and about 7km. wide at the widest point. The range lies between Thirlmere and Ullswater. On the west side the slopes are steep but rounded in the typical 'upturned basin' shape of the Lake District fells, the steepest slopes being nearest the valley bottom. On the east side the hard rock is deeply indented into craggy valleys as a result of glaciation, and there are several 'combes', high indentations, scooped

out of the higher slopes by lingering ice, two of them holding sizeable mountain tarns: Grisedale Tarn and Red Tarn. RED TARN is dramatically situated between two arms of the mountain – arêtes – with narrow edges. The northern arm is known as Swirral Edge, the southern arm, and most popular line of ascent, is STRIDING EDGE, so called because walkers are obliged to stride over gaps in the serrated edge if they keep to the ridge, though for most of the route there is a lower side path. Striding Edge is for experienced and well-equipped walkers only, and is dangerous in iced conditions and in high wind. Swirral Edge is slightly easier and is a popular line of descent for walkers returning to Glenridding and Patterdale.

From the Thirlmere side the popular approach to the summit is from Wythburn church: this is the easiest line but it is a long slog, taking about three hours for an average walker in no particular hurry. Another line is by the 'whitestones' route from the inn at Thirlspot (King's Head), called 'whitestones' because traditionally the path is annually waymarked with whitewash by the landlord of the inn. This practice was established many years ago when there was rivalry between the inns at Thirlspot and at Wythburn; the object of the King's Head was to tempt the travellers away from the Wythburn inn, the popular Nag's Head. The rivalry no longer exists: in spite of strong protests the Nag's Head was closed down by Manchester Corporation Waterworks, and is now demolished.

Another approach to the summit is from Grasmere via Grisedale Tarn. This way, between the Helvellyn and Fairfield ranges, was once a busy pack-horse track between Grasmere and Patterdale. The path up Helvellyn leaves it just north of Grisedale Tarn at a point known as Brothers Parting (qv).

The southernmost peak of the Helvellyn range is DOLLYWAGON PIKE. The origin of this strange name is unknown, though 'Helvellyn' appears to be Celtic. The height here is 856m. Below it, to its north and east, steep cliffs drop to Ruthwaite Cove, about 225m. below, occupied by a small tarn, Hard Tarn. The northern arm of the cove, or combe, is occupied by the next peak, Nethermost Cove, the northern wall of which is Striding Edge. NETHERMOST COVE holds the winter snows a long time and is popular with snow and ice climbers. The peak above the centre of the cove is Swallow Scarth (868m.).

Where the Striding Edge path reaches the summit plateau is the Gough memorial, erected in 1890 to honour a dog. Gough was the name of an unfortunate gentleman who died while crossing the mountain in winter; when his body was eventually found three months later it was still guarded by his faithful but emaciated dog. Both Scott and Wordsworth wrote some lines about this remarkable event; the lines are quoted on the monument. On the approach to the summit there is another monument, to celebrate the first landing of an aircraft, an Avro Alpha in 1926, on a mountain summit. (The monument is undecipherable at time of writing, but replacement is contemplated.)

Just below the summit is a cruciform wall shelter built in the nineteenth century, and restored by NP Wardens in 1968. Cliffs drop from the summit on the eastern side to a combe containing Red Tarn. On a clear day all the major fells of the Lake District can be seen from the summit, the highest peaks being between south-west and west. Morecambe Bay may be seen to the south, and the Solway Firth, with the fells of southern Scotland, to the north-west. The north wall of Red Tarn Cove is Swirral Edge, and at the far end of the edge is an impressive pointed peak oddly named Catstycam (889m.) (spelt on some old maps 'Catchedecam'). After Swirral Edge ends, the Helvellyn summit ridge crooks westwards to Lower Man (924m.), then north again to the next peak, Whiteside (863m.). From that peak a pony track zig zags eastwards into Kepple Cove below, the track eventually passing the old mine workings on the way to Glenridding.

From Whiteside the ridge again bends to the northeast and RAISE (880m.); the slopes below are now less craggy. The northern-facing fell-side of the eastern flank of Raise holds snow well and in good winters is much used by skiers. The local club has a ski hut, and a tow is operated. Between Raise and the next peak to the north, Stybarrow (840m.), a pass – Sticks Pass, 747m. at its highest point – crosses the mountain. It was once an important pony track but is now reduced to a rough footpath, linking Stanah at Thirlspot with Glenridding, via the waste heaps of the old mines.

The northern reach of the range, wild, open, and less interesting, is broken by the peaks of the other Dodds – Watson's (788m.) and Great Dodd (855m.) – and drops to the bleak moors of Matterdale and Threlkeld. The range is on the northern boundary of the Borrowdale Volcanics; to the north are the Skiddaw Slates. Such junctions often provide interesting geological features: there are extrusions of granite, profitably quarried and largely used for roadmaking, and other minerals are also evident, including iron, lead, and some garnets.

Helvellyn is a great attraction for botanists and is listed by the Nature Conservancy as an Area of Special Scientific Interest. Wet areas on the barren mountain sides (flushes), fed from low-ground sources, leach out minerals to the surface and provide rich plant habitats. Where these are out of reach of grazing sheep some interesting alpine plants can be found, but the botanist needs to be something of a rock climber. Schelly, a freshwater whitefish common in Ullswater, is also found in Red Tarn.

Rock climbing on the Helvellyn range is largely centred on two points. CASTLE ROCK, on the north-western flank above Legburthwaite, at the foot of St John's in the Vale, is very popular, some of the climbs requiring a special skill. This is the crag that Scott

named The Castle Rock of Triermain, the castle being pure imagination, though clearly suggested by the shape of the crag. The second attraction to rock climbers is EAGLE CRAG, east of Nethermost Pike and hanging above Grisedale.

Helvellyn is served by four mountain-rescue teams. Patterdale in the south-eastern part, Ambleside/Langdale team in the south-west, Keswick team in the north-west, and the Ullswater Outward Bound School in the north-east.

Hesket Newmarket   3D1   *(pop.* 415)
East of Caldbeck is a quiet, off-the-beaten-track hamlet of old white houses, built of the local carboniferous limestone, ranged around a green. Until the world passed it by, Hesketh Newmarket was an important market-town. Charles Dickens stayed here with Wilkie Collins in 1857, and in an article in *Household Words*, 'The Lazy Tour of Two Idle Apprentices', he wrote of the area and described a climb up Carrock Fell. HESKET HALL (not open to the public) is architecturally interesting for its circular roof and cubic shape, with full-height porches front and back, and projecting wings at each side to accommodate staircases. It is locally suggested that the twelve corners thus formed make an effective sundial.

High Raise   High White Stones   3C4
High Raise (762m.) is the summit point of a fell area known as High White Stones, directly north of Langdale Pikes and east of Lang Strath, and near to the central point of the Lake District fells. It is largely a featureless plateau of nardus grass and bog, with a stone cairn and a survey column marking the highest point. The old boundary between Cumberland and Westmorland crosses the peak, and the line is marked by the remnants of an iron fence. In mist, following the fence is the easiest way off the fell: it can be followed northwards to the 'crossroads' at Greenup Edge, from whence tracks go eastwards to Grasmere, north-westwards to Borrowdale, and north-eastwards to Wythburn.

High Street   3D3/D4
The Lake District's High Street is not a shopping precinct but a fell ridge, reaching a height of 828m. and surmounted by a Roman road, between the valleys of Ullswater and Haweswater. An obvious question is why a Roman road on the fell spine when less steep routes through the dales could be used? But it has to be remembered that the present-day landscape has been transformed by man since the Roman occupation. In Roman times the fell sides were thickly forested and the valleys boggy and inhospitable, and likely places to suffer ambush. A glance at the map shows that the route along the High Street ridge is almost on a direct line from the Roman fort at Brougham, Penrith, to Troutbeck, near Windermere, where it is assumed that it met the road from Watercrook fort, Kendal, to the Roman

The Langdale Pikes

The Solway Firth: near Anthorn looking out across Moricambe Bay

High Street ridge above Haweswater's head. Blea Water is left centre

fort at Ambleside. The Roman road almost certainly followed a route used by Britons; it is a 'road-improvement' job with no elaborate works.

The highest point on the High Street range is directly east of Hartsop, and its eastern face towers craggily over the wild head of Haweswater, with cliffs of 310m. As a contrast to its savage eastern flank, the top is grassy and even; and, having the advantage of easy, though long, approaches from the north and south, it was until the nineteenth century an annual meeting point for shepherds, where stray animals could be claimed and an excuse easily found for revelries. Shepherds from Mardale, Troutbeck, Martindale, Patterdale, Kentmere, and Longsleddale took part. There was a fair, casks of ale were consumed, and there was horse racing, wrestling, and games. The summit plateau is still named Race-horse Hill. There could be no finer setting for such rustic fun on a summer's day.

At the range's northern end, rising south-east of Howtown, is Loadpot Hill: the summit (671m.) is an uninteresting, grassy area, with the ruins of a shooting-lodge rising about heather moors and peat bogs. The Roman road approaches from the long, easy climb from MOOR DIVOCK, part of Askham Fell, in the north-west. Moor Divock is a wild, open area roamed by wild ponies. There are many signs of Iron Age settlement, including cairns and a small stone circle.

South of Loadpot is Weather (Wether) Hill (674m.),

equally featureless on the summit; the ridge rises to High Raise (803m.) and the path goes south-west before turning south for High Street summit.

South from High Street is THORNTHWAITE CRAG (783m.), which has the most distinctive summit cairn in Cumbria: a stone column 4m. high. Who built it and why they went to such elaborate length is not known, though it is on an old boundary line. From Thornthwaite the Roman road leaves the range to descend southwards to Troutbeck. This section of the route is known as Scots Rake, named, it is said, because this was the route that the Scottish raiders used. Although there is no evidence of defensive houses in Troutbeck, it is certainly likely that raiders used the easy High Street route. There are excellent views from various points on Troutbeck's summit: the best view is that looking towards Windermere.

Southwards, the ridge continues with Froswick (719m.), then ILL BELL (Hill Bell on some maps) (755m.). Both these fells have a distinct peaked appearance when viewed from the south-west. The sides overlooking Kentmere Reservoir are cragged. There are several cairns on the summit of Ill Bell, a fell that offers one of the finest, if not the finest, of views over Windermere.

The last peak on the ridge is YOKE (703m.): it appears as a green hill from the Troutbeck side, but on the Kentmere side it is riven by the sheer crag of Rainsbarrow, the haunt of rock-climbers, and, in days past, peregrines.

Holker Hall: the main hall; the cantilevered staircase is behind

The quarries at the foot were once very active. The southern part of Yoke falls evenly to Garburn Pass – the track between Troutbeck and Kentmere – and the southernmost end of the High Street range.

High Stile and **High Crag** 3B3
Behind Buttermere, and on a still day reflected in the lake, are the steep walls of a crag-topped fell, its base beautifully wooded, its summit jutting with sheer crags. The fell is an indispensable part of the Buttermere scene, often thought to be the finest landscape in the country. Directly above the lake are two buttresses surmounted by two peaks: the lower one, on the left, is High Crag (745m.) and the one on the right is High Stile (806m.). To the left (east) of High Crag is Ennerdale (qv).

In the cove between High Crag and High Stile is Burtness (Birkness) Comb, a popular rock-climbing area. The cove to the right of High Stile, Bleaberry Comb, contains a small tarn, Bleaberry Tarn; behind the tarn is the summit of Red Pike (qv).

The High Stile ridge-walk demands a steep ascent and descent and should only be attempted by the fit and well-booted.

Holker Hall 3D6
Situated in a beautiful setting, near Cark, on the road between Grange-over-Sands and Haverthwaite (B5278), Holker Hall is an outstanding 'stately home' open to the public. The site belonged to Cartmel Priory until the Dissolution, and was acquired by the Preston family in 1556; a hall was built very early in the seventeenth century. Later in the same century the hall was passed over to the Lowther family when a Preston heiress married

Sir William Lowther of Marske in Yorkshire. In 1756 the property passed to the Cavendish family when a later Sir William Lowther died childless and a nephew, Lord George Augustus Cavendish, second son of the third Duke of Devonshire, inherited. (As an M.P. he became 'father' of the House of Commons, and was nicknamed 'Truth and Daylight'.) The hall has remained Cavendish ever since. Over the years the seventeenth-century hall has had Georgian and Victorian additions and alterations. The west wing was destroyed by fire in 1871 and later replaced by a copy of the original.

The light and friendly atmosphere and lay-out of the interior is a delight. The owners, who live in a wing of the hall, have managed to do without restrictive barriers, which too often spoil a good effect.

The library contains 3,500 volumes, among which are books by the son of the second Duke, Henry Cavendish, the discoverer of the properties of hydrogen. The Cavendish Laboratory at Cambridge is named after him.

There are beautiful examples of classical furniture in every room, and some rare paintings, including a cartoon by Van Dyck, and a caricature by Sir Joshua Reynolds. There is a screen embroidered by Mary Queen of Scots. The FIREPLACES are all superb: one has some fine carvings in Carrara marble and another an imposing oak surround made by local craftsmen. The staircase, built on the cantilever principle, is a masterpiece of local work. There are some beautiful antiques and *objets d'art*, but the most lasting impression left with visitors is probably of the exquisite décor of each room: the Wedgwood Room, for example, is in sensitive shades of pale green, pale blue, and white. Other rooms offer other effects.

Honister Pass

The beautiful gardens are at their best in early summer. The monkey-puzzle tree (chile pine), planted in 1851, is reputed to be the oldest surviving example in the country. When the tree was blown over in a storm in the 1890s it was pulled upright, with the help of chains and seven carthorses, and replanted. There are also an old tulip tree and some fine, unusual specimens of conifers.

In the grounds there are herds of fallow deer, red deer, and sika. There are also wild roe deer on the estate, but these are shy and, except early and late in the day, rarely seen.

Holme Cultram Abbey *see* **Abbey Town**

Howtown *see* **Ullswater**

Honister Pass   3C3
Honister Pass (358m.) links Seatoller, near the head of

Borrowdale, with Buttermere. It is nowhere difficult, although a little narrow in places; in winter the Buttermere side is sometimes impassable. The Honister Quarries continue in production and the slate, of very high grade, is in constant demand. Like other successful slate quarries in the Lake District, the slate consists of a hard volcanic stone formed over the ages from a dust laid down in water and subjected to great pressures. Some of the slate is finely marked and suitable for facing buildings. Much of the slate on Honister is 'mined' as the high-quality material is often deeply bedded. Honister has been worked from at least as far back as the mid eighteenth century, though the transport problems in that era must have been acute. The slate used to be sledged down from the higher sites to the roads on wheelless barrows with a 'jockey' positioned between the shafts to steer the contraption.

The fell above the quarries is Fleetwith Pike and the

fell on the opposite side of the hause is the handsome DALE HEAD (754m.), the sides of which were also once quarried.

Irton Cross 3B5 N of Ravenglass

In the churchyard of Irton church, well off the beaten track in west Cumbria, is a near-perfect Anglian cross that has stood for over a thousand years. Irton church is found by taking a minor road towards Santon Bridge from the A595 at Gubbergill, 4km. north of Ravenglass. Just over 1km. down this dead-straight road there is a lane to the left, leading to the church. The cross is on the far side of the church among a mass of modern gravestones. (A cross in a corner is a modern copy.) The sandstone cross has the intricate decorations of the period: interlacing and complicated knot work; the Runic inscription on the west side has weathered away. The cross was probably made in the late ninth century.

The nineteenth-century church, built on the site of an earlier structure, offers little of historical or architectural interest.

Keld *see* **Shap**

Kendal 4E5 *(pop.* 21,595)

Kendal was the largest town in the old county of Westmorland, and remains an important Cumbrian centre and market town. It contains some administrative offices, including those of the Lake District National Park, although it is a few metres east of the Park's boundary. The town occupies a strategic position on the A6, a road connected with the A591 leading into the Lake District; it is served by a spur from the M6 and a branch line from the mainline railway between London and Glasgow.

Kendal is largely built of the traditional grey limestone on which it stands. And, although the town has been altered since the war, it still retains, in places, the 'yards' construction system: examples are to be found at the end of alleyways leading from the town centre. Buildings were traditionally built round a communal yard in many old Cumbrian towns. One theory is that this was a defensive system, the gates being closed when necessary; but the Scots raids were long since past when the yards were built, and the pattern is common in the eighteenth-century development. Some of the older buildings are timber-framed, the timber usually concealed behind rendering and roughcast, but typical jettied upper storeys can be seen (e.g. Fleece Inn, Highgate).

The town stands by the River Kent, which takes water from a considerable watershed – from Kentmere, Longsleddale, and Shap – flooding after prolonged rains. The river is spanned by six bridges. On a hill on the east bank are the remains of KENDAL CASTLE, a motte-and-bailey castle built by order of William Rufus. In 1543 it was in the ownership of Thomas Parr, father of

Irton Cross: W side

*Kendal Castle: curtain wall and three towers C13. On the NE
are the remains of a range of the C14*

Katherine Parr, one of the wives of Henry VIII.
Katherine was born in the castle. By 1583 the castle was
recorded as being in decay, and little now remains
standing. One of the town's more durable properties is
Castle Dairy, Wildman Street: it is of Tudor design and
was restored in 1564.

Kendal's parish church, HOLY TRINITY, dates from the
thirteenth century, but was built on the site of an earlier
church. It has five aisles, contains various monuments
and brasses, and retains the three chapels of the notable
local families: the Parrs, Bellinghams, and Stricklands.
Near the Bellingham Chapel hang a sword and helmet
traditionally belonging to 'Robin the Devil', a Major
Phillipson of Windermere serving in the Royalist Army,
who sought revenge of a Cromwellian Colonel Briggs.
He rode into the church one Sunday morning in a vain
search for the Colonel and was thrown from his horse
when attempting to leave by a door smaller than the one
by which he had entered.

Kendal has been of importance since Roman times.
There was a fort south of the town at Watercrook; only
its platform is now visible. The fort was named ALAUNA
and archaeologists have evidence that it was occupied
from around AD 80 to the fourth century. It is assumed
that it commanded a road from Lancaster: northwards,
perhaps, to Ambleside and to Brougham, and north-east
to a main north–south road at Low Borrow Bridge, near
Tebay; the roads have not been effectively traced.

After the Norman conquest the town was subject to
numerous border raids, one of the most destructive oc-
curring in an attack of 1210 led by the Earl of Fife. In the
more settled days of the fourteenth century Flemish
weavers settled in Kendal and there began a woollen
trade that flourished for six centuries. Kendal Green, a
heavy cloth, became famous and is mentioned by Shakespeare in *Henry IV*. Kendal's main business is now in shoe
manufacture and insurance.

The town has a fine Museum of Life and Industry and

TOP: *Kentmere Hall: N front. C14 pele tower; attached farm building C16*

BOTTOM: *St John's church, Keswick, with Blencathra (Saddleback) in the background. Keswick town is to the left of the church*

an art gallery at Abbot Hall, near the parish church. There is also a good natural-history museum near the station.

There is an annual festival of music, the Mary Wakefield Music Festival, that attracts a great deal of attention.

Kentmere 3D4/D5

The dale that contains the source of the Kent, a river that gave the name to Kendal, is Kentmere. The dale no longer has the 'mere' that once occupied the flat fields south of the church and the road head: in the nineteenth century it was only a small, shallow lake and an area of reeds (it was referred to as a 'tarn' but was technically a lake); the outflow was subsequently cleaned out and the land drained for agriculture. All that remains is a swelling of the river where dredging now takes place for diatomous earth to supply the processing plant down-valley at Waterfoot, the old lake foot. In 1955 a wooden boat believed to be of tenth-century construction was uncovered in the course of the dredging operations; it was presented to the National Maritime Museum.

Although the 'mere' has disappeared there is a piece of water at the high valley head, Kentmere Reservoir, dammed last century to supply a constant head of water for valley mills. Round the reservoir the head is impressive, faced on the west with the steep crags of the High Street range, Froswick and Ill Bell. The ridge ending in Harter Fell (qv) is on the east with KENTMERE PIKE (730m.), a rounded summit, south-east of the reservoir. The pass of NAN BIELD (640m.) west of Harter Fell is the way out of Kentmere for Mardale and Haweswater.

Above the disused quarries south of the reservoir is RAINSBARROW CRAG, a climbing crag. Below this is a quiet, curving valley, descending to Kentmere village, a scattering of farms and houses. The grey church of St Cuthbert has existed at least 400 years, but there is little left of the original structure beyond the roof beams, apparently reused when restoration work was done in 1866.

The road up-valley is only 'public' as far as the village. There is a public road, GARBURN PASS, leaving westwards for Troutbeck, but this has been reduced to a footpath. The path reaches a height of 442m., and the walk gives a pleasant view over the Troutbeck Valley. A number of other pleasant walking paths leave the village. One goes south-westwards to Ings via an ancient British settlement. Several others go eastwards into Longsleddale over the wet moors that hold SKEGGLES WATER, a high tarn.

KENTMERE HALL (not open to the public), west of the village, is the oldest remaining building in the valley. The defensive pele tower is a fourteenth-century structure, the attached farm building of the sixteenth century replaced an earlier one. The defensive measures were, as ever, against the Scots raiders and were commissioned by the de Gilpin family. Bernard de Gilpin, who was born here, became Archdeacon of Durham, and as a champion of the Reformation became known as the 'Apostle of the North'. It is said that the great 9m.-long beam of the house was lifted into position by strong-man Hugh Hird, 'The Troutbeck Giant', after ten men had failed to move it.

Keswick 3C3 (pop. 5,183)

Keswick was once a small mining town. It is now a tourist's town crowded in the season with jostling holidaymakers. But there are no bingo halls and amusement arcades. The tourists come for the magnetic and magnificent setting: superlatives are unnecessary, it is impossible to be oblivious to the obvious. High fell and crag wall the little town on three sides, and at its open end is the wide expanse of Derwent Water backed by the highest mountains in England.

Almost the whole town is Victorian; it was built with the coming of the railway from Penrith, a railway that once offered one of the most pleasant rides in England. The railway is, alas, no more, and instead the town is served by an unlovely fast highway, the A66, spurred from the M6. The buildings in Keswick are of the local stone so the town looks as if it belongs. The MOOT HALL, in the town square, was built in 1813 on the site of an earlier structure; it is now an information centre. The town's oldest building is the parish church at Crosthwaite ('the clearing of the cross') at the north-west corner of the town, dedicated to ST KENTIGERN, otherwise St Mungo, the patron saint of Glasgow. The oldest fabric is to be found in the foundations of the north-aisle wall, and is assumed to date from 1181, but, with the exception of this fabric and the fourteenth-century north chapel, St Kentigern is a Late Perpendicular church. Additions and alterations were made in the fourteenth, seventeenth, and nineteenth centuries. There are ancient relics, but one of the main objects of interest is a white-marble memorial to Robert Southey, Poet Laureate and once presiding genius of Keswick. The epitaph was composed by his friend Wordsworth.

The town's small MUSEUM on Station Street, between the greenery of Lower and Upper Fitzpark, contains manuscripts and letters of the great Lakeland writers and poets. There are also geological exhibits, and the famous musical stones: carefully tuned pieces of volcanic rock mounted in a bizarre musical instrument that includes steel bars and bells; the musical stones were played by royal command at Buckingham Palace in 1848.

There are many fine viewpoints around the town, including Friars Crag (see Derwent Water), Castle Head, and Latrigg.

Although copper was one of the chief minerals mined in the neighbourhood, largely by German miners (who left their surnames among the early populace), Keswick was famed for its 'wad', or black-lead, mines. The town's pencil industry survives from those times, though the lead is now imported.

For a fortnight in July, Keswick becomes the home of

the Keswick Convention, when evangelists from home and abroad gather for meetings and services.

Keswick Stone Circle *see* **Castlerigg Stone Circle**

Kirkby Lonsdale 4F6 (*pop.* 1,505)
Kirkby Lonsdale is one of those delightful slightly off-track country towns that has not had its character too assiduously 'developed'. It has two distinct personalities. On Thursday, market-day, it bustles with activity as farmers and families from scattered communities converge for business and a 'crack' to catch up on local news. There are stalls in the market square and folk jostle in the narrow street; but walking through the churchyard to an alley in the south-east side of the town you are walking on cobbles into the eighteenth century, into the quiet square of the horsemarket amongst oddly-named streets of neat old houses.

The town is on a high bank overlooking a bend in the River Lune. The views over this area of the LUNE VALLEY are pleasant: Ruskin was particularly enthusiastic about them (it is 'one of the loveliest scenes in England – therefore in the world') and Turner painted a prospect from the churchyard. The old BRIDGE over the river, now closed to traffic, dates from the thirteenth century, and like many old bridges that have unnaturally survived the ravages of time, it is known locally as the Devil's Bridge.

The church of ST MARY THE VIRGIN stands near the site of a Saxon church. The oldest parts date from the twelfth century: among such survivals are three lovely arches and columns on the north side of the nave, the diamond patterning on the columns being a fine example of a style current between 1096 and 1130. The design was no doubt directly inspired by the work at Durham. The less splendid remaining arcading has given rise to some conjecture. Did the builders run out of funds? During restoration work in 1866 it was seen that the Norman arcading extended beyond the present structure, and evidence was found of an old fire. This burning probably dates from the period of the Scottish raids in the fourteenth century. There are signs of other additions and alterations and there is an explanatory plan fixed to a pillar. The usual damage was inflicted by the nineteenth-century 'restorers'; but this church's interior still presents one of the most impressive Early Norman displays in Cumbria.

Country market towns sometimes give the impression that they cannot make up their minds whether they are town or village: 'God made the country; man the town; the devil the country-town'. Here the devil only made the bridge.

Kirkby Thore 4F3 (*pop.* 800)
BRAVONIACUM, 'The Place of Querns', was a Roman cavalry fort guarding the Stainmore Pass. The site now lies partly under the houses of Kirkby Thore: the stones

Inspiration from Durham. Diamond patterning on a column in the church of St Mary the Virgin, Kirkby Lonsdale. W side of N arcade of nave

were looted long, long ago for building. The fort is also thought to have been a checkpoint and depôt for the lead coming south from the mines around Whitley Castle (Alston) for transport to York. At this point the Maiden Way leaves the York road for Alston.

Kirkoswald 4E1 (*pop.* 670)
Kirkoswald is a neat picture-book village with a small market square and clusters of old, well-kept buildings. The village has possessed a market charter from the

TOP: *Church of St Mary the Virgin, Kirkby Lonsdale, from the SW*   BOTTOM: *Kirkby Lonsdale: the C13 Devil's Bridge*

thirteenth century, allowing it a fair day and, on Easter Monday, a sports day. But the tradition has died and the village is now left in peace.

The church of ST OSWALD is built in a hollow and the bell-tower, probably for acoustic reasons, is placed separately on a hill. Reason for the odd siting of the church dates back to the seventh century when it is said that St Aidan, observing that the local pagans worshipped a well there, built a Christian church on top of it. The early wooden church was replaced with a stone one in 1130. All that can be seen of that Norman stone church is the base of the chancel arch and a portion of the square piers in the arcades. In the fourteenth century the Scots burned the village but the church seems to have been spared. Alterations in the sixteenth century brought the church to its present shape. Chancel aisles were pulled down and windows were added, and the wooden porch, still surviving, was erected. When the church's foundations were strengthened in 1970 it was found that the original foundation was constructed using oak piles.

The COLLEGE with its very beautiful late-seventeenth-century entrance is opposite the church. In 1590, after the Dissolution, the State sold college and lands to Henry Featherstonehaugh of Southwaite, near Dacre.

A pleasant path flanked by an avenue of limes starts opposite the college and leads down to the church. The well, mentioned earlier, is under the nave, but an outflow is in the west wall. There are some interesting stones in the churchyard, including Saxon grave-covers.

The present bell-tower dates from 1897, replacing an earlier wooden structure of 1747.

Kirkoswald's CASTLE, built by Ralph Engayne in 1200, is a complete ruin. A tower survives with remains of a spiral staircase; other fragments have to be sought in undergrowth. The castle was wrecked in the seventeenth century.

Kirkstone Pass 3D4

Kirkstone Pass is crossed by the road to Ullswater, reaching a height of 450m. The route from Ambleside to the summit of the pass is the steepest, the upper portion being called The Struggle: in the days of the horse-carriage, passengers had to leave their vehicle and walk up, and on the descent, it is said, the local drivers used to take the horses down at the gallop to terrify the tourists.

The route from Windermere is a steadier climb, though all the delightful views are on the downhill journey, with aèrial views down into the green valley of TROUTBECK. The uphill views are marred by the great scar of KIRKSTONE QUARRY.

On the Ullswater side the climb is not too steep but some steeper sections catch motorists napping, and at busy periods there are sometimes hold-ups caused by stalled vehicles.

At the pass summit is one of the North's highest inns, well known from earliest tourist days. At the summit,

too, seen against the sky on the approach from Ullswater, is the huge block of stone suggesting the shape of a dales' church and giving the pass its name.

Lanercost Priory 6E5

The ruins of Lanercost sit below Hadrian's Wall northeast of Brampton. The priory was dedicated to St Mary Magdalene and was founded as an Augustinian house by Robert de Vaux in 1166. Inevitably, being so near to the Border, the building was used and misused by armies and thieves from both sides. Edward I, 'Hammer of the

ABOVE: *Lanercost Priory: choir and clerestory*

RIGHT: *Lanercost Priory: looking SW from the sanctuary*

Scots', stayed at the priory three times. During the
Dissolution the priory was devastated and the monks
executed for their part in the Pilgrimage of Grace. The
buildings were granted to Sir Thomas Dacre in 1559, the
north aisle of the old church being retained as a parish
church. Much of the stone from the rest of the priory
was robbed for other buildings.

The oldest parts of the church are of the thirteenth
century. The remains of the monastery include part of
the transept tower and choir walls. Some Roman stones
can be identified, including altars.

The priory is open to the public daily except Sunday
mornings, closing time varying according to the time of
year.

Langdale *see* **Great Langdale** and **Little Langdale**

Lang Strath Borrowdale Fells 3C4
At the head of Borrowdale a deep valley from the south-
east joins the main valley at Rosthwaite. Down this
subsidiary valley, through low fields scarred by flooding, flows STONETHWAITE BECK. The paths through
woodlands on either side of the beck take the walker to a
split in the valley, with a great hump of crag, Eagle
Crag (503m.), at the division. The right-hand, southwards, valley is Lang Strath. Through it flows Langstrath Beck; a path along its bank leads up a wild valley
overhung by crags. At a point where a wall crosses the
beck is Blackmoss Pot, a deep pool in a deep gorge. A
main path, Stake Pass, eventually leaves the beck due
south, rising to 480m. before descending to Langdale. A
path continuing with Langstrath Beck to its source ends
at Esk Hause (759m.) (*see* Eskdale), a 'crossroads' of the
fells, with routes to Eskdale, Wasdale, and Langdale.

Latrigg 3C3
The nearest eminence to Keswick, on its northern side
crowned with battered pines, is Latrigg, 367m. high and
looking impossibly steep. But there is an easy 'back-
door' approach to the summit offering a superb viewpoint. Starting from the road behind the Keswick
Hotel, the way cannot be missed, though the pleasant
approach of yesteryear is marred by a view of the new
highway, the A66 'improvement' Keswick by-pass. The
track climbs to the back of the fell and is there met by
another track ascending at a steep angle. The view over
Derwent Water commands the attention but it is also
possible on a clear day to see most of the high Lake
District fells.

Latterbarrow 3D5 s of High Wray
From Hawkshead, a hill to the north-east, crowned by a
prominent cairn, draws the attention. The slim, tall
cairn also identifies the hill from Langdale to Kirkstone.
A notable viewpoint, Latterbarrow is in the care of the
NT and can be approached from the minor road linking
Colthouse to High Wray. The summit commands a view

Levens Hall: detail of the carving in the drawing room

of a large area of high fells, from Old Man of Coniston
round to High Street. It is necessary to walk a little way
north-westwards for a splendid view of the head of
Windermere.

Levens Hall 4E6 SE of Levens
Connoisseurs of gardens and landscaping should not miss
a visit to the gardens of Levens Hall, 7½km. south of
Kendal on the A6. The design of the gardens has not
changed since it was created in 1690 by Monsieur Beaumont, a gardener to many peers and great landowners of
the day. Beaumont was in great demand but chose to
spend no less than forty years of his life, from 1690 until
his death in 1730, with Levens Hall. To walk in the
grounds today is to enjoy garden design on a grand
scale, to find a mixture of formality and curiosity, perspective and quiet seclusion. The very strange TOPIARY
with large yew trees clipped into odd shapes has remained
substantially unchanged through a succession of eight
gardeners; for generations visitors have been trying to
see a meaning in them. As every turn in the garden is
explored there are vistas that bring an immediate response to the imagination; there is a dream-like handling
of form, almost a drift from reality. A meeting with the

Levens Hall: the hall ceiling, c. 1580

celebrated ghost of the 'grey lady', reputed to haunt the grounds, might not surprise! The garden is not large, but the impression it leaves is in inverse proportion to its size.

The present Levens Hall was originally a defensive pele tower built in 1300 by the de Redmans, a family who obtained the land by charter from William de Lancaster in the twelfth century. The tower was built to withstand the Scottish raids and its remains form the oldest part of the hall. The hall stayed in the de Redman's ownership until it was sold to the Bellingham family in the late sixteenth century; James Bellingham, during a long life there, extended and improved the hall, panelling and plastering some of the rooms. When a grandson of James Bellingham inherited he lost the estate in gambling debts and a kinsman, Colonel James Graham, acquired the property. It was during Graham's ownership that Beaumont was employed to set out the garden and park. By marriage, the estate next passed to Henry Bowes Howard, Earl of Suffolk, and from the Howards, again by marriage, to the Bagots. The present owner is Oliver Robin Bagot, well known for his unusual hobby of making harpsichords.

The hall contains some fine antiques, portraits and miniatures, and relics of Waterloo. There is an unusual and fine oak FIREPLACE OVERMANTEL in the south drawing room bearing carved personifications of the four elements, the five senses, and the four seasons. On some of the walls of the hall is a covering of decorated goatskin leather dating from the late seventeenth century.

In an outbuilding there is a fine collection of working models of steam-engines.

The owners open the hall on three and a half days each week (details from information centres); the gardens are open daily.

Lindale 3D6
Lindale is a village at the junction of the Grange-over-Sands road with the Levens Bridge–Ulverston road.

Just down the Grange road from the village is a particularly ugly iron OBELISK, a memorial to that engineer and eccentric JOHN WILKINSON (1728–1808). Wilkinson, probably the first man to launch an iron boat successfully, floated a prototype model on the nearby Winster in 1786, a year before his full-scale attempt near Broseley. A great iron-master, Wilkinson's seat was at Castle Head, near the village, though he worked and lived mainly in south Staffordshire. Before he died he

Levens Hall: late-C17 topiary

had an iron coffin made, directing that on his death he was to be buried in it in his garden at Castle Head. This was done, but new owners of the property had his remains removed to the churchyard.

The obelisk, which bears a relief likeness of Wilkinson, has been slightly damaged by lightning.

Little Langdale   3C4   s of Langdale

From the Coniston road, the A593, Wrynose Pass is reached by a very narrow road going through Little Langdale, a dale parallel with, but south of, Great Langdale. It is almost possible to pass through the HAMLET – a few houses, a pub, and a post office – without being aware of it. Just after the hamlet a track crosses left to right: down on the left the track goes by Birk Howe Farm to an ancient bridge, SLATER'S BRIDGE, a masterpiece of delicate stone work. Up-river from it is Little Langdale Tarn, a small lake fed by many waters: by the Brathay river from Wrynose, Greenburn Beck from the Old Man of Coniston range to the south, Bleamoss Beck from Blea Tarn to the north, and by innumerable becks from Lingmoor.

Much of the property here is in the ownership of the NT, including Busk Farm – where in times of stronger belief fairies took on the night shift, churning butter when the family were in bed – Birk Howe Farm, and Slater's Bridge. The dale ends at the foot of Wrynose, at Fell Foot, another NT farm. Behind the farm is a man-made terraced hillock thought to be a 'Thing Mound' where the Viking settlers met to settle disputes and administer justice.

Little Salkeld *see* **Great Salkeld**

Long Meg and Her Daughters   Little Salkeld   4E2

> A weight of awe, not easy to be borne,
> Fell suddenly upon my Spirit – cast
> From the dread bosom of the unknown past,
> When first I saw that family forlorn.

(*The Monument Commonly Called Long Meg.*)

Such was Wordsworth's reaction to the remarkable stone circle lying between Cross Fell and the Eden, near

Long Meg (and Her Daughters)

Little Salkeld. The circle is very large and some of the stones are massive. It is oval in plan, its dimensions are 110m. by 91m., and twenty-seven stones of a probable total of about sixty are still standing. A farm track passes through the circle and trees have been planted.

Long Meg, the tallest stone, is about 3m. high and carries carvings of some of the mysterious cup-and-ring symbols. There is a gateway with exterior standing stones. One can merely guess at the significance of this stone family and feel the 'weight of awe': if only at the effort required, in 1500 BC, to move and erect the massive lumps of stone.

The circle is sometimes wrongly referred to as 'Druid'. It long preceded the Celtic settlement.

One thing is certain: if Long Meg and Her Daughters were not so remotely situated they would be much better known, the lush green grass on which they stand would probably be beaten bare, or, alternatively, carefully mown and tended by the staff of the appropriate ministerial department. As it is, the odd family broods in silence.

Long Sleddale   4E4/E5

Long Sleddale is 10km. long and, like its neighbour Kentmere, has all the attributes of a typical Lake District dale except a lake. The dale is the course of the River Sprint, which joins the Kent to flow through Kendal. The beauty and interest in the valley are the broadleaf woodlands – two of the natural oak woods are listed as Areas of Special Scientific Interest – and in the cragged and wild head, leading upwards to Gatescarth Pass (594m.), the old way to Mardale and Haweswater, now only a footpath. The fells on the eastern side of the valley are seldom walked.

Sadgill, at the end of the public road, is a mere building or two and there is only a scattering of farms and dwellings in the whole valley.

Lorton   3B3   (*pop.* 235)

The road from Crummock Water to Cockermouth (B5292) passes through the green valley known as Lorton Vale. There are two hamlets in the vale, High Lorton and Low Lorton. Near the latter is LORTON HALL, part of which is a pele tower dating from the fifteenth century; most of the rest is also medieval but is completed by a neoclassical frontage of the seventeenth century. In 1653 Charles II stayed as the guest of the Lady of the Manor, Mary Winder, when secretly rallying support in the area. It is said that at the Restoration she planted one of the King's favourite trees, a beech. The tree still survives. The house contains some fine oak panelling.

The house and gardens are opened on Bank Holidays, and at other times by prior arrangement.

The village hall at High Lorton is called Yew Tree Hall, and behind it is the celebrated yew tree referred to by Wordsworth in his poem on that subject:

THERE is a Yew-tree, pride of Lorton Vale
Which to this day stands single, in the midst
Of its own darkness, as it stood of yore.

(*Yew-Trees*)

It is from the yew that George Fox, founder of the Quakers, preached pacifism to a large gathering that included soldiers.

The Whinlatter Pass (318m.) links the valley with Braithwaite and Keswick.

Loughrigg   3D4   w of Ambleside

Loughrigg, an unpretentious fell at the head of Windermere and close to Ambleside, appears to be a flattish hump of land with no visible summit. Its biggest attraction is that it overlooks four lakes – Windermere, Rydal Water, Grasmere, and Elter Water – and has its own modest water, Loughrigg Tarn, for good measure. It is endowed with a mass of paths and, on closer inspection, a fair number of summits and viewpoints. Between Rydal village and Grasmere is one of the most famous paths in the Lake District: LOUGHRIGG TERRACE, an easy, made-up track offering some excellent views.

The network of paths on Loughrigg allows almost any number of walk permutations. Todd Crag, on the southern end of the fell, offers the best view of Windermere head and of the Roman fort of Galava. The highest point on the fell is on the north side overlooking Grasmere (336m.).

On the Rydal side of the fell are abandoned quarry workings that once produced some highly-valued decorative slate bearing ripple and 'raindrop' patterns.

Loughrigg Tarn is at the foot of the fell's western side; there is no public access to the tarn but a lane overlooks it.

Lowes Water   3B3

The small lake of Lowes Water is delightfully set in woodlands cared for by the NT. Unlike the other lakes, the water from it flows inwards towards the central valley system (and also into Crummock Water). The fishing rights are owned by the NT and boats can be hired locally.

Best views are up-lake to the daunting crest of MELL-BREAK (511m.). The ascent is particularly enjoyable when the heather is in bloom, but care is needed and the paths should be used. It is necessary to move around the summit ridge for the best views, which are all good.

Lowther   4E3

The Lowther estate has been in Lowther possession for 700 years. The first LOWTHER HALL was built in the early thirteenth century.

Sir Richard Lowther was a supporter of Mary Queen of Scots but managed to survive the indiscretion. In the late seventeenth century Sir John Lowther fared better, for he was a supporter of William and Mary and, in

recognition of his good judgement, was granted the title of first Earl of Lonsdale. Sir John extensively rebuilt the hall, but in the 1720s it was struck by a disastrous fire.

The present Lowther Castle was designed for Sir Hugh Lowther, the fifth earl, by Robert Smirke, designer of the British Museum. The building was started in 1806 and work finished in 1811. Unfortunately, the castle's proportions proved too extravagant for the twentieth century and it was pulled down, leaving some of the shell. The unique and spectacular façade, not approachable by the public, is 128m. long.

The church of ST MICHAEL, across the park to the north, offers an intriguing dichotomy between the seventeenth-century exterior and the essentially medieval interior. The capitals in the north arcade have some interesting decorative tooling, although much of this has been subsequently reworked. Restoration work was carried out on the church in the late seventeenth century. The curious Lowther Mausoleum (1857) is in the churchyard.

There are two Lowther villages. Lowther New Town is near the church and was designed to replace the original village. The other Lowther village is to the east: this was another specially-designed village – attributed to Robert Adam or James Adam, his younger brother – and was built between 1765 and 1775.

LOWTHER WILD LIFE PARK, a more recent venture, attracts thousands of summer visitors. It is not a 'safari park' in the accepted sense because the choice of animals has been confined to European species: it is possible to see otters, badgers, foxes, the wild boar – an animal once common in England – red, fallow, and sika deer, Highland cattle, and the old English longhorns, an ancient and now rare breed. There is also a collection of birds.

The management lays much emphasis on the educational use of the park and school parties make regular use of it.

Lyth Valley   3D5/D6

In May weekend crowds flock to the Lyth Valley, at the south-east end of the NP, to see the damson bloom. The older residents will say that the sight is not what it was, the damson orchards having been reduced since the last war; but if the brief glory is caught on time it is still an unforgettable experience. The chemistry of the Lyth, sheltered and set between the limestone scars of Whitbarrow and Underbarrow, suits damsons well, and damson jam and damson wine still figure prominently in southern Lakeland fare.

Mardale *see* Haweswater

Martindale   3D3/D4

Martindale Common takes up an area on the south-east side of Ullswater and is owned by the Dalemain Estate. It contains an important, carefully conserved herd of

Lowther Castle : the grand staircase from the W , now demolished :
only the castle façade remains

red deer. The red deer is more naturally an animal of open woodland, but will adapt to moorland conditions such as those at Martindale, though the different type of feeding produces a lighter animal with much lighter antlers. As the area is not open to the public, and is in any case rather inaccessible, the deer are able to wander without disturbance. An area of 1,327ha. has been designated as an Area of Special Scientific Interest.

The red deer, particularly in winter, are often seen in the larger area outside the common, such as the shores of Ullswater, and above Kirkstone. In the rutting season the 'roar' of the stags carries over long distances.

MARTINDALE HAUSE is the pass summit between Howtown and Martindale. A church is on the pass summit; but beyond and below, at the head of Martindale itself, is the old CHAPEL. This is worth a visit. The interior of the chapel is starkly simple with no old stone effigies or memorials. The walls were built in 1633 upon foundations that had probably already been in existence for several centuries. The holy-water stoup, heavily scored by arrow-head sharpening, is of the fourteenth century. The yew tree in the churchyard is several centuries old.

Maryport   3A2   *(pop.* 11,613)

Maryport is a small industrial town, once a port, at the south of the Solway. Originally it was a small village named Ellenfoot, but was renamed after landowner and developer Humphrey Senhouse, following Sir John Lowther's example at Whitehaven, began to build and extend the town in 1749. He named the town after his wife. The new town's prosperity was built upon the extensively-worked coal and iron mines. In 1777 it was recorded that the port owned between seventy and eighty vessels and that there were three shipyards. Prosperity continued, and the town was linked to Carlisle by rail in 1846.

The town and port now show, only too sadly, the results of the severe depression of the 1930s. The harbour closed in 1961 and dereliction is grimly evident, although it is being dealt with. The buildings around the old harbour – an eccentric conglomeration – are of interest and it is to be hoped that they will enjoy preservation and a facelift. An intention eventually to develop the town as a tourist centre has been expressed, and a number of industries have recently started in the area.

During the Roman occupation Maryport was of strategic importance in defence against raids from Scotland and as a supply port. ALAUNA, the fort, was north of Ellen River and immediately north of the present town. Traces of the foundations of the fort, facing the sea, can still be seen. At first the fort may have been established of turf and wood during Agricola's north-west campaigns, and later rebuilt of stone. Altars found in the nineteenth century record some of the fort garrisons, and there is evidence that the fort was occupied until well into the fifth century. A coastal road must have left the fort from two sides, but only a few traces are apparent. A road also left the castle south-eastwards to

King Arthur's Round Table, near Eamont Bridge

the fort at Papcastle (Derventio), a little over 10km. away; a straight section of the A594 uses the route, and the last 1½km. to Derventio is a public footpath.

Mayburgh and King Arthur's Round Table
Eamont Bridge 4E2

Mayburgh is near to Eamont Bridge in the island formed by the M6, the A6, the B5320, and the River Eamont. It is a henge monument, thought to date from Late Neolithic times. It is unusual: the stone circle consists of a bank of water-worn cobbles rising to a height of about 4½m. and enclosing about half a hectare of land. There is a single standing stone within the circle, but it was recorded in the eighteenth century that there were three others near the position of this one and two more stones standing at the gap assumed to have been the entrance. A broken stone was found near this entrance in 1879.

Nearby and down-river is another henge thought to be of about the same period and known as King Arthur's Round Table. This is a circular area surrounded by a mound and ditch with two entrances, both about 18m. in diameter. This henge has been greatly damaged by road works.

The purpose of these constructions can only be guessed at, but one can wonder at the wealth of historical remains in this area. There was, for instance, a Roman crossroads on this site, at a spot now taken by old roads, motorway, and railway.

Mickleden see Great Langdale

Milburn 4F2 (pop. 155)

Milburn is an interesting village because it has not changed appreciably from its twelfth-century form; it follows the traditional Cumbrian pattern: houses built round a central green or yard with narrow entrances that can be blocked off. It is usually said that this form made it more readily defensible against raiders; it is as likely that it was designed to contain cattle.

On the green, a large oblong one, is a maypole set in the base of an old cross. The village is featured in R. W. Brunskill's *Vernacular Architecture of the Lake Counties* (1974).

The Norman church of ST CUTHBERT was heavily renovated in 1894.

Millom 3B6 (pop. 7,100)

West of Duddon Sands and sitting below Black Combe is a sea-washed peninsula with a sandy beach that would make many popular holiday resorts green with envy.

In a corner, sheltered from the westerly winds, is Millom, once a tiny village. In the nineteenth century it struck iron in a big way: it boomed; it grew; and then it fell into decline. It is sad to see such places, all too common in west Cumbria. They hang on to life like grand old men who have fought through hard times and will not let a minor trial like old age beat them.

The iron ore was discovered in 1843 at HODBARROW, south of the town; several shafts were sunk and the boom began. An annual output of 343,194 tons was recorded in 1880 and the town was growing rapidly. To prevent the workings being flooded by the sea a timber barrier was constructed, followed, in 1890, by a sea wall. In 1905 another barrier, over 1½km. long, was built. In the 'twenties came the fall. Now the site looks like a huge playground left by tired children.

A visit to Millom's enterprising town MUSEUM will tell something of the story of the local industry.

MILLOM CASTLE is now a farmhouse. The original structure was of wood, but, like so many of the district's fortified towers, was strengthened after the grim experience of the Scottish raids that followed Bruce's victory at Bannockburn. At this time the castle was owned by the Hudleston family. The castle was severely damaged in 1460 during the Wars of the Roses, but was subsequently restored. During the Civil War the Hudlestons were Royalists, and the castle was at one point besieged by Parliamentarians.

HOLY TRINITY church has remnants dating from the twelfth, thirteenth, and fourteenth centuries; but most of the detail of the church belongs to the Victorian restorations.

Milnthorpe 4E6 (pop. 1,635)

Milnthorpe was once a reasonably important centre. It was a small port and a market town from the thirteenth century, and for a short time in the nineteenth century it became a modest watering-place. The Kendal–Lancaster canal (1819) and the Furness Railway (1857) passed it by. The busy A6 gave it some sense of bustle until the M6 took away the long traffic queues normal on the hill north of the town. Nevertheless, there is still some lively activity on market days around the eighteenth-century market cross.

DALLAM TOWER, built in 1720 on the site of an earlier structure, is a house to the west of the village. It is not open to the public but it is possible to admire the herd of fallow deer in the park from the surrounding roads and paths.

Miterdale 3B4/B5

Miterdale is missed by Lake District tourists, who pass it by without knowing of its existence. It is perhaps as well: the access road from Eskdale is very narrow and peters out after a short distance; Miterdale is really a walkers' valley. The Mite rises in a hollow below Burnmoor Tarn and disappears underground for a short length before making a descent through Eskdale Green to flow by the side of the Ravenglass and Eskdale Railway into Ravenglass.

The dale was once on a pack-horse route from Eskdale to Ravenglass until the expansion of the port of Whitehaven put it out of business. Once there was even an inn. Now there are a couple of ruins and few farm buildings,

Muncaster Castle, by Salvin. Built 1862–6

and the memory of a violent death, the story of which is told so well in *English Lake Country* by Dudley Hoys. A farmer's wife at the lonely farm at Miterdale Head was alone while her husband had gone on an over-night journey to market, and a strange-looking woman called at twilight, said she had been lost on the moor, and asked for shelter. It was readily given and the woman, overcome by the hot fire, fell asleep in a chair: her head dropped, jaw sagged, and the headscarf slipped off to reveal that this was not a woman but an ugly man. Being sure that he was a robber using a disguise to gain access, and having no hope of fleeing in the night with her child, the farmer's wife on impulse took a ladle of scalding fat out of a pan (from which she was making tallow candles) and poured the stuff down the man's throat. When the farmer returned next morning he found a demented wife and a choked corpse. The farmer buried the corpse and did not tell the story until long after the family had left the farm.

At the valley foot are Forestry Commission planta-tions: a pleasant footpath goes through them and over

Irton Fell before getting terribly bogged down above Nether Wasdale. A turning north-westwards along the ridge before this point takes the walker along WHIN RIGG and ILLGILL HEAD – the top of Wast Water Screes – one of the finest ridge walks in the country.

Morecambe Bay *see* **Grange-over-Sands**

Muncaster Castle 3B5
Just east of Ravenglass are the beautiful gardens of Muncaster Castle, famed for rhododendrons and azaleas.

Like many northern houses, Muncaster Castle is built onto a defensive pele tower. The tower dates from 1325 and, like most towers of its type, was designed, in troubled times, to house cattle on the ground floor and human occupants on the upper floors. In the mid nineteenth century Anthony Salvin, well known for his work in adapting castles and old houses into elegant, comfortable, and tasteful modern dwellings, was com-missioned by the fourth Lord Muncaster to rebuild (1862–6). The present building is the happy result.

Naworth Castle: the narrow courtyard between original building and late extension

of the castle hill, with sudden views up Eskdale, is only lacking for trumpets and choirs of angels.

The castle is open three days weekly and on bank holidays between Easter and September; the gardens are open daily between Easter and June, then three days weekly in July and August. Details are available at information centres.

Naworth Castle   6E5

In the early seventeenth century Naworth Castle was the home of 'Belted Will' (Lord William Howard) to whom Walter Scott refers in the *Lay of the Last Minstrel*:

> His Bilbao blade by Marchmen felt
> Hung in a broad and studded belt.

The oldest part of the structure to be seen today is the early-fourteenth-century Dacre Tower, the old pele tower. The building – the castle was converted to a mansion by Lord William – was severely damaged by a fire in 1844 but was skilfully restored by Salvin. The 30m.-long GREAT HALL contains heraldic shields and oak carvings said to have been brought from Kirkoswald Castle by Lord William. Lord William also brought from that castle a splendid mid-fourteenth-century timber ceiling, now in a room on the third floor of Lord William Howard's Tower.

Parts of the castle are divided into residential flats and the public are only admitted to the other parts by arrangement.

Near Sawrey   3D5

On the Windermere-ferry road from Hawkshead, after passing Esthwaite, are two small villages, Near Sawrey and Far Sawrey. There is nothing remarkable about

Hill Top, Near Sawrey, home of Beatrix Potter

Salvin gave the house an uncluttered symmetry, balancing the pele tower with a second tower.

The house has an immense variety of classical furniture, and paintings by Kneller, Reynolds, and Gainsborough. Each old castle has its legend. Muncaster's is unlikely, but just possible. The story tells that Henry VI, on the run after his defeat at the battle of Towton, fled through Cumberland and arrived near Muncaster, exhausted. He was brought to the castle by shepherds and was given hospitality for nine days while he recovered. As a token of gratitude the King gave his host a green glass bowl bearing gold and enamel decoration, 'The Luck of Muncaster', and with it the blessing that so long as the bowl was unbroken the family would prosper. From the 'King's bedroom' at the castle can be seen a 'pepperpot' monument on a nearby hill, supposed to mark the spot where the King was found.

At rhododendron time the gardens are magnificent, and an exotic contrast to the starkness of the highest fells in England seen in the background, sometimes still topped with snow. The terrace walk round the contours

ABOVE, LEFT *and* RIGHT: *Beatrix Potter: original drawings*

either, although both are quite attractive; but at Near Sawrey is HILL TOP, the farm cottage and home of Beatrix Potter, the writer and illustrator of those children's classics, the 'Peter Rabbit' books. The house, with its faithfully preserved interior, is owned by the NT and is open to the public from Easter to November. Beatrix Potter enthusiasts from all over the world visit the cottage: the more dedicated among them explore the area to identify the scenes that Beatrix Potter so faithfully copied in her books.

Newlands 3C3

The most direct way from Keswick to Buttermere village is by Newlands Pass, though the approach to the summit of the pass (335m.) from the Keswick side is steep and, in winter, sometimes dangerous.

The road for Newlands leaves the A66 at Portinscale. East of the Newlands Valley are the fells of Cat Bells and Maiden Moor, the sides of both providing Newlands with its mines. Lead and copper were once profitably worked here and at one time German miners were engaged to work the mines. Goldscope Mine – 'Goldscope' being a corruption of the German *Gotes Gab* (God's gift) – was brought into production in 1565 and was the most profitable; it is situated by the Newlands Beck some way south of the hamlet of LITTLE TOWN. Yewthwaite Mine, near Little Town, enjoyed a briefer prosperity than Goldscope, producing, in the eighteenth century, lead and iron pyrites at an annual profit of £3,000. The mine workings are now dangerous.

There are a few charming old buildings at Little Town, with which readers of Beatrix Potter's books will be familiar (*The Tale of Mrs Tiggy Winkle*). The small church enjoys a magnificent setting and is worth a visit.

The valley is bifurcated at Little Town by the fells of Hindscarth (727m.) and Robinson (736m.), the Newlands Pass road taking the westerly fork by Keskadale Beck. On the fell-side above Keskadale is KESKADALE OAK WOOD, an Area of Special Scientific Interest, said to be the only remains of the original Cumbrian oak forest. Unfortunately the wood was damaged by fire many years ago and the specimens are not good.

By the summit of the pass (Newlands Hause) a waterfall, MOSS FORCE, can be seen in the crags to the south.

Newton Arlosh (Long Newton) 5C5

Newton's name derives from 'New town': the new town in question was built to replace Skinburness, washed away by the sea in 1301. The CHURCH was founded by the abbot of Holme Cultram Abbey and built in 1304. In such a strategic position on the Solway any building could expect to take a hammering from border raids. And so, like a few other churches in the area, this one was

OPPOSITE, BOTTOM: *Beatrix Potter's Dolls' House, at Hill Top, Near Sawrey*

built with a heavy defensive tower; it has no outer doorway and the windows are high and narrow. Dedicated to St John the Baptist, it was the parish church for Abbeytown until after the Dissolution, when the abbey church was adopted instead. It became ruinous and was restored in 1844.

Old Man of Coniston range 3C5

The Old Man of Coniston range is the southernmost of the major central fells of the Lake District and is prominently seen from most of the main viewpoints. From the eastern shore of Coniston Water its great spread cuts into the skyline like a huge defensive wall. This was Ruskin's view of it from his home at Brantwood. 'Mountains', he wrote, 'are the beginning and the end of all natural scenery'.

Old Man of Coniston has been extensively mined since Norman times. An elderly inhabitant of Coniston remarked that the mountain was so full of holes that it was like 'a maggoty old cheese'. The main workings were directly up Church Beck above the village in Coppermines Valley. When the mines became uneconomic the slate industry expanded to compensate. The slate quarries of Bursting Stone, all too clearly seen from the lake's eastern shore, and Broughton Moor, at the southern end, continue to prosper. Like the slate of Honister and Kirkstone, Coniston Slate is tough and takes a high polish; it is in demand all over the world for faced buildings.

Five tarns sit in the mountain's high coves. Above the village is LEVERS WATER: once enlarged by a dam to serve the mines, it now provides water for part of south Lakeland. By the easiest, and very popular, footpath to the summit, and above the old quarries, is Low Water. Viewed from the summit this is often a startling blue, and photographers who capture it on colour film are often accused of using faulty stock. Goats Water sits in a dramatic cove under Dow Crags and on the southern shoulder of the crag is Blind Tarn, a small tarn without a visible outlet. On the fell's western flank, and enlarged by a dam to provide water for the larger towns of south Cumbria, is Seathwaite Tarn.

The highest point is the Old Man himself at 803m. The name may refer to the summit cairn: cairns are sometimes referred to as 'men'. The walk to the summit from Coniston is one of the most heavily-trodden ways in the fells. It begins up the Walna Scar road to the fell gate, then goes right to the old quarries and Low Water. To this point it is easy, if rough, but the last pull to the summit from here has greatly deteriorated and is loose and uncomfortable. The view from the summit on a clear day is glorious, taking in not only the major fells of the Lake District, but also a wide seascape. The nearby rounded peak is Brim Fell (796m.).

The north-eastern flank of Old Man of Coniston is WETHERLAM (762m.). It is a great hulk of a fell dominating the views westwards across Windermere. Behind it, and closer to the summit, is another peak, Swirl How

Summit of Old Man of Coniston

(802m.) with Great Carrs (785m.) just beyond. Overlooking the Duddon from the mountain's north-western arm is the less frequented Grey Friar (773m.).

The most striking peak – to say the least – is DOW CRAG (779m.) (NP), its great rugged cliffs towering 180m. above Goats Water. This is where rock climbing began and it remains a great attraction to large numbers of climbers every year; its degrees of challenge range from 'difficult' to 'severe'.

Starting from Coniston village and skirting the southern flank of the mountain to Seathwaite in Dunnerdale is the ancient road of WALNA SCAR. It was once possible to take a cart over this road but it has deteriorated beyond recognition during this century: it is nothing better than a rough footpath in places.

Old Man of Coniston is a fell full of interesting features for climber, walker, geologist, mineralogist, archaeologist, botanist, naturalist, and industrial archaeologist. There is even a religious society that believes that a certain rock of the Old Man has been 'charged' with spiritual energy: the fell has become a place of pilgrimage for its members. It must also be of interest to those who just want a measure of peace and solitude.

Papcastle   3B2   (*pop.* 445)

The Roman fort of DERVENTIO is now buried in the fields near the village of Papcastle, on the edge of Cockermouth. The stones were long ago taken for the building of Cockermouth Castle. Derventio was a strategic

cavalry camp, able to despatch reinforcements to the Solway defences, to the west coast, or to the western part of Hadrian's Wall. The area of the fort is 3ha., and there is evidence of a large vicus (village) outside it. The fort seems to have been occupied from Flavian times to the end of the fourth century.

Part of the village contains some old houses. The manor of Papcastle belonged to the Lords of Egremont. 'The Boy of Egremont' who fell into the Strid near Bolton Abbey and was drowned, referred to in Wordsworth's poem *The White Doe of Rylstone*, was the son of Ochtreda of Papcastle, heiress of the Lord of Egremont.

Patterdale *see* Ullswater

Penrith   4E2   (*pop.* 11,381)

The old red-sandstone town of Penrith has welcomed weary travellers going north or south since the days of the first Bronze Age settlers. And until the coming of the tourist industry, except to the inhabitants of the surrounding countryside, its primary importance was as a staging post. By the 1960s the constant stream of heavy traffic on the A6 had made life in the town centre almost intolerable, and it was hoped that the building of the motorway would give back to Penrith some of its old identity. Most of the heavy commercial vehicles have gone, but on market days care is still needed to cross Penrith's busy streets.

The Romans built their fort some 6½km. to the north

'View from Rydal Park' by Francis Towne (City Art Gallery, Leeds)

Thirlmere

Penrith Castle: S wall with remains of NE Red Tower on right. The design is quite unlike that of other Cumbrian castles

of the present town and called it Voreda; it was roughly half way, therefore, between the important forts at Brougham and Carlisle.

In post-Roman Britain it was an easy journey to Penrith for marauding Scots. In 1314, after Bannockburn, the town was burned: it suffered the same fate in 1345, at the hands of 'Black' Douglas, and in 1382. Licence to crenellate a DEFENSIVE TOWER was given either to Bishop William Strickland (later Archbishop of Canterbury) or to Ralph Neville, first Earl of Westmorland. It was at first a simple tower, but when Ralph Neville received the town and manor of Penrith from Richard II he made improvements and extensions.

A later Neville to occupy the castle was Richard, Earl of Warwick and Salisbury (1428–71), Warwick the Kingmaker. Later, Richard Duke of Gloucester was made Lord of the Western Marches and, spending some time in the Borders, made improvements to the castle. He married Anne Neville, the Earl of Warwick's daughter. As Richard III he made further improvements, including the addition of a large banqueting hall and comfortable apartments.

The castle deteriorated after Richard's death at Bosworth Field and in the sixteenth century became a free 'quarry' for town buildings. Today the south wall still stands to some height, together with the east tower and remains of the south-east tower. The land is now a public park.

Churches suffered no less than the rest of the town at the hands of the Scottish raiders. There was possibly a chapel on the site of the present ST ANDREW's church in Saxon times. A church served by Augustinian friars was in use in 1133: the great thickness of the Early Norman tower walls ensured the tower's survival; the rest was largely rebuilt between 1719 and 1722. On the northwest corner of the tower are the arms of the Earl of Warwick (bear and ragged staff). A plaque in the church is a memorial to those who died of the plague brought into the town by travellers in 1597.

In the churchyard is the peculiarity known as THE GIANT'S GRAVE. A popular tradition, maintained until recent generations, suggested that this large stone mound with two high stones at each end was the grave of Owen Caesarius, King of Cumbria from c. 920 to c. 937. Actually the group consists of two Angle or Norse crosses, with hogback gravestones of the same period. Another standing stone in the churchyard, known as the Giant's Thumb, is a pre-Norman cross, now headless.

The town-houses overlooking the churchyard are of considerable interest. Queen Elizabeth Grammar School is one: it was founded in 1564 and continued as a school until 1915. On the west side of the churchyard is a building of 1563 in which Dame Birkett kept a school: this is assumed to be the school where the infants William and Dorothy Wordsworth started learning at the ages of seven and six respectively when living with their grandparents in Devonshire Street.

The TOWN HALL at first glance might look like any

other town hall. In fact, it is a 1906 adaptation of two houses attributed to Robert Adam; sadly, only two chimneypieces survive as Adamish features.

There are two inns of note. The Two Lions dates from the sixteenth century. The Gloucester Arms, Great Dockray, has stood from at least the fifteenth century, but the earliest feature on the building is Elizabethan; Richard of Gloucester is said to have occupied the inn for a period. Other buildings of interest in the town include the Mansion House (1750) behind the parish church and the George Hotel, where the Young Pretender stayed during the '45 rebellion.

PENRITH BEACON was once a link in the country's communication chain. Now it is the great local viewpoint: the views over the Lake District hills are superb.

Pillar 3B4

Pillar, a fell at the head of Ennerdale, is usually seen by the ordinary traveller from a distance. A near view is possible only after a long approach on foot up the Ennerdale Valley, or from Wasdale by Black Sail Pass. The fell itself is a large, bulky, and buttressed fell reaching a height of 893m. It is a formidable object in itself but has acquired its name from a detached, gnarled, and riven rock standing 180m. high on the Ennerdale side. Reckoned to be the tallest mass of vertical crag in England, the rock is enough to make any climber drool. It was first climbed, in 1826, by John Atkinson, a local man; it quickly became a strong attraction to pioneer climbers. Many of the climbing routes are now listed in climbers' guides; the routes vary in difficulty from 'moderate' to 'very severe'. Walkers can approach the crag's foot and gaze on it with awe, but it is strictly for roped climbers.

The views from the summit of the fell, easily approached by paths, are everywhere magnificent. The High-Level Route from the summit of Black Sail departs from the direct climb to the summit for Pillar Rock on the 600m. contour. A rough path from Pillar Rock continues to the summit.

Place Fell 3D3

Across Ullswater from the Glenridding steamer pier is the tall spreading fell of Place Fell (657m.), a hummocky, steep-sided, crag-faced fell, the haunt of foxes and buzzards (even of hunting golden eagles) and scattered groups of the Martindale herd of red deer. The views from the summit are exhilarating. To the south of the peak there is a subsidiary peak, Round How; and to the north are the two peaks of The Knight and Birk Fell.

The usual fell-walkers' line of approach to the summit of Place Fell is from Patterdale up a track on the southern end of the fell to Boardale Hause (see Bore Dale), a

crossroads of paths. From this point a path ascends northwards to the summit ridge.

Pooley Bridge see Ullswater

Port Carlisle 5C5

The businessmen of Carlisle financed the construction of a canal, 18km. long, from the city to Fisher's Cross, near Bowness-on-Solway. Work began in 1819 and the canal, containing eight locks, was opened in 1823. It meant that passengers and small cargo from Carlisle could reach Liverpool by sea in one day. The journey down the canal took an hour and forty minutes and was made in small boats. The project was assumed a success and there were plans to connect Carlisle to Newcastle by water! But within six years the canal was beginning to run into financial difficulty: the expansion of the railways sealed its fate.

Rannerdale 3B3 E of Crummock Water

Crummock Water is narrowed by a hard knoll of rock known as Rannerdale Knotts, a good viewpoint for scramblers. Behind the knoll a small uninhabited dale runs eastwards. Apart from offering a delightful and secluded walk, it offers some puzzles of ancient origin. There are man-made tracks that appear to lead nowhere. Higher up valley there is an ancient ditch-and-wall enclosure. Was it defensive or merely a well-constructed cattle enclosure?

In his novel *The Secret Valley* Nicholas Size puts a few known facts together, adds conjecture and imagination, and comes up with a good story. He speculates that the local Norse 'capital' was in this area, that the strange tracks were built to confuse the Norman invaders, and, in the absence of Norman reports of a victory over the Norse inhabitants, that a determined Norman effort to penetrate the settlement was met by a bloody defeat in Rannerdale.

Ravenglass 3B5 (pop. 310)

Ravenglass, 27km. south of Whitehaven, is a small village on the Cumbrian coast in the mouth of the Esk and is served by the west-coast railway. Before silting, centuries ago, it served as an important port for the earliest inhabitants, for the Romans, and for the Saxon and Norse settlers. The Romans built a fort here, GLANNAVENTA, 'the town on the bank', but although the settlement must have been extensive little now remains: those parts of the site that are not covered by a plantation are crossed by the railway. One remnant, though, and a remarkable one at that, is the bath house, known as Walls Castle, with walls that stand to a height of $3\frac{1}{2}$m. This is in the woodland to the east of the fort. Close vegetation must have protected it over the centuries and one must fear for its continuing safety.

Ravenglass is the starting point for the Ravenglass and Eskdale Railway (see Eskdale).

LEFT: *On Pillar Mountain, with Great Gable in the background*

The single village street ends in a launching ramp, but launching is only possible within three hours of high tide. Muncaster Castle (qv) is within walking distance by public footpaths.

Across the river estuary is a stretch of sands scheduled as a Nature Reserve and containing the largest black-headed-gull colony in England.

Ravenstonedale   4F4   (*pop.* 535)

Ravenstonedale village used to have a refuge bell. If a criminal wishing to avoid just retribution could run to the bell-tower – then separate from the church – and toll the bell he was free from arrest. Incredibly this dodge was allowed to continue until the early seventeenth century. The present CHURCH, built in 1744, replaces an earlier building, although a very few features are retained from the original structure (the thirteenth-century chancel arch, for example). The church is worthy of a visit for its several interesting features, among which is the three-deck pulpit – saved from the old church – with a sounding board and, behind the top tier, a seat for the parson's wife. (Do the modern spouses avail themselves of the facility?) The box pews, too, are notable for the typically Georgian arrangement that allows the two halves of the congregation to face each other. A window in the east wall is a memorial to the last woman to suffer death in England in the cause of the Protestant faith. The woman, Elizabeth Gaunt, was burnt at Tyburn in 1685 after sentence from Judge Jeffreys.

Red Bank   Grasmere   3D4

A narrow road, with 1-in-4 inclines in places, leaves Grasmere southwards for Loughrigg and Elter Water. This is Red Bank, in the early days of the motor car a severe test for some vehicles. Now only misguided caravaners get stuck. The top of Red Bank is a starting and finishing point for the Loughrigg Terrace walk (*see* Loughrigg), which overlooks both Grasmere and Rydal Water.

Red Pike, Buttermere   3B3

sw of Buttermere village

Looking across Buttermere from the public road the stirring backcloth is a craggy ridge with the two peaks of High Crag and High Stile. To the right, and directly over the village of Buttermere, is a third peak with the conical shape that one expects of much higher mountains. Viewed from Crummock Water it blocks off the sight of higher peaks behind and appears more dominant. This is Red Pike (756m.), a popular fell-walk from Buttermere. The foot of the pike is pleasantly wooded and is an area of interest to botanists. Falling through the wood from the steep fell above is Sour Milk Gill, a stirring sight (and sound) after heavy rain. The ghyll falls from BLEABERRY TARN, which is cupped in a hanging valley below the pike's summit.

The way to the summit through the wood is a steep slog; worse, the descent is a nasty, slow scramble on loose stones. To get the most enjoyment out of the fell-walk it is probably best to make a day of it, to climb direct, taking suitable rests, then from the summit to do a ridge walk over High Stile to Scarf Gap, descending to Gatescarth Farm and the road by the lake head.

Red Pike, Wasdale   3B4   SSE of Steeple

Wasdale Red Pike's crags are seen from the track up Mosedale, on the way to Black Sail Pass from Wasdale Head. The pike (801m.) is usually taken in on the long fell-walk known as the Wasdale Horseshoe, with the fells of Steeple and Pillar. But it is worthy of a visit for its own sake and at one time was very popular; visitors now seem to concentrate on the better-known, more glamorous fells in the area. A part of Red Pike's attraction in the days of its popularity was a cairn near the summit built in the form of a chair, complete with back and arm rests. THE CHAIR was better known than the fell itself. It is still there, and indeed has been there for so long that it ought to be listed as an ancient monument.

Red Screes   3D4   NNW of Kirkstone

Red Screes (774m.) is the most prominent fell to be seen from Kirkstone Pass. It closes in the western sky and its rough side walls the way down to Brothers Water. From the pass a beaten track ascends for a distance up the lower slope of the fell on very rough, broken rocks: the path has been made by motorists wanting to stretch their legs or find a viewpoint; some of them imagine the summit of the fell to be within sight and easy reach. In fact the summit cannot be seen from the pass and there is a 300m. climb. The descent, too, is cruel on this side. The easier, if longer, ascent is from Ambleside by Sweden Bridge and Scandale Pass (*see* Scandale).

Raven Crag is a rock face near the summit of Red Screes; Snarker Pike is a subsidiary summit to the south; and Kilnshaw Chimney is a rock-filled gully below the main summit. These are all part of the same fell, though on some maps they appear to have greater prominence than the summit itself.

Stock Gill, which falls as Stock Ghyll Force near Ambleside, has its source on Red Screes. On the eastern-facing slopes of the fell are the quarries for Kirkstone Green Slate.

Robinson   3C3   NE of Buttermere

A fell with the odd name of Robinson walls in the Buttermere Valley on the east, its summit (737m.) behind and invisible. All the attention at Buttermere focusses on the lake and the craggy fells at the western side; Robinson is too often taken for granted. The view of the fell on the ascent up Newlands Pass from Newlands, the best approach, is quite different: from that direction the fell appears as a mass of crags and waterfalls. A frequently-used line of ascent from Buttermere village is beaten out and is reasonable, but it crosses a bog, BUTTERMERE MOSS, passable if there is no deviation from the track, but straying here in mist can lead walkers into waist-deep mud.

The summit is a plateau and to enjoy the valley views it is necessary to walk about. Robinson is a fell to avoid in bad weather.

Rosehill Theatre   Moresby   3A3

Cumbrian industrialist Sir Nicholas Sekers converted a large barn in the grounds of his house near Moresby into a well-appointed concert hall. The Rosehill Theatre is now well known and attracts international artists.

Rosthwaite *see* Borrowdale

Roudsea Wood   3D6   sw of Haverthwaite

To the east of the Leven Estuary two ridges of differing rock – carboniferous limestone and Silurian Bannisdale Slate – form an island of varying habitats – salt marsh, raised bog, and peat – for plants and animals. Oak grows on the acid soil, yew, ash, and hazel on the alkaline, and birch and pine colonize the peat. The animals in Roudsea Wood include roe deer, red deer (transient), and red squirrel. The whole area has been given the status of a National Nature Reserve and is being studied by scientists from the Merlewood Research Centre, the Nature Conservancy headquarters at Grange-over-Sands. Access is by permit only.

Rusland   3D6

Rusland is one of the southern lakeland valleys that must have changed but little over centuries. It lies in the Coniston Slate area midway between the southern reaches of Coniston Water and Windermere, and is largely deciduous woodland and moss. The lower area may at one time have been a shallow lake. Through the valley runs the river known as Rusland Pool, which empties into the Greenodd Estuary. It is fed by waters from Grisedale and Dale Park. At the valley head is Force Beck where there was once a profitable forge owned by the Rawlinson family; it was this family that built Rusland Hall in the sixteenth century.

RUSLAND HALL has seen several restorations and several owners since. The present building owes much to the restoration and extensions in 1845 by Charles Archibald and the design is essentially Georgian. The present owners (1975) have opened the house and the classically-laid-out gardens to the public. The house contains a collection of mechanical music machines and other antiques, including a statue of the Three Graces, originally from Senhouse at Maryport.

RUSLAND MOSS is listed as an Area of Special Scientific Interest by the Nature Conservancy. The native pine growing in the area was a source of seed for pine plantings in the seventeenth and eighteenth centuries and foresters have shown that the species here has different characteristics to the common Scots pine. Naturalists are interested in the area because it is an example of a largely undamaged moss with characteristic plants and fauna.

THE RUSLAND BEECHES, lining the secondary road to Haverthwaite, attract a number of visitors, especially in autumn when they are a blaze of colour. The trees may originally have been planted as a hedge, although one that was neither cut nor laid. They are now in the care of the NP.

Rydal   3D4

'Rydale' has its head in a cove below the summits of Fairfield and Hart Crag. Rydal Beck does not in fact flow into Rydal Water, but directly into the River Rothay below the lake. Rydal, as most people, particularly Wordsworth enthusiasts, know it, is the lake and its environs.

Rydal is a modest little lake set in reeds between the crags of Nab Scar on its north and Loughrigg Fell on its south. Alas, the A591 runs close along its northern shore, destroying the peace that the great poet knew. WORDSWORTH'S SEAT, the poet's favourite viewpoint, is a rocky, tree-covered knoll with stone steps by the roadside at the eastern end. The lake is only 17m. deep and is the first of the lakes to freeze after a period of continual frost; needless to say, when this happens it attracts crowds of skaters. A lake-side path, stretching for a good part of the southern side of the lake, is approached by a footbridge from Rydal village and a path through the wood. The lake-side path rises at the western end to Loughrigg Terrace, above Grasmere's lake, and the walk around both lakes is one of the most trodden in the Lake District.

Church of St Mary (1824), Rydal

Rydal Water in winter

Rydal village is a church and a few houses, and is up a lane northwards from the A591. The church was built in 1824 and Wordsworth helped to choose the site for it, but was not too enthusiastic about the final outcome. The Wordsworth pew was in front of the pulpit. Behind the church, and approached through the yard, is Dora's Field, given by the poet to his daughter. It is a mass of daffodils in spring and is now NT property. RYDAL MOUNT is at the top of the lane and on the left. Wordsworth lived here from 1813 to 1850, though his best work had all been written, and mainly at Dove Cottage (qv). At Rydal Mount he was at the peak of his fame and he received many visitors, sometimes a hundred in a day. The house, subsequently acquired by a trust, inspires a kind of pilgrimage during the months that it is

open to the public (from April to December, except Mondays). It is furnished in the style of the period and includes some of Wordsworth's pieces and some of the family possessions. The poet's bedroom has views over the lake, his daughter Dora's room has a spartan simplicity. The garden is still laid out as it was in Wordsworth's day.

RYDAL HALL, below Rydal Mount and on the opposite side of the lane, was the home of the Le Flemings, who originally lived at Coniston Hall. The Fleming family were important landowners and the estate still owns much of the property around Rydal. The hall, not open to the public, is essentially a seventeenth-century building, although the south front is Early Victorian; it is owned by the Carlisle Diocese of the Church of England,

Portrait of Wordsworth, Rydal Mount: copy by Inman for Dorothy Wordsworth

and is a conference and study centre. The lovely tree-fringed fields (RYDAL PARK) below the hall are the scene of the famous Rydal Sheepdog Trials held each August.

West of the village, and close by the side of the A591, is NAB COTTAGE, a farmhouse with a diamond-shaped date-plate ('1702') above the door. This building is associated with another writer, Thomas De Quincey. De Quincey, after the Wordsworths had left, lived at Dove Cottage, but it was to Nab Cottage that he came courting, eventually marrying the farmer's daughter, Margaret Simpson. The Wordsworths did not fully approve the match. Later, Hartley Coleridge, elder son of Samuel Taylor Coleridge, lodged at Nab Cottage for about twelve years until his death in 1849. He, too, was a noted writer, but as his father was addicted to laudanum, so was he addicted to drink. In spite of his failings he was regarded by Wordsworth as an adopted son and they were frequently in each other's company. The house is now privately owned.

At the western end of Rydal Water, below the road, is WHITEMOSS COMMON, an old quarry site turned picnic area (NT); through it, before entering Rydal Water, flows the River Rothay from Grasmere. On the opposite side of the A591 a secondary road leaves to climb a hill above the common: this is the old road to Grasmere, via Dove Cottage, and there are good views over Rydal

from its summit. Beyond the summit there is a road junction, and the road to the right (no through road for vehicles) is the old road to Rydal village: a most pleasant walk entering the village by Rydal Mount.

St Bees 3A4 *(pop.* 1,335)
If St Bees were more accessible it might by now have become a very popular holiday resort, and its quiet charm would have been ruined. As it is, it is tucked modestly behind its high sandstone cliffs south of Whitehaven, and it is mainly the Cumbrian folk who enjoy the fine sands and the airy walks with views across to the Isle of Man and the hills of Galloway.

St Bees village is assumed to have got its name from the nunnery of St Bega. Tradition has it that St Bega was an Irish noble-lady who fled to Cumbria to escape an undesirable marriage, asked the local lord for some land for a nunnery, and got the dusty reply that she could have as much as could be covered by snow on midsummer day. Snow duly fell on midsummer day, miracles being relatively more common in those times. The Benedictine nunnery, founded *c.* 650, was later destroyed by the Danes, but the Normans founded a PRIORY on the same spot in the early twelfth century. The priory grew wealthy, owning land and rights in Eskdale, Ennerdale, and the western dales, and owning salt pans, coal mines and quarries, and the port of Whitehaven. St Bees stone was shipped from Whitehaven in the twelfth century for the building of St George's Chapel, Windsor. The priory itself was severely ravaged by the Scots in 1314 after their victory at Bannockburn; but it survived until its dissolution in 1538. The parish church of ST MARY is a surviving portion of the priory. There is a superb Norman doorway, *c.* 1160; the rest of the church is the usual mixture of original and not-so-original details. William Butterfield contributed to the latter in his restoration of 1855–8. There remain stone fragments and inscriptions dating back to the twelfth century, and one stone between the churchyard and the vicarage, thought to be eighth-century, may have its origin with the nunnery.

The village itself is quaint but unlovely, the beach being the best feature, and the cliffs of ST BEES HEAD to the north, 90m. high, the crowning glory. There are cliff-top walks for the sure-footed. The head is topped by a working lighthouse built in 1867.

St John's in the Vale between Thirlmere and Threlkeld 3C3
A minor road leaves the A591 north of Thirlmere and is a link with the A66 at Threlkeld. Travelling north on this minor road through the Vale of St John there is a magnificent view of the massive bulk of BLENCATHRA (qv): by some peculiar trickery of the landscape it is made to look larger than life, particularly if there are summit snows. The best and most photographed viewpoint has the delicate arch of Sosgill Bridge, about a third of the way up the valley, in the foreground.

Travelling southwards down the valley there is another view with a few surprises. The subject is CASTLE ROCK, otherwise known as Castle Rock of Triermain, which is at the southern end of the valley, east of the road. In the Romantic period of tourism it was fashionable to imagine that this natural rock was a castle, complete with towers, battlements, and a keep; it was the inspiration of Sir Walter Scott's poem *Bridal of Triermain*, in which King Arthur sees it as a fairy castle. Modern visitors are less romantic, many among them seeming to prefer it for rock climbing.

St Sunday Crag   3D3   sw of Patterdale
Why the fell rising above Patterdale and taking up the whole of the southern wall of the Grisedale Valley was called St Sunday is not known. Its appearance from every viewpoint is impressive. The summit is at 840m. but the highest point does not offer the best views: it is necessary to walk about the summit to find them. St Sunday Crag is a popular walk from Patterdale, offering a round walk of 11km. and an ascent of 700m.

Saddleback *see* **Blencathra**

Sca Fell   3C4
Sca Fell (964m.) is now accepted as a completely separate mountain from Scafell Pikes, the highest mountain in England. Sca Fell towers above the eastern flank of Wasdale Head, and the fell-walker using the popular route from Wasdale Head – by Lingmell Gill and Brown Tongue towards Scafell Pikes – is confronted by the north face of Sca Fell, 300m. of savage rock architecture, the most awesome crags in the Lake District. This wrinkled and fissured face has offered the greatest challenge to rock climbers since the pioneers of the sport claimed it early in the century; but the crag has also made its claims and some of the victims lie in the churchyard at Wasdale Head.

The great crag is split by the three main chasms of Deep Gill, Steep Gill, and Moss Gill. The only route up the crag for walkers is by a diagonal east-to-west scree-gully, known as Lords Rake, crossing the foot of Deep Gill. But this is a rough scramble and is dangerous when the gully is filled with snow and ice. By comparison, the summit of the mountain can be easily reached via the smoother slopes of the west side.

Separating the mountain from Scafell Pikes is a short, steep ridge known as MICKLEDORE. The step down to Mickledore from Sca Fell is Broad Stand, a short but treacherous overhang. It is not advisable for the ordinary fell-walker to try to move directly between the two mountains. Going up Broad Stand onto Sca Fell requires a blind grope, a little faith, and some contortions; its

LEFT: *Norman W doorway of St Bees church, c. 1160, a rich and powerful display*

negotiation up and, worse, down has caused many accidents, though arguably the fatalities have mainly occurred through walkers trying to avoid the trap and finding themselves in even greater difficulties. Strangely, the earliest recorded ascent of Broad Stand is that by Coleridge, who accurately described the climb to Wordsworth in an account of 1802.

On the east side of Mickledore is EAST BUTTRESS, another climbing crag. Walkers with steel nerves can find viewpoints from various parts of the summit. The highest point, set back in tamer surroundings, gives extensive views, but much of the north-eastern aspect is chopped off by the summit of Scafell Pikes.

Scafell Pikes   3C4
On the Scafell range, completely separated from Sca Fell by the gap of Mickledore, are a number of 'pikes'. One of them, popularly known as Scafell Pike, is, at 977m., the highest point in England. An inscription on the summit cairn records that the peak was taken into the care of the NT as a memorial to those who died in the 1914–18 war. The rest of the Scafell range, down to the then 2,000ft. contour, was presented by three donors, including the Fell and Rock Climbing Club, in the 1920s.

After Helvellyn, Scafell Pikes attracts more walkers than any other high fell. Although a few slightly lesser peaks offer more attractive walking, the highest of all has the glamour. Alas, its accident rate is high, including, over the years, many fatalities. It is not a more dangerous mountain than any other: it is an easy excursion on a fine day. But the number of walkers is high and a proportion is bound to include the unwise, the unprepared, the ill equipped, the late starters, and the foolhardy. The weather is the enemy. It is often extreme on the Pikes when in the valleys it is mild; and walkers are often surprised to find a covering of snow – frozen hard or wet and slushy, it is equally dangerous without an ice-axe. Mist clamps down swiftly and frequently to make it one of the easiest fells to get lost on.

The highest point is often busy with visitors and attracts all the traffic to the exclusion of the other Pikes: Broad Crag (931m.) to the north-east, Ill Crag (927m.) to the east, Lingmell (808m.) to the north-west, and, at the northern end of the summit ridges, Great End (909m.), which holds snow in its north-facing gullies longer than any other fell and receives a lot of attention from climbers in winter.

All the routes to the high point of the Scafell Pikes are heavily used. The shortest way is from Wasdale Head by Lingmell Gill and Lingmell Col, an ascent of 914m. and walk of 6km. The most exciting walk is from Seatoller in Borrowdale to Styhead Pass, then by a superb rough and airy walk along the western side of the mountain – the Guide's Route, otherwise known as the Corridor – a climb of 914m. and a walk of 10km. Those not familiar with the path used to find it difficult to keep to, but it is

From the summit of Pavey Ark in the Langdale Pikes, looking towards the Scafells and (left) Bow Fell

now well walked and worn (except, perhaps, on the wetter ground near Styhead, where it is still indistinct).

The summit ridge of the Scafell Pikes is a bleak mass of bare block scree and detritus, grim and uninspiring in poor weather; but on a clear day the views are magnificent, taking in all of Cumbria's fell tops. The wise fell-walker will start early in the day to avoid the crowds.

A more level area south-west of, and below, the highest point is the site of a Neolithic stone-axe factory, though most of it is covered by detritus.

Between Lingmell and the main massif is the deep and treacherous gully of Piers Gill, which the Corridor route crosses at its top. In 1921 a fell-walker fell into the gully and broke both his ankles. He lay there for eighteen days before being found by climbers. Unusually warm weather and a supply of water close by had kept him alive.

Scafell Pikes, though central, is one of the more remote mountains and several mountain-rescue teams serve it, participation depending on the location of the incident. The teams are in Wasdale, Borrowdale, Eskdale, and Langdale, and other teams lend support when required.

Scale Force   3B3   w of Crummock Water

Scale Force, 38m. long, is usually reckoned to be the longest waterfall in the Lake District, though its claim clearly rests on a particular definition of a fall: some becks on the high fells must exceed this length. The feeder beck for Scale Force falls northwards in a geological fault from a cove between Red Pike and Starling Dodd. Many people turn back from the path to the falls (signposted at Buttermere village) because of the extremely boggy ground. Other, less tremulous, adventurers who make the foot of the falls are disappointed to discover that a good view of the falls is seemingly impossible. Nerveless scramblers assuage this disappointment by clambering about the wet rocks to take photographs. Scale Force is really for dedicated waterfall-seekers only.

Scandale   3D4   N of Ambleside

Scandale and Scandale Pass is the walkers' way between Ambleside and Brothers Water. The first section from Ambleside, as far as HIGH SWEDEN BRIDGE, is a popular evening stroll. The top of the pass is at a height of 533m. Red Screes (qv) walls in the dale on the east and the

Fairfield range, together with Little Hart Crag, does likewise on the west.

Scout Scar (Underbarrow Scar) 4E5 w of Kendal
Opposite Kendal Town Hall, Allhallows Lane joins a road past the hospital. The road continues westwards by limestone quarries to Scout Scar, a hill crest. An iron kissing-gate leads on to the limestone scar, a scar that makes an admirable viewpoint for the Lake District fells: nearly all the major fells are visible and distance lends its usual enchantment to the prospect. A mushroom-shaped shelter on the summit of the ridge (230m.) once had a diagram painted on its roof indicating the features that could be seen; this has not been maintained and the shelter is now a useless ornament. Botanists will enjoy plant-searching on a very good example of limestone pavement. Although everyone calls this viewpoint Scout Scar, it is often shown as Underbarrow Scar on maps; such maps show Scout Scar at the southern end of the ridge.

Seascale 3A5 (*pop.* 2,105)
Seascale grew around the railway and most of it is little more than a century old. It is an attractive seaside town, far enough away from Calder Hall and Windscale to hold the modern industry at bay but close enough to give its inhabitants employment at the works.

As a holiday resort, and in spite of its small size, Seascale is impossible to fault. The sands are excellent, the beach fine and uncrowded, the shopkeepers helpful, and there is access to some of the best country in the Lake District; indeed the Scafells and Great Gable can be seen from some points in the village.

Seatoller *see* **Borrowdale**

Seathwaite (Borrowdale) *see* **Borrowdale**

Seathwaite (Dunnerdale) *see* **Dunnerdale**

Seat Sandal 3D4 e of Dunmail Raise
Looking north from Grasmere, Seat Sandal, taking up the eastern side of Dunmail Raise, is a fell much in the picture. There are two popular fell paths on either side of the fell. To the south a path up TONGUE GILL ascends to Grisedale Hause and Grisedale Tarn. To the north a path from the top of Dunmail Raise ascends to Grisedale Tarn via Raise Beck. From the tarn a path can be taken to Patterdale, or, by Dollywaggon Pike, up to Helvellyn.

The fell summit (736m.) is less frequently visited than most.

Sedbergh 4F5 (*pop.* 2,741)
Almost like an alpine village, Sedbergh is but 113m. above sea-level. It stands below the Howgills, and Brant Fell (Brant means steep) soars above the village streets. Sedbergh is properly Yorkshire, and indeed is in the YORKSHIRE DALES NATIONAL PARK; it was annexed by

Cumbria during the boundary revisions. Sedbergh has some seventeenth- and eighteenth-century buildings and a largely thirteenth-century church (ST ANDREW), which retains evidence of an earlier building.

Any visitor to the village will probably notice quite a number of young students in school uniform. SEDBERGH SCHOOL, a boys' school for over four centuries, is almost a local industry. The old school building, built in 1716, is now the village library; the present school is to the south of the village.

Sergeant Man 3C4 N of Stickle Tarn
Sergeant Man (736m.), a peak on High Raise, is as near dead centre of the Lake District fells as one could get. It is conspicuous from many parts of the Langdale Fells. A hollow below the peak, on the Stickle Tarn side, holds the snows after winter, sometimes for long periods.

The only really good view from the summit column is over the Langdales to the Old Man of Coniston range.

Shap 4E3
Shap is the high fell unavoidably climbed by the A6, the railway, and, more recently, the M6 motorway. It is a bleak, wild area given to winter gales and snow, and Shap village, before the advent of the M6, occasionally resembled a refugee camp as stranded lorry drivers waited for the road to be ploughed. Shap could tell a tale about the travellers who have been its way: Romans, Scottish raiders, the Bonnie Prince (who was overcharged at a local hostelry), and 'Butcher' Cumberland. Some visitors are daunted by the open scenery. Others like it. When John Ruskin wrote about a wild alpine scene that he had admired he stated: 'Ever since I passed Shap Fells, when a child, I have had an excessive love for this kind of desolation'. Shap village is at 245m., though the highest point over which the railway passes is at 279m.

Shap was extensively settled in Neolithic times. A stone circle near the village-centre of Shap, approached by an avenue of stones, is of that period, though the assembly has been destroyed by the railway. There are still a number of standing stones and cairns in the area. The village itself boasts nothing of great historical interest, though the church of ST MICHAEL retains twelfth-century portions and has a pleasant atmosphere.

West of the village, approached by a narrow road, is SHAP ABBEY. The site, low down on the banks of the Lowther, seems oddly chosen. But the sudden appearance of the tower, through trees and below, is rather thrilling. The abbey is in the care of the Department of the Environment and is open to the public. Although there is little standing except the heavy tower, it is possible, following excavations, to see the lay-out. The abbey was founded by Premonstratensians (White Canons) at Preston-in-Kendale in 1150 and in 1199 moved to its present site; it was dissolved in 1540. After the Dissolution many of the abbey's stones were taken

THE SOUTH-EAST VIEW OF SHAPP-ABBY, IN THE COUNTY OF WESTMORLAND.

Shap Abbey: C18 engraving

for the building of Lowther Castle (*see* Lowther).

South-east of the abbey, across fields, is the hamlet of KELD. The hamlet has a small sixteenth-century chapel (NT) of a type that must once have been common.

The QUARRIES that produce the granite for which Shap is famed are 5km. south of the village. The stone is much used for road building and cement products; but the handsomest type with pink crystals, from a quarry opened in 1868, is used for ornamental building stone. Stone from here can be seen in some London buildings. Garnets are found in some of the granite.

Shopford *see* Bewcastle

Silecroft 3B6 (*pop.* 370)
There is little to Silecroft village, on the south-west Cumbrian coast, except a good inn, a shop, and a post office. The approach to the beach is tatty. The caravan site is only partly screened as the winds and inhospitable soil will not support trees. But the beach itself is superb, and is very popular for sea-bathing. The pebbles on the tide line are a collector's treasure-house; the varieties of stone include pink and grey granite, black and grey slates, quartz, and volcanic tuffs. Below the tide line the sands are of high quality and extend far north and south. The hills of the Isle of Man are visible on a fine day.

Silloth 5B5/6 (*pop.* 2,660)
Silloth dates from last century when it was selected to be the new port of Carlisle. It also aspired to be a fashionable holiday resort. It never quite made either: the railway made a port less necessary and the position was not quite right for a holiday resort. Yet it still serves these two functions in a modest way.

The sea front and promenade are well made, and the views across Solway fine. The buildings facing the sea are not obtrusive and are solid and business-like; in front of them, and before the promenade, is a large expanse of grass. The buildings, including the flour mill at the port end, are not too ugly, the shopkeepers friendly, and the main visitors apparently natives of Cumbria. The beach is stony and not to be recommended, and the Solway is not as clear-looking as the open sea off the west coast. The bathing is dangerous on an ebb tide. The impression is of a traditional seaside resort out of season. Some people like it that way. Silloth should not be ignored.

Silver How 3C4 w of Grasmere
Any walker staying at Grasmere climbs Silver How (393m.) sooner or later. Looming large to the west on the Blea Rigg ridge, it is a pretty fell with many paths, hollows, groves, and gullies to explore. The summit is

Sizergh Castle: front view. The pele tower, c. 1340, is one of the largest of its kind

best approached from Grasmere by Allan Bank (Wordsworth's family home from 1808 to 1811), following a path to Long How, north of the summit, to reach it from behind. The views over Grasmere are the best and need a long savouring.

Sizergh Castle 4E6

Sizergh Castle hides away west of the A6, 5km. south of Kendal, and has been the home of the Strickland family for 700 years and twenty-seven generations. The land was granted to Gervase Deincourt in the twelfth century by Henry II, passing by marriage to the Stricklands in 1239. Like other landowning gentry in Cumbria, the Stickland's had, in the fourteenth century, to replace the original house by a pele tower to withstand Scots raids. The tower still stands, 18m. high, with walls 3m. thick.

The Stricklands were long involved in fighting the Scots. In 1297 Walter Strickland recruited 1,000 men to assist Edward I with the invasion of Scotland. He evidently fought well for several years, for he was made a Knight of the Bath and was granted a Charter of Free Warren, which gave him the exclusive right of killing game on his land, a prerogative normally reserved for the King. (Miraculously the charter has survived and is together with other ancient manuscripts, on display in the castle.) A Strickland later fought at Agincourt. But the losing cause was served by the family in the Wars of the Roses and they had to seek a pardon from Edward IV for any 'illegalities and excesses'. The family were not treated so leniently after their support of the Royalists in the Civil War: for their Stuart sympathies they were exiled for eleven years.

The GREAT HALL of Sizergh Castle was built onto the

157

Chimneypiece, 1564, in the dining room, Sizergh Castle

158

Second floor of pele tower, Sizergh Castle

north-east wall of the pele tower in 1450. There were later Elizabethan additions and alterations. Oak panelling in some rooms dates from this period and there are a number of very fine benches and five most remarkable CHIMNEYPIECES. Pevsner comments: 'No other house in England has such a wealth of Early Elizabethan woodwork of high quality. Moreover, it was one carver or one group of carvers that must have been at work over twenty years'. Some of the inlaid panelling of a bedroom has been taken for display in the Victoria and Albert Museum.

Also worthy of note is the second floor of the pele tower with adze-hewn oak beams. The house contains many fine examples of antique furniture and paintings, and the little museum on the top floor of the pele tower is full of interest.

The gardens are carefully tended and the castle and grounds are owned by the NT. Opening times are subject to revision and details are available from the NT and information centres.

Skiddaw 3C2

Skiddaw looms large in the northern landscape of the Lake District and towers over Keswick. At 931m., it is the fourth highest fell in Cumbria. Its great angular outline, lacking the dramatic crags and shattered aspects of its brothers up Borrowdale and Thirlmere, is explained by its different geology. Most of the central fells are of volcanic rock; Skiddaw's rock – Skiddaw Slate – is sedimentary and much older: it is a rather crumbly

material, quite unlike the slate the builder knows. The high volcanics overlay the Skiddaw Slate beds in central Lakeland, the Skiddaw Slate appearing again at the south-west corner: Black Combe is composed of this material. Skiddaw, then – some 400 million to 500 million years old – is the 'old man' of the Cumbrian hills and is not to be ignored. Skiddaw is sometimes scorned: the paths are 'like motorways', it 'lacks character', it is is 'like a giant slag heap'. But Skiddaw, used to such uninformed slanders, retains its popularity. For some people it offers the first fell-walk: the usual ascent from Keswick is recommended for this; the path is good and it is hardly possible to go astray. The walk from the town centre to the summit should take an average walker, taking his time, a little over three hours.

The common approach from Keswick is by the track beside Latrigg: a short walk by a field side, then a straight, unrelenting climb. The first peak to loom up is Little Man (865m.). This deceives some people into thinking that they have made the top and they turn aside to it; but the path continues to a short summit ridge. High Man, the summit, is at the northern end and is marked by a triangulation column. The views are tremendous and, apart from the Lake District hills, include the Pennines, the Isle of Man, and, across the Solway, Scotland.

The other peaks of Skiddaw are also worth climbing. Carl Side, to the south-west of the summit, offers fine views over Derwent Water; to the north-west are Longside Edge, craggy on one side, and ULLOCK PIKE, carpeted

Sty Head Tarn, with Great End on the right

with heather and offering the finest view of all; and to the south-west is LONSCALE FELL (714m.), with superb southern views.

On the north-east side of Skiddaw, Dash Beck falls down DASH FALLS (Whitewater Dash): these waterfalls are worthy of a visit after rain. An old track past the falls takes one round the fell and back to Keswick via a high, tree-screened shepherds' house, Skiddaw House, at the 450m. contour.

Steel Fell   3C4   sw of Dunmail Raise
Steel Fell towers over Dunmail Raise on its western side. When there was room for ample car parking nearby (the area is now fenced off) the fell was attempted by many people, most of whom did not persevere in the struggle up the steep side. The best approaches for walkers are from the back: from Grasmere, by Far Easedale, Green-burn, and Calf Crag, or direct from Gill Foot.

Steeple   3B4
SCOAT FELL (841m.), Wasdale, is hardly known. A pointed rock protruding largely from Scoat Fell on its

northern side is Steeple (819m.). From some viewpoints it appears to have been well named and from a distance seems impregnable; but in fact it does have an easy slope up to the summit on a side generally hidden from view. The superior way of ascent is by the long walk up Ennerdale to Low Gillerthwaite and through the forestry plantation. The usual way is from Netherbeck Bridge, Wasdale, by the wild Scoat Tarn to Scoat Fell; or by the left bank of Mosedale from Wasdale Head to the col between Red Pike and Scoat Fell.

In some directions the views from the top are extensive; but perhaps more impressive is the atmosphere in the midst of a conference of peaks and crags.

Strands *see* **Wasdale**

Sty Head Pass   3C4
'If you stand on Sty Head Pass summit long enough all the mountaineers in the world will walk past you'. So it used to be said when mountaineering was still a pre-dominantly British occupation. It is still almost true. Sty Head is the great crossroads of the high fells, with its

summit at 490m.; paths leave the top for the Scafells, for Great Wasdale, Esk Hause, Eskdale and Langdale, and Borrowdale. STY HEAD TARN, set below the summit, is a pleasant resting place: fell campers make use of the level ground offered at its banks.

Swarthmoor *see* **Ulverston**

Swinside Stone Circle   3B6   w of Duddon Bridge
Situated up a minor road that runs from the west side of the Duddon Bridge–Millom road is the stone circle of Swinside. Well off the beaten track, it is in some ways more impressive than the popular circle at Castlerigg near Keswick. The circle at Swinside is a tighter one than that at Keswick, containing fifty-five stones, and is a more regular circle. The size is similar, with a diameter of about 26m.

It is difficult to decide why the stone circle was sited at this spot; being hidden by hills, it is far from prominent. Circles of this kind are reckoned to be about 3,500 years old.

The circle can be seen from a public path, but it is in a private field.

Tarn Hows   3D5   NW of Hawkshead
In 1974 a count of visitors to Tarn Hows, one of the most popular beauty spots in England, showed that in the year three quarters of a million people made the pilgrimage. The NT, the owners, are taking urgent and continuing steps to combat the erosion to footpaths caused by such heavy use.

Tarn Hows is properly the name of a farm below the tarn that now enjoys its name. The tarn is situated on high ground in woodland between Hawkshead and Coniston and can be reached by car. The view of the tarn, framed in pines and larches, is a classic one and has appeared on innumerable calendars, chocolate boxes, greetings cards, and murals. Popularity does not lessen its beauty; it is, though, sometimes marred by the sheer volume of people who come to enjoy it. Only the crippled and infirm can enjoy a view of the tarn from their cars; other visitors have to leave their cars in car parks decently hidden in woodland. The walk around the tarn is fairly level and most enjoyable, though in wet weather it is a wellington-boot walk. To the west of the tarn is TOM HEIGHTS, a delightful viewpoint.

Tarn Hows was presented to the NT in 1930 by the Scotts, a local family, in memory of Sir James and Lady Scott.

In winter, because of its height, and shallowness, the tarn often freezes and provides good skating.

Taylor Gill Force   3C4   sw of Seatoller
From Borrowdale there is the choice of two routes up to Sty Head. The usual route is past Seathwaite Farm, by the east side of the ghyll to Stockley Bridge, across the bridge, and up the old pack-horse route. The alternative

– for scramblers – is to cross the ghyll by a bridge at Seathwaite Farm and to follow the opposite bank: this is rather indistinct at first, but opposite Stockley Bridge it turns up the side of a ravine. Down this ravine falls Taylor Gill Force, considered by many people to be the most spectacular waterfall in the Lake District; it is not so much the height of it – over 30m. – nor the volume of water, but, rather, its wild and craggy setting and the view of it from the high path.

Temple Sowerby   4E2   (*pop.* 275)
Temple Sowerby is a neat and attractive village by the A66 east of Brougham. The village gained its odd name from the early owners of the manor of Sowerby, the Knights Templars. After their suppression in 1308 the manor was transferred to the Knights Hospitallers. The manor-house, ACORN BANK, largely a seventeenth- and eighteenth-century building, was bequeathed to the NT in 1950. The gardens, but not the house, are open to the public.

The village, containing some seventeenth- and eighteenth-century buildings, is scattered around a large green.

Tilberthwaite Gill   3C5   N of Coniston
When leaving Coniston on the Ambleside road the first narrow road on the left after Yewdale Wood runs to Tilberthwaite, a dead end. Near the road-end a waterfall comes steeply down the fell slopes below Wetherlam.

Before the last war it was possible to walk up the ghyll by a series of bridges and catwalks for close views of the falls, which come down in several steps. But during the war the system of bridges and paths was wrecked by the army in training. The replacement costs in the 1960s, when the ghyll was taken over by the NP, were astronomical; a compromise solution produced a built-up path and a viewpoint bridge for the lower falls. A path from the top of the ghyll down the ravine, though technically a right-of-way, is suicidal.

The path up to the falls crosses the waste-heaps of an old quarry; these have weathered and grow lichens and ferns, and are not unpleasant. Higher up, larch trees are naturally regenerating on the slopes. The impressiveness of the fall from the viewpoint bridge depends upon the volume of water: after heavy rain the fall is thunderous, at other times the visit just makes an enjoyable walk.

Troutbeck   Windermere   3D4   (*pop.* 455)
An interesting, unspoilt hamlet with largely seventeenth- and eighteenth-century buildings and farms. The road from Windermere to Kirkstone just passes it by in the lower part of the hamlet. The main part of the hamlet is perched on a hillside among an interesting and purposeful network of roads and tracks, the buildings in groups like small conversation pieces. The groupings are a result of the practicalities of sharing communal water supplies; some of the wells, obviously sunk in more pious

times than our own, are dedicated to various saints. A student of the vernacular architecture could browse here for hours.

The CHURCH sits rather oddly below the main village, by the Kirkstone Road. There are two old but restored inns, The Mortal Man being well known for its advertising doggerel: 'Oh mortal man that lives by bread, what is it makes thy face so red? Oh silly ass that looks so pale, 'tis from drinking Sally Birkett's ale'. (Sally Birkett and her ale have long since gone.)

Several of the farms in the area were at one time owned by 'statesmen' – farmers owning a small amount of land, usually struggling to maintain a subsistence living. Among them was the father of William Hogarth. It is fortunate that the survival of one of the more prosperous farms, TOWNEND, allows us some insight into the life-style of a statesman. Townend, owned by a local family – the Brownes – for many generations, is now owned by the NT and is open to the public (weekday afternoons except Mondays). The design of the building is typical of a standard farmhouse added to in times of growing prosperity. The house has the cylindrical chimneys common to the older local properties. The core, the original seventeenth-century house, is divided into the usual two sections: the 'down house', where the work of the farm was done and the 'fire house', or living quarters:

ABOVE: *Townend, Troutbeck. The bed and cot are examples of the homemade oaken furniture*

LEFT: *Townend, probably 1626*

the area around the fire was lit by a small 'fire window'. Further wings and a dairy were added. The original homemade oaken furniture, with intricate carvings, is still in place. The little guide-booklet by W. Rollinson is invaluable.

TROUTBECK PARK is a tongue of land in the valley bottom, breathtakingly revealed to travellers up the Kirkstone Pass from a high bird's-eye view. The farm was once owned by author-turned-farmer Beatrix Potter. (Farm not open to the public.) On the tongue itself are remnants of an ancient British settlement, and a track on its eastern side leads to the Roman road on High Street. Some historians have speculated that the Roman road from Brougham to Ambleside fort came this way and through what is now the village of Troutbeck.

Ullswater 3D3

Ullswater was the lake of L'Ulf, a Norse settler. It is popularly regarded as the Lake District's most beautiful lake. The serpentine shape of Ullswater is a result of the varying degrees of hardness in the rock strata resisting by different amounts the pressure of a retreating Ice Age glacier. The geological contrasts also account for the varying types of scenic beauty along the lake's length. Its head, walled by Place Fell on the eastern side and the fell buttresses of Fairfield and Helvellyn on the west, is extremely dramatic. In the middle reaches the harsh, austere crags of the Borrowdale Volcanics give way to the angular shapes of the softer Skiddaw Slate. And from the foot the comparatively flat landscape of limestone and sandstone stretches to Penrith and the Eden Valley.

Ullswater is fed from a host of fast-flowing mountain becks. At its southern end the waters of Kirkstone, Hartsop, and Caudale flow through Brothers Water before being joined by the waters from Hayeswater and Deepdale to make Goldrill Beck, Ullswater's main source. The beck from Grisedale Tarn, fed from Fairfield and Dollywaggon, pours down Grisedale through Patterdale to the lake. From the heart of Helvellyn, through Red Tarn, Glenridding Beck also flows into Ullswater. This beck was once dammed to provide water power for the Greenside Lead Mines, above Glenridding village, but in 1927, during a great storm, the dam burst and devastated the settlement; miraculously there were no fatalities. The only sign left of the disaster is a stony peninsula formed from flood debris: a pier has been built here and a steamer service operates from it. Further waters from Helvellyn flow through lovely Glencoynedale and, further to the north, down the Aira Beck to the vertical cascades of Aira Force.

On the eastern shores the becks of Bannerdale, Bore Dale, and Fusedale pour to the lake through the old deer forests of Martindale.

Ullswater is a public highway and is therefore open to anyone who can put a boat on its surface, though like any highway it has speed-limit areas and safety rules. The lake is policed by the NP Wardens. A regular 'steamer' (now, alas, diesel) service plies between Glenridding, Howtown, and Pooley Bridge; the whole journey takes an hour.

PATTERDALE (*pop.* 615) is at the head of the lake. The name was no doubt originally 'St Patrick's Dale' (tradition has it that the Saint once came this way). By the roadside approaching the Glenridding boat-landing from Patterdale is St Patrick's Well, once reputed to have healing properties.

GLENRIDDING, only a kilometre away but at the foot of the next dale, was a mining town until, in 1962, it became uneconomic to continue to work the lead vein that had brought a degree of prosperity for about 300 years; the mine's production was at its height in the early part of the nineteenth century. When the mine was finally closed it was packed with explosives and used to test instruments designed to detect underground nuclear explosions. The mine buildings, well up-valley, are almost all gone, the few remaining now being mountain huts and a youth hostel. The 'tailing' dams of waste material are still ugly, though, just before the mine closed, some success was achieved in experiments to grow grass and pines on one of the faces. A public access area by the lake shore at Glenridding is now the centre for boat-hire.

On the west side of the lake there are no further settlements for 8km. Just north of Glenridding the fine woods of GLENCOYNE clothe the steep sides of Glenridding Dodd and the road squeezes round the crag face of Stybarrow at one of the lake's deepest points.

At Glencoynedale is a row of miners' cottages known as Seldom Seen: being round the valley corner, they are well named. The beautiful woods in this area – the land is in the care of the NT – reach down to the lake shore. As the road goes down-lake the interesting views are across to Place Fell, only 657m. high, but close, steep, and rough. With binoculars it is often possible to pick out part of the herd of Martindale red deer: on still October nights the roaring of the challenging stags can be heard.

Just after the road from Matterdale joins the lakeside road, Aira Beck enters the lake through pleasant woods cared for by the NT. It was the lake-shore fields at this point that inspired William Wordsworth to write his poem on daffodils. The waterfalls of Aira Force cannot be seen from the roadside: a walk from the public car park is necessary. The falls are, of course, best seen after a period of rain, but at any time the walk up the wooded ravine of this beautiful beck is very rewarding. There are two viewpoint bridges, one above the other. Aira Force was the scene of Wordsworth's *The Somnambulist*, an unlikely story with all the tear-jerking ingredients demanded by the Victorians (or some of them, at any rate): noble knight, faithful lady awaiting her lover's return, a reuniting marred by tragedy, and moving death scene.

Next to Aira Force Wood is Lyulph's Tower, not open to the public. It was the Duke of Norfolk's shooting lodge early last century and was built upon the site of an earlier tower; the name is said to be a derivative of L'Ulf, the first Lord of Ullswater, though some authorities suggest that the original name was Wolf's Tower.

Beyond the tower is Gowbarrow Park (NT), once a deer park. The road runs alongside the lake for a further 3km. with public access points to the lake shore provided by the NP; at Gowbarrow Bay the road leaves the lake by the Outward Bound School and does not approach it again until the lake foot. Close to the lake foot is a rounded, wooded hill, Dunmallet (Dunmallard) Hill: the 'Dun' suggests an ancient fortification, and, although the hill is not in public ownership, a footpath leads upwards to the remains of a pre-Roman ditch-and-bank fortification. Stone battle-axes have been found there. It has been suggested that the fortification may have continued in occupation until after the Roman departure. There is no view from the high point as all is obscured by trees.

POOLEY BRIDGE village is beyond. EUSEMERE, at the far side of the bridge, was the home of Mrs Clarkson, wife of Thomas Clarkson, the anti-slave-trader. She was the most intimate friend of Dorothy Wordsworth and the Wordsworthian excursions in this area were based on Eusemere.

The eastern shore of Ullswater is only accessible by road, and a very narrow one at that, for half its length. A public road goes to HOWTOWN, a small hamlet served by the steamer service; and from there to the lake head a public footpath skirts the lake shore. This is one of the finest walks in the Lake District and the popular way of doing it is to take the morning steamer from Glenridding Pier to Howtown and to walk back; the more energetic will feel inspired to take in the climb of Hallin Fell, above Howtown and at the foot of Martindale, to enjoy some most exciting views.

Ullswater is 12km. long and is over 1km. across at its widest point; it is over 60m. deep off Glencoyne, its deepest section. The water is not biologically rich, but supports perch and trout. Records show that the lake once held char but this fish is now absent: it is possible that as deep-water fish they suffered from the lead-ore washings coming from the mines through Glenridding Beck. There is no pike at all in Ullswater, but the lake has a whitefish, the schelly, sometimes called the freshwater herring. At one time the schelly was caught by net – spread across the narrowest point of the lake, below Hallin Fell – in huge quantities: the northern promontory opposite Hallin Fell is appropriately called Skelly Neb.

The lake's few small islands are all in the southern reaches, in the area of the hard Borrowdale Volcanics. Ownership of the lake is mainly shared between the NT, the NP, and the Dalemain Estate. Water from Ullswater is pumped, via a completely hidden underground pumping station at the lake's northern end, by pipeline to the reservoir of Haweswater. This arrangement came into effect after a hard-fought battle in the 1960s between the Manchester Corporation, which owned Haweswater, and the joint opposition of the NP and the conservationists. The arrangement made is a sound compromise: Ullswater remains what it was, a completely unspoiled and very beautiful lake.

Ulpha *see* **Dunnerdale**

Ulverston   3C6   (*pop.* 11,907)

Ulverston is a friendly market town that has had its ups and downs like any other Cumbrian industrial town; a few scars show and the town is not pretty, but it was never meant to be. New local industries have brought a lease of life: a local pharmaceutical processing plant is one of the world's major producers of penicillin. Ulverston is a very old town and was once the most important one in southern Cumbria, taking over from Dalton, it is said, when that town was stricken by the plague in 1631. Ulverston market became so popular that it took all the trade from surrounding market towns in the early nineteenth century, virtually killing the markets of Broughton, Cartmel, and Hawkshead. The late eighteenth and early nineteenth centuries made Ulverston a boom town. There were good natural resources: iron ore at Newlands, on the town fringe; charcoal for the furnaces from the woodlands of nearby High Furness; and water power. To this was added another, less natural, advantage. In 1795 a scheme was launched to link the town with a mile-long canal to the sea. The great engineer John Rennie, master dock and bridge builder, directed the work, and in 1796 the canal was opened with a grand procession led by a fiddler and a piper. The canal made Ulverston the unchallengeable capital and port of Furness. In 1847 it was recorded that the port of Ulverston was capable of taking vessels of '400 tons burthen which are discharged on the extensive wharfs erected close to the town, where there is a capacious basin'. The average number of vessels cleared was about 600 a year. A maritime colony grew up around the basin, shipbuilding became a new industry, and ships' ironmongery – chains, bollards, anchors – were made locally. The town also had many mills, and manufactures included cotton, linen-check, canvas, sailcloth, sacking, hats, and spades. Slate from the area's quarries was exported from the port, along with local leather, grain, butter, wool, and gunpowder. By the mid nineteenth century the population had increased to 50,000. There was a lively social life and the local theatre played to packed houses. The view of Ulverston from Hoad Hill was undoubtedly one of animation, though it was often obscured by smoke from the countless works and chimneys.

The boom – as is the nature of such things – proved to be rather ephemeral. The development of more efficient coke furnaces outstripped the technology of those in Ulverston. And the railway, in a reversal of its popularly conceived rôle, brought decline. The railway came in 1856 when the iron financiers were already seeking to exploit new resources and when the rapid expansion of Barrow-in-Furness was firmly planned. It soon became evident that the builders of the railway, the Ulverston and Lancaster Railway Company, were taking trade away from the port. The port's fate was sealed when the railway company was acquired by the Furness Railway, which also bought the canal. As trade declined, the company allowed the canal to silt up. All eyes were then on Barrow. Some of the small companies in Ulverston survived, but the small blast furnaces acquired by the big companies were considered to be uneconomic and were eventually closed. Ulverston lost its greatness and many of the townsfolk migrated; the town was particularly vulnerable when the general slump came in the 'twenties, and, until the coming of vigorous new industries after the last war, Ulverston was a place of ghosts.

SIR JOHN BARROW (1764–1848), Under-Secretary to the Admiralty for forty years, deserves a mention as one of Ulverston's more famous inhabitants. Born in a cottage still preserved in the south of the town, he went off to sea when nineteen, later becoming a teacher of mathematics at Greenwich. He made some long voyages and the books he wrote, including the *Life of Lord Macartney* (1807), the *Life of Lord Howe* (1838), and *Voyages of Discovery and Research within the Arctic Regions* (1846), became classics of the time. His monument is erected on Hoad Hill (132m.) and a 30m.-high imitation of the Eddystone Lighthouse can hardly be missed. The hill, which is easily climbed by a winding path, gives a good view.

Due south of the village is SWARTHMOOR. This part of the town was the scene of some excitement in 1487 when Lambert Simnel and his mercenaries camped here after their landing at Barrow, on the way to claim the throne from Henry VII.

At Swarthmoor is the remaining portion of the sixteenth-century SWARTHMOOR HALL, visited by many people because of its connexions with George Fox, founder of the Society of Friends (Quakers).

George Fox was a fearless preacher who believed passionately that there was 'that of God in everyman'. He disagreed with paid clergy, and regarded churches as unnecessary (he called them 'steeple houses'): anywhere where Christians gathered together, he maintained, was a place of worship. He argued that a prescribed order of worship was an obstacle to worship itself, he was against the taking of oaths, and was a pacifist. Such a man, with enormous energy and strong personality, won thousands of converts, but he also made enemies. Ulverston did not treat him well: he was set upon and beaten more than once. But Judge Fell, the owner of Swarthmoor Hall, was a fair man, if not one wholly convinced by Fox's philosophy, and the preacher and his friends were always welcome at his home. Swarthmoor Hall became a base for Fox's Cumbrian missions, and the 'headquarters' of the Society. Eleven years after Judge Fell's death in 1658, Fox married his widow, Margaret, a convert to the Society; but he was hardly at the hall, for he was either on his travels or in prison for his convictions. Margaret, too, had her share of prison. The hall has been restored; Judge Fell's room with the seventeenth-century fireplace, oak floors and panelling, and the unusual oak newel staircase can be seen. (Open mid March to mid October except Friday and Sunday.) SWARTHMOOR MEETING HOUSE, the seventeenth-century Quaker meeting hall, is down the lane to the east.

Signs of Ulverston's former shape can still be seen. The town has not been excessively 'developed'. The market square remains much as it was. St Mary's church is Ulverston's oldest building, with some twelfth-century stonework. 'La'al Oosten's' Thursday market is still a lively affair with stalls spilling from the square to Market Street.

Urswick   1D1

The church of ST MARY AND ST MICHAEL at Urswick is one of the most interesting in the area, and lovers of good wood carving – the Chipping Campden Guild are responsible for some of the carving – will find much to admire. The present church largely replaces a pre-Norman structure, but there still remain fragments of a ninth-century Anglo-Saxon cross and fragments of a Viking cross with Runic inscriptions. The painting of the Last Supper is by James Cranke (1707–81), a local man and Romney's early master. A rushbearing ceremony, a tradition dating from the days when the church had an earthen floor, takes place every September.

Urswick, Great and Little, is spread about a tarn, URSWICK TARN, that has associations with an odd legend about a sunken village. The story goes that a priest, tired of the constant complaints about the lack of water for the village cattle, and the suggestion that he was worthless for doing nothing about it, turned his back on the village and induced an earthquake that destroyed the settlement and replaced it with a tarn. The story is ridiculous. But why is the church sited so far from the present village?

To the west of the village is URSWICK STONE WALLS, the remains of a pre-Roman settlement.

Walla Crag (Wallow Crag)   3C3
E of Derwent Water
Above Great Wood on the eastern shore of Derwent Water is a wall of crags only 376m. high but offering grand views over the lake. There are two safe approaches to this ridge. From the south, from the Watendlath road, the ascent can take in the summits of High Seat (608m.) and Bleaberry Fell (589m.), which, with Walla Crag, are all part of the fell known as Castlerigg Fell. From the north an approach can be made from Rakefoot Farm.

At the southern end of Walla Crag is Falcon Crag, a climbing crag. Between this crag and Walla is CAT GILL, a source of much interest, and some controversy, among geologists. It is a fault between Skiddaw Slate and the Borrowdale Volcanics and contains some purple explosion breccia.

Through LADY'S RAKE, a gap on Walla Crag, it is said that the Countess of Derwent Water escaped with her jewels when the Jacobite Earl was arrested for high treason in the aftermath of the unsuccessful 1715 rising.

Walney Island see Barrow-in-Furness

Wansfell   3D4
To the east of Ambleside, and above Stock Ghyll Force, are Wansfell Pike, one of the best viewpoints for Windermere, and Wansfell. The usual approach is by Stock Ghyll Force, up a lane beyond, and over an iron stile; the climb is unrelenting and is not for a hot day. The summit of Wansfell Pike (482m.) is a mound to which the path directly leads. The summit of Wansfell (502m.) is along the wall to the north-east, but it is hardly worth the effort of reaching: its view is inferior. There is no direct descent to Ambleside except by the route described. The only other legal right-of-way off the Pike is eastwards to Troutbeck via a track known as Nanny Lane.

SKELGHYLL WOOD (NT), on the lower western slopes, above Waterhead, is a mixed one, providing varied habitats; the narrow band of Coniston Limestone evident in the wood is of interest to geologists. JENKIN CRAG is a point in the wood where there is a rocky knoll; it is reached from Ambleside with little effort and gives an extremely fine, tree-framed view.

Wasdale (Wastdale), Wast Water   3B4
Most travellers first see Wasdale from the road that leads into mid dale from Gosforth. The view is stark and startling: in front and below is a wide, dark, rock-girt lake and directly behind is a huge wall of loose scree, the famous 600m.-high WAST WATER SCREES, from this angle looking near-vertical and about to descend bodily into the water. For some people the atmosphere is too austere, even hostile; but at the same time it has an irresistible, haunting quality. Visitors sometimes have confused memories of the dales but they never forget Wast Water and The Screes.

Yet if one were to approach the lake from the south by public footpath to the NT wood south of the Youth Hostel, a completely different impression would be gained. The foreground is framed by handsome trees, The Screes are seen edge-on, showing a lesser angle, and way across the lake, softened by distance, are the great banks of mountains, Yewbarrow, Kirk Fell, Great Gable, and Lingmell. If the reflections are right and if there is snow on the summits touched by the sun, there is probably no finer view in the world.

TOP: *Wast Water Screes*

BOTTOM: *Wasdale, with Wast Water in the foreground and Great Gable in the centre background*

Wast Water is the deepest lake in England. The Screes continue their angle of slope down to the lake-bottom, a depth of about 80m. The Screes occasionally slide into the water; in the spring, especially, there are often rock avalanches, continuing a process that has gone on since the last Ice Age. (The glaciers, then thrusting down from the high fells, combined to scoop out the lake-bed and undermine a fell side.)

The only village, really a scattered hamlet, is STRANDS, on the Irt, west of the lake foot. It has a beautiful dale church, built like a barn and full of atmosphere. There are texts on its ornate ceiling and panelling and there is carving from York Minster. The Royal Arms are those of George III. A maypole on the green was erected in 1897 to celebrate Victoria's sixtieth year of reign.

The road from the village to the lake passes WASDALE HALL (NT), now a Youth Hostel. It was once reputed to be haunted by a previous owner's wife whose child was drowned in the lake in the 1820s. The ghostly figure has

been seen, it is said, walking around the lake edge. Up-lake, beyond the Gosforth turning, two becks, Nether Beck and Over Beck, flow down waterfalls into the lake, but the falls have to be sought out by walking up the banks.

Much of the head of the dale is owned by the NT. The NT has made a camp site within a tree screen at the lake head, which has effectively done away with the un-sightly camping that used to be scattered along the lake shore. East of the site, by Lingmell Gill, is the commonly-used way of ascent for Scafell Pikes or Scafell Crag. The narrow road beyond the lake head finishes at Wasdale Head near the smallest church in Cumbria, a tiny dales' church beloved by many. There is a memorial window to Queen Victoria and in one window is a little panel with the words 'I will lift up mine eyes unto the hills'. It is sometimes claimed that the church's rafters were made from ships' timbers. This could be true: Cumbrians are thrifty and pieces from a breaker's yard would not have

Looking towards Great Gable from Wasdale Head

come amiss. But the tradition that such rafters came from a Norse ship probably gained some credibility from the Viking habit of building roofs like ships' hulls or even of using upturned boats.

In the churchyard are buried some climbers who died on the local mountains.

Nearby is the Wasdale Head Hotel, home, in the last century, of Will Ritson. It was said of Wasdale that it had the highest mountain, the deepest lake, the smallest church, and the biggest liar in England. Will Ritson was the king of liars, famed for his tall stories. During a lie-telling competition at a local sports day he listened to many tall stories and when it came to his turn he asked to withdraw; he was asked why and replied, presumably with a straight face: 'Because I can't tell a lie'. He won the competition.

Behind the hotel is a fine example of an arched pack-horse bridge. Crossing this and following the left bank of Mosedale Beck, the path reaches the attractive Ritson Force; to get a good view of the waterfalls some scrambling is required.

The old track up Mosedale to Black Sail is on the other side of Mosedale Beck. This is the route to Ennerdale and is the fell-walkers' route to Pillar. Beyond the church the track joins the Sty Head path, the route to Borrowdale. The present path is a recent one, made earlier this century; the older way is on the south side of Lingmell Beck. A plan to make a highway over the Sty Head route mercifully never materialized. Great Gable towers over the head of the Sty Head track to its north; to the south are Lingmell and Scafell Pikes.

The little school at Wasdale Head is now, alas, disused. Nearby there was once a farm with the attractive name of Down-in-the-Dale; this has now been demolished and the stone put to good use to build a pumping station, in tune with its surroundings, at the foot of the lake; its function is to supply water to west-Cumbrian factories.

WASDALE HEAD, in its amphitheatre of great fells, is a masterpiece of landscape. The view down-lake provides a contrast in scenery accounted for by the change in geology: the high fells, including Illgill Head, the fell to which The Screes belong, are all of the Borrowdale Volcanics, while the lake foot is mainly Eskdale Granite. The granites, though very hard, break down in a different way to the other volcanic rocks and have yielded to the accumulated pressure of an Ice Age glacier. The dry-stone walls, built of material close to hand, make an interesting study. At Wasdale Head they are mainly rounded beck-bottom boulders, often of massive thickness. In the lower, Nether Wasdale, area the walls are largely of granite blocks and boulders.

The high fells around Wasdale are popular. The lower fells north-west of Wast Water (Copeland Forest) are hardly walked but offer some reward to seekers of solitude; the fells include Yewbarrow (627m.), the great hump west of Wasdale Head, High Fell (615m.), and

Seatallan (690m.). Among these fells are three tarns worth seeking out: behind High Fell, and the source of Nether Beck, is Scoat Tarn; further south, and feeding Over Beck, is Low Tarn; in an eastern hollow of Seatallan Fell is Greendale Tarn, reached by a pleasant path alongside Greendale Gill.

Wast Water is a clear, pure lake. So much so that it holds little natural food to support freshwater life. It does, though, contain char and brown trout.

Watendlath 3C3 NE of Rosthwaite
The narrow road to Watendlath leaves the road up Borrowdale at Ashness Gate, and given that there is no press of traffic, for which the road was never designed, the journey to the hamlet is a rare feast. First one crosses the little humped bridge, ASHNESS BRIDGE, one of the most photographed viewpoints in the country; then, climbing through the woods, the road comes to the edge of a precipice, SURPRISE VIEW, a breathtaking, bird's-eye view of Borrowdale and Derwent Water; and the road, between narrowing dry-stone walls, comes to Watendlath itself, with Watendlath Tarn in the background. Readers of Hugh Walpole's novels will associate Watendlath with *Judith Paris*; Judith's house stands by the tarn.

At weekends and busy holiday times Watendlath is to be avoided. The walk up the road has been ruined by the motor car; and the motorist has no time to enjoy the journey: he is too busy avoiding other cars and dry-stone walls. The walkers' way, avoiding the road, is directly upwards from the village of Rosthwaite, or on the path by Lodore Falls.

The hamlet of Watendlath

Wetheral   6E6   *(pop.* 105*)*

South-east of Carlisle is the attractive village of Wetheral, well known to fishermen, now largely a dormitory for Carlisle. There are celebrated walks through woods owned by the NT. A Benedictine PRIORY, founded *c.* 1100 by Ranulph de Meschines, stood near the river at the south side of the village: only a remnant of the fifteenth-century gatehouse remains. Nearby are caves cut into the sandstone of a gorge: they are known as St Constantine's Cells or, alternatively, the Wetheral Safeguards. Their purpose is not really known but one suggestion is that they were a hiding place for the priory's treasures during Scots raids.

The church of the HOLY TRINITY was restored in Victorian times but the exterior is still essentially early-sixteenth-century and there are thirteenth-century piers and some fifteenth-century glass. A sculpture by Nollekens of the dying Lady Maria Howard (d. 1789 at the age of twenty-three), with her dead baby in her lap, greatly affected Wordsworth; the sculpture is one of Nollekens' major works. There are two alabaster effigies, of Sir Richard Salkeld and his wife Jane.

The WETHERAL VIADUCT, north of the village, was one of the first major railway viaducts in the country. It was built in the 1830s, has five arches, and is about 30m. high.

St Constantine's Cells (Wetheral Safeguards), Wetheral. The caves are each about 7 × 3 × 3m.

Wet Sleddale   4E4

Wet Sleddale is a small dale running south-westwards from Shap Summit. A reservoir has been constructed by the late Manchester Corporation. It is a bleak, high-moorland area suited only to solitude seekers with a preference for the austere.

Whinlatter Pass   3B3/C3

The easy way to Lowes Water, Crummock, and Buttermere from Keswick is the westwards route by Whinlatter Pass (318m.) on the B5292. From Braithwaite it starts steeply through THORNTHWAITE FOREST, thick conifer plantations of the Forestry Commission. From lay-bys at the hill brow there are fine views over Bassenthwaite (qv). On the descent westwards, on a bend, there is a signpost to SPOUT FORCE WATERFALL: a path from here leads along the banks of Aiken Beck through woodlands. The less nimble taking it will probably suffer the frustrations that beset most waterfall viewers in the Lake District.

The fall is down a tree-surrounded gorge. Photographers will probably need a telephoto lens.

After this point the road falls elegantly into the Vale of Lorton.

Whitbarrow Scar   3D6

Whitbarrow (White Hill) is a long, prominent limestone scar much sought out by keen naturalists. An area of 1,010ha. is listed by the Nature Conservancy as an Area of Special Scientific Interest. The Lake District Naturalist Trust also has a nature reserve on the land. The ridge has the largest area of limestone pavement in the Lake District and there are uncommon and interesting contrasts in habitats.

Whitehaven   3A3   *(pop.* 26,724*)*

Whitehaven is a coastal industrial town struggling, apparently successfully, to heal some of the scars of depression. On market day at least, it bustles as it has done for the last two centuries.

It is now difficult to believe that the port of Whitehaven was once second only to London, having twice the tonnage of the ports of Liverpool and Bristol. Prosperity came from trading in tobacco and coal: the former from Virginia, the latter from Whitehaven's own mine. Now the only reminder of the tobacco trade is the tobacco snuff mill in Kendal, and the coal mining has declined. The large amount of trade once handled by the port is accounted for by the fact that much of it was with Ireland, Whitehaven providing a quick turn-round for shipping. Ireland obtained nearly all its coal from the Whitehaven coalfields.

In 1778 there was a rather bizarre episode in Whitehaven's history: an American invasion. The invasion was led by JOHN PAUL JONES, a well-known figure in the American War of Independence; Jones had served his apprenticeship as a seaman at Whitehaven before settling in the New World. In 1777 he obtained the command of the privateer *The Ranger*, and it was with this ship that he attempted a raid on Whitehaven, his intention being to fire the ships in the harbour. The raid was hardly a success. The winds were too light for *The Ranger* to come close inshore and the raiders, in two ships' boats, had a long journey to make against an unexpectedly strong tide: by the time they reached the ships in the harbour dawn was beginning to rise. John Paul Jones's party raided the fort and, meeting no resistance, spiked the thirty-six cannon of the fort and battery. At this point the other boat inexplicably returned to *The Ranger* without having accomplished anything. John Paul Jones continued with his plan to fire the boats, but the candles he had brought had burnt out and a light had to be obtained at a watch house on the quay. There was difficulty in starting the fire at all and ultimately only three ships were damaged. Jones retreated hastily at 8.00 a.m. under the fire of three guns obtained from ships in the harbour. The attack, understandably, caused a great deal of stir in the town and a public subscription took only four days to raise £857 5s 3d for repairs and improvements to the port's defences. Within ten years firepower was increased to ninety-eight cannon in four batteries.

The decline of the port began in the early nineteenth century, when Liverpool was being developed and railways were expanding. Coal mining also declined as the mines became less economic. Whitehaven has had its share of pit disasters: between 1910 and 1941 ninety-five men were killed; the biggest disaster of all occurred in 1947 when, after an explosion in William pit, 107 men were trapped behind heavy falls: only three of these entombed men escaped alive.

Some mining continues yet.

The harbour is still maintained and used. A slipway in the south harbour is available to the public at all times, except low tide. The port is still served by a coastal rail link through Barrow to the main line at Carnforth.

Whitehaven has further links with the American Revolution – less traumatic than the connexion with John Paul Jones – in the graveyard of St Nicholas, the parish church: for here is buried the grandmother of George Washington. In 1699, as a widow and mother of three children, she married George Gale, a merchant trading from Whitehaven with the colonies of Virginia and Maryland. Her two sons, born in Virginia, attended school at Appleby. On her death the two sons returned to Virginia, and one of them, Augustin, married and eventually became the father of George Washington, first President of the United States.

St Nicholas was heavily damaged by fire in 1971, and the site is now a pleasant open space and garden with only the church tower preserved.

The church of ST JAMES crowns a hill near the town centre. The Georgian exterior is impressive but the inside is a gem and is beautifully kept. The altarpiece –

Whitehaven: the earliest post-medieval planned town in England

The altarpiece, a Transfiguration, by Procaccini, St James's church, Whitehaven

said to be from the Escorial – represents the Transfiguration and is by Giulio Cesare Procaccini; it was presented by the third Earl of Lonsdale.

Whiteheaven is an interesting example of early town planning and it is pleasing to record that generally the modern development fits quite pleasantly into the old plan.

Windermere   3D4/D5/D6

Many people feel that the lake of Windermere has been vulgarized by its popularity. And undeniably Windermere *is* the Lake District in the minds of some of its many visitors. The lake has all the ingredients for the gregarious

pleasure-seeker: boats, steamers, villages with many hotels and guest-houses, parks and pleasure-gardens, and a backcloth of dramatic scenery. Visitors who appreciate solitude tend to go elsewhere at the height of the holiday season.

Windermere is not only the largest lake in England (nearly 18km. long and, at its widest point, 2km. across), it is also one of the most beautiful. The shores of the southern reaches are well wooded with hardwoods: these are glorious in spring and breathtaking in autumn. Wooded islands straddle the middle reaches with the wooded heights of CLAIFE (NT) on the western shore and, across the lake, high-pasture viewpoints. At the head of Windermere the landscape is dominated by the imposing and craggy ring of the volcanic mountains of the central Lake District.

The lake basin was scooped out by glaciers ploughing southwards from the central fells. The upper reaches were cut to below sea-level (the lake is 61m. deep at this end) but less impression was made on the middle reaches: these are much shallower and indeed Belle Isle almost divides Windermere into two lakes. Below mid-lake the ice, accelerated by further glaciers from the edges, bit deeper into the rock; the lake in its lower reaches is 45m. deep.

From the time of the earliest settlements Windermere must have served as a highway. When the Romans were building GALAVA, near Ambleside, they brought their quarried stone up-lake; iron ore was similarly transported for smelting at primitive bloomeries in the charcoal-producing woods (clinker from the old hearths can still be found on the lake shores). By the mid nineteenth century purely functional uses of the lake were being superseded by 'pleasure sailing': two competing steamer companies, in perhaps the first of many affronts to the lake's dignity, fought for custom with cut-rate fares and brass bands. These companies were bought out by the Furness Railway Company when the line was built to Lakeside. British Rail inherited, but the line to Lakeside was abandoned and is now in the hands of steam enthusiasts; the boats – bearing the names of the original craft – were kept and still operate. *The Raven*, an old steam cargo vessel once owned by the Furness Railway Company, is still on the lake after restoration by Mr G. Pattinson of Windermere. It is reputed to be the oldest registered steam vessel afloat.

The western shore of the lake has no villages and the few houses are usually hidden in woodland. A public footpath follows much of the lake shore from the foot of the ferry landing. (A car ferry connects Bowness-on-Windermere with a steep road leading to Hawkshead, a way often trodden by Wordsworth.) To the north of the ferry a quiet lane leads up to the upper lake shore and the grounds of the Victorian extravagance of WRAY CASTLE (NT). (*See* Wray.)

The east shore bears the brunt of Windermere's popularity. FELL FOOT, a Country Park at the southern

Skating on Lake Windermere, 16 February 1895

end of the lake, is 7ha. of pleasant ground in the care of the NT; the outbuildings in the park belonged to an imposing Georgian house that, sadly, was demolished late last century. The park contains car parks, picnic areas, facilities for the hire and launching of boats, furnished chalets, and a site for touring caravans.

The old Roman village at the lake head, near Ambleside, has gone; the modern Ambleside is built back from the lake and Waterhead – the site of the Roman occupancy – consists of hotels, a car park, a steamer pier, and boat landings.

It is BOWNESS that is the tourists' honeypot. There are no amusement arcades on the promenade and, so long as Windermere remains in a National Park, there is little likelihood of them appearing. But otherwise Bowness is as crowded as the front of any small seaside resort, with commercialization raising not *too* ugly a head.

Between Bowness and the lake head the only public access is at Brockhole (qv).

The monks of Furness Abbey once reaped the fish harvest of Windermere. The lake is famed for its char,

a deep-water trout; potted char was a great delicacy on the tables of the aristocracy in the seventeenth and eighteenth centuries: Sir Daniel Fleming, a local landowner, wrote that he made the char 'an instrument of social diplomacy' with which he 'sweetened intercourse with politicians and friends at Court'. Char fishing – the fish is caught on a spinner – is for the expert angler. Pike also give fine sport.

It takes many years to explore Windermere fully, it has so many 'nebs' and 'neuks' (bays and promontories). It is full of surprises and even at the height of the holiday season, with the peace broken by the noise of motor boats, solitude can still be successfully sought in the wooded hems.

Windermere (town) 3D5 (*pop. 6,082*)
Windermere is a small town and popular resort just over a kilometre from the lake on the eastern side. It is 13km. from Kendal and 7km. from Ambleside on the A591. It is served by a branch railway line from Oxenholme, a station on the main Glasgow line.

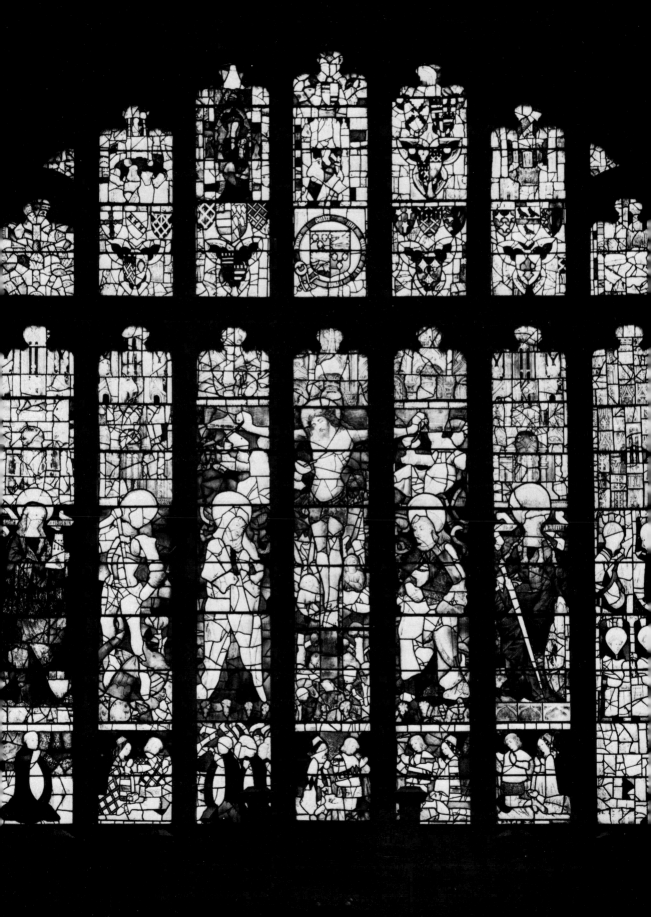

Windermere was formerly the village of Birthwaite until the building of the Kendal and Windermere Railway in 1847. From that time most of the town has been built and developed as a resort. The original intention was to continue the railway to Ambleside, but this was prevented by preservationists and local landowners. The growing town was renamed Windermere for obvious commercial reasons, though the lake is only reached after a journey westwards through the nearby village of Bowness-on-Windermere. As the town grew rapidly from the middle of the last century there is little of historical interest. Many of the larger houses, built originally by railway-commuting industrialists, are now hotels and guest houses.

ORREST HEAD is a superb viewpoint reached from a lane opposite the turning into town off the A591. A half-hour's climb finishes at a knoll. On the knoll there is a stone plinth bearing an indicator from which all the surrounding fells may be named: arranged from left to right over the lake are: Old Man of Coniston, with Wetherlam, its northern shoulder, in great prominence, Crinkle Crags and Pike o'Blisco, and if the air is clear there is a distant view of Scafell Pike, the highest point in England. Nearer and to the right again, Bowfell, and right and beyond, the northern part of the Scafell range, Great End. The Langdale Pikes come next, followed by High Raise and Ullscarf and the Fairfield horseshoe. Right again and almost due north is the High Street range. To the east lie the Yorkshire fells with the flat top of Ingleborough recognizable. SCHOOL KNOTT, east of the town, is also a good viewpoint.

Windscale see Calder Hall

Winster Valley   3D6

The beautiful valley of the Winster runs parallel with Windermere on its lower eastern side, but is separated from it by Gummers How and the hills of CARTMEL FELL. It is an area of low woodland with dispersed farms and houses, some of them old. The hamlet of Winster is at its head. The little post office is much photographed and is probably one of the most delightful in the county; it was built c. 1600. The Brown Horse used to be a typical village pub but has been modernized. Down a road opposite the pub is Holy Trinity church. It is not an old building (1875) but the setting and atmosphere are near perfect.

The narrow road from the church goes with the River Winster, passing houses great and small, to the hamlet of BOWLAND BRIDGE. Here a road goes westwards for Gummers How and Newby Bridge or, going south, there is a choice between a road on the east side of the river or

LEFT: *St Martin's church, Bowness-on-Windermere: E window, late-C15, which may come from Furness or perhaps from Cartmel*

one on the Cartmel Fell side, on the west. The latter gives access to Cartmel Fell church, ST ANTHONY'S O' THE FELL, well worth the trouble of seeking out. It is a sixteenth-century church and built like a heavy barn. The setting is perfect. Following the higher road south, a seventeenth-century Quaker Meeting House (now a private residence), with a walled burial ground opposite, is passed at The Heights. The Winster flows into Morecambe Bay east of Grange-over-Sands.

Workington   3A2   (*pop.* 28,431)

Workington is rather overshadowed by Whitehaven, her larger southern neighbour. Considering the short distance between the two towns, the character of each is quite different. Workington has the same Industrial Revolution buildings and shows signs that she too has seen bad days and good, but the pace is a little slower and quieter. The town lacks the straight-line grid plan of the Whitehaven streets. Its pride is Portland Square, long and narrow, with two rows of trees, and surrounded by streets laid out around 1780. It makes up for much of the drabness.

Leland, writing in the reign of Henry VIII, described Workington as 'a pretty fysher town': the estuary and the River Derwent were famed for salmon. By 1688 the fishing was estimated to be worth £300 per annum.

But, like Whitehaven, Workington's prosperity came from coal and shipping. Coal was being mined as early as 1650. The invention of steam engines made deeper mining possible and in 1750 four mines were being exploited; by 1792 fourteen mines were working and Workington had 160 ships, averaging 130 tons, employed in export. Boat building and the manufacture of sailcloth and cordage were developed in the expanding town. And iron ore, brought in by sea from Furness, was being smelted: following the invention of coke furnaces this industry grew rapidly, the first large ironworks being developed at Seaton in 1763. There were two blast furnaces, a rolling mill, a double forge, a foundry, and several small furnaces. Cannons were a speciality. With the prosperity continuing, Workington received its Charter of Incorporation as a municipal borough in 1888; the decline came in the twentieth century.

Sir Gilbert de Curwen obtained licence to crenellate in 1379 from Richard II. Only a trace now remains of the fortification, which was incorporated into a noble HALL in the fifteenth century: the features of the present structure are mostly of 1782–1828. In 1568 Mary Queen of Scots, fleeing from her defeat at Langside after escaping from Lochleven Castle, landed in Workington and was welcomed to Workington Hall by Sir Henry Curwen before she moved on to Carlisle. In 1678 the hall, boasting a herd of fallow deer, was described as one of the fairest in the country; but, after changing hands many times over the last few centuries, the hall is now the property of the town and is a ruin.

The parish church of ST MICHAEL was originally a

sixteenth-century building, but was rebuilt in 1770 and again, after a fire, in the late 1880s. It contains some Norman masonry of unknown origin and effigies of a knight and his lady, thought to be Lord and Lady Curwen and dated about 1450. The lady has two angels by her pillow and two puppy dogs are biting her skirt.

Wray 3D5

WRAY CASTLE, set among some beautiful trees, is seen prominently from Windermere's upper reaches, particularly from the north-east shore. From a distance the tower appears medieval, but in reality it is a Victorian extravaganza built for Dr James Dawson, a Liverpool surgeon, between 1840 and 1847. Sham 'ruins', some now demolished in the interests of safety, were also erected in the vicinity. Wordsworth could hardly have approved, though he planted a mulberry in the grounds. The owner also built a church alongside the castle and for a time this was served by Canon Rawnsley, later at Crosthwaite, Keswick, champion of the Lake District and one of the founders of the NT. Wray Castle is now owned by the NT, the castle being tenanted by a Merchant Navy training school. The grounds give access to the lake shore where, before its harassment by water skiers, there was one of the few safe bathing points on Windermere. A lake-shore path can be taken from Wray all the way to the Windermere ferry.

There are two hamlets, Low Wray near the castle

Wray Castle, by H. P. Horner, 1840–7

with the nearby nature reserve of Blelham Tarn, and High Wray to the south, where there is access to paths and bridle-ways onto CLAIFE HEIGHTS.

Wrynose Pass 3C4

Wrynose Pass is notorious for its steepness and narrowness, almost matching the conditions on Hard Knott Pass, onto which it leads. The pass, leaving the narrow road at Little Langdale to climb 393m., can cause difficulties on days of heavy traffic: there are long sections where it is impossible for two vehicles to pass and passing places – sometimes abused by motorists who *park* their cars in them – have to be used. Before 1939 the road was unsurfaced, but became so heavily worn by army training during the war that it was reinstated and surfaced, largely with concrete.

At the summit is THREE SHIRE STONE, until the county-boundary changes a meeting point of Lancashire, Westmorland, and Cumberland. This point is a well-used starting place for access to Crinkle Crags and, by Wet Side Edge, from which there are good views of the pass, to the Old Man of Coniston range.

The valley on the western side of the pass is Wrynose Bottom; Wrynose ends, and Hard Knott Pass begins, at Cockley Beck.

The Roman road from Ambleside to Hardknott fort can be traced in places over Wrynose: in Little Langdale it is mainly on the upper side of the present road; on the descent from Wrynose summit it takes the left-hand side of the road; but at Wrynose Bottom it is largely on the right-hand side, on what is now shown as a public right-of-way.

Yanwath 4E2 *(pop. 210)*

Yanwath is a small village near the motorway and railway south of Penrith. Close to the south bank of the River Eamont is YANWATH HALL: the large, heavy, well-preserved pele tower is of the early fourteenth century and was built by John de Sutton. The hall came to the Lowther family via the Dudleys in 1671. It is now a farmhouse.

Wordsworth's great friend Thomas Wilkinson (1751–1836), a Quaker, lived in Yanwath and it is to him that the poet addressed *To the Spade of a Friend* (1806).

Yanwath Hall: S front. Pele tower early-C14, hall and kitchen C15

Further Reading

General

Hoys, Dudley. *English Lake Country* (1969).

Millward, Roy, and Robinson, Adrian. *The Lake District* (1970).

The National Trust in the Lake District (NT 1975).

Nicholson, N. *The Lakers: the adventures of the first tourists* (1955),
    Portrait of the Lakes (2nd edit. 1972).

Pearsall, W. H. and Pennington, W. *The Lake District* (1973).

Poucher, W. A. *The Lakeland Peaks* (1960).

Smith, K. *Cumbrian Villages* (1973).

Sylvan's Pictorial Guide to the English Lakes (1847).

Wainwright, A. 'Pictorial Guide to the Lakeland Fells' series:
    The Central Fells (1960),
    The Eastern Fells (1960),
    The Far-Eastern Fells (1960),
    The Northern Fells (1962),
    The North-Western Fells (1964),
    The Southern Fells (1960),
    The Western Fells (1966).

Wordsworth, W. *Guide to the Lakes* (1810).

Architecture

Brunskill, R. W. *Vernacular Architecture of the Lake Counties* (1974).

Pevsner, Nikolaus. 'Buildings of England' series:
    Cumberland and Westmorland (1967),
    North Lancashire (1969).

Geology

British Regional Geology: Northern England (4th edit. 1971).

Dudley Stamp, L. *Britain's Structure and Scenery* (1946).

Marr, J. E. *The Geology of the Lake District* (1916).

Shackleton, E. H. *Lakeland Geology* (1967).

History

Gambles, R. *Man in Lakeland* (1975).

Garlick, T. *Romans in the Lake Counties* (1972).

McDonald Fraser, G. *The Steel Bonnets* (1971).

Marshall, J. D. and Davies Shiel, M. *Industrial Archaeology of the Lake Counties* (1969).

Rollinson, W. A. *A History of Man in the Lake District* (1967),
    Life and Tradition in the Lake District (1974).

Williams, L. A. *Road Transport in Cumbria in the Nineteenth Century* (1975).

Natural history

Evans, A. L. *The Naturalist's Lakeland* (1971).

Hervey, G. A. K. and Barnes, J. A. G. *The Natural History of the Lake District* (1970).

Pearsall, W. H. *Mountains and Moorlands* (1950).

Photograph and Map Credits

Conversion Tables for Weights and Measures

The figures in bold type can be used to represent either measure for the purposes of conversion, eg 1in. = 2·540cm., 1cm. = 0·394in.

kilometres		miles
1·609	**1**	0·621
3·219	**2**	1·243
4·828	**3**	1·864
6·437	**4**	2·485
8·047	**5**	3·107
9·656	**6**	3·728
11·265	**7**	4·350
12·875	**8**	4·971
14·484	**9**	5·592
16·093	**10**	6·214
32·187	**20**	12·427
48·280	**30**	18·641
64·374	**40**	24·855
80·467	**50**	31·069
96·561	**60**	37·282
112·654	**70**	43·496
128·748	**80**	49·710
144·841	**90**	55·923
160·934	**100**	62·137

centimetres		inches
2·540	**1**	0·394
5·080	**2**	0·787
7·620	**3**	1·181
10·160	**4**	1·575
12·700	**5**	1·969
15·240	**6**	2·362
17·780	**7**	2·756
20·320	**8**	3·150
22·860	**9**	3·543
25·400	**10**	3·937
50·800	**20**	7·874
76·200	**30**	11·811
101·600	**40**	15·748
127·000	**50**	19·685
152·400	**60**	23·622
177·800	**70**	27·559
203·200	**80**	31·496
228·600	**90**	35·433
254·000	**100**	39·370

hectares		acres
0·405	**1**	2·471
0·809	**2**	4·942
1·214	**3**	7·413
1·619	**4**	9·884
2·023	**5**	12·355
2·428	**6**	14·826
2·833	**7**	17·297
3·237	**8**	19·769
3·642	**9**	22·240
4·047	**10**	24·711
8·094	**20**	49·421
12·140	**30**	74·132
16·187	**40**	98·842
20·234	**50**	123·553
24·281	**60**	148.263
28·328	**70**	172·974
32·375	**80**	197·684
36·422	**90**	222·395
40·469	**100**	247·105

metres		yards
0·914	**1**	1·094
1·829	**2**	2·187
2·748	**3**	3·281
3·658	**4**	4·374
4·572	**5**	5·468
5·486	**6**	6·562
6·401	**7**	7·655
7·315	**8**	8·749
8·230	**9**	9·843
9·144	**10**	10·936
18·288	**20**	21·872
27·432	**30**	32·808
36·576	**40**	43·745
45·720	**50**	54·681
54·864	**60**	65·617
64·008	**70**	76·553
73·152	**80**	87·489
82·296	**90**	98·425
91·440	**100**	109·361

kilograms		av. pounds
0·454	**1**	2·205
0·907	**2**	4·409
1·361	**3**	6·614
1·814	**4**	8·819
2·268	**5**	11·023
2·722	**6**	13·228
3·175	**7**	15·432
3·629	**8**	17·637
4·082	**9**	19·842
4·536	**10**	22·046
9·072	**20**	44·092
13·608	**30**	66·139
18·144	**40**	88·185
22·680	**50**	110·231
27·216	**60**	132·277
31·752	**70**	154·324
36·287	**80**	176·370
40·823	**90**	198·416
45·350	**100**	220·462

Index

Map Section

GEOLOGY OF CUMBRIA

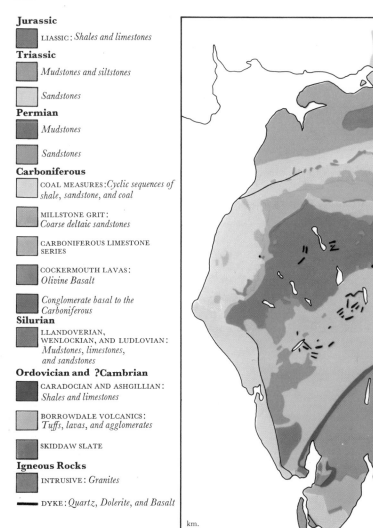

KEY

Jurassic
LIASSIC : *Shales and limestones*

Triassic
Mudstones and siltstones

Sandstones

Permian
Mudstones

Sandstones

Carboniferous
COAL MEASURES : *Cyclic sequences of shale, sandstone, and coal*

MILLSTONE GRIT :
Coarse deltaic sandstones

CARBONIFEROUS LIMESTONE
SERIES

COCKERMOUTH LAVAS :
Olivine Basalt

Conglomerate basal to the Carboniferous

Silurian
LLANDOVERIAN,
WENLOCKIAN, AND LUDLOVIAN :
*Mudstones, limestones,
and sandstones*

Ordovician and ?Cambrian
CARADOCIAN AND ASHGILLIAN :
Shales and limestones

BORROWDALE VOLCANICS :
Tuffs, lavas, and agglomerates

SKIDDAW SLATE

Igneous Rocks
INTRUSIVE : *Granites*

—— DYKE : *Quartz, Dolerite, and Basalt*

—— FAULTS

km.

0   10   20

Column headers: A B C D

Map labels (top right, Barrow/Ulverston area)

Silecroft
Whicham
Kirksanton
Kirkby-in-Furness
Beck Side
The Duddon Sands
Soutergate
Broughton
Beck
Greenodd
Arrad Foot
Milom
Ireleth
ULVERSTON
Canal Foot
Haverigg
Rodbarrow Pt.
Askam
Marton
Lindal
Bardsea
Haverigg Pt.
The Duddon Sands
Roanhead
DALTON in Furness
Little Urswick
Urswick
Baycliff
Scarth Chan.
Stainton
Newton
Scales
Aldingham
Nth. End
Abbey
Dendron
Nth. Scale
Leece
Roosecote
Roosebeck
BARROW
Vickerstown
Sth. Vickerstown
Mort Bank
WALNEY ISLAND
Rampside
Ulverston Chan.
Biggar
Piel Pier
Sheep I.
Piel I. Cas.
Foulney I.
Hilpsford Pt.
Haws Pt.

Right side lower

FLEETWOOD
Rossall Pt.
Cleveleys
Lit.Bispham
Norbreck
BLACKPOOL
North Shore
South Shore
SOUTHPORT

KEY

M11	Motorway
Interchange	Interchange
25	Limited Interchange
25 S.A.	Service Area
Under Construction	Under Construction
Projected	Projected
Dual Carriageway	Dual Carriageway
A 142	'A' Road
B 1438	'B' Road
A 134 B 113	Single Track Road
Other Serviceable Road	Other Serviceable Road
Mileage (between circles)	Mileage (between circles)
Track	Track
Path	Path
Other Ferries and sea routes	Other Ferries and sea routes
Principal Civil Airport	Principal Civil Airport
Railway (Passenger) L.C. Level Crossing	Railway (Passenger)
Canal	Canal
Church	Church
County Boundary	County Boundary
▲ 2450 ·167	Height (in feet)

SCALES OF FIFTH-INCH SECTIONS

Statute Miles
0 1 2 3 4 5   10

Kilometres
1 0 1 2 3 4 5   10   15

CONTOUR COLOURING

| Feet | Below sea level | Sea Level | 100 | 500 | 1000 | 2000 | 3000 | Feet |

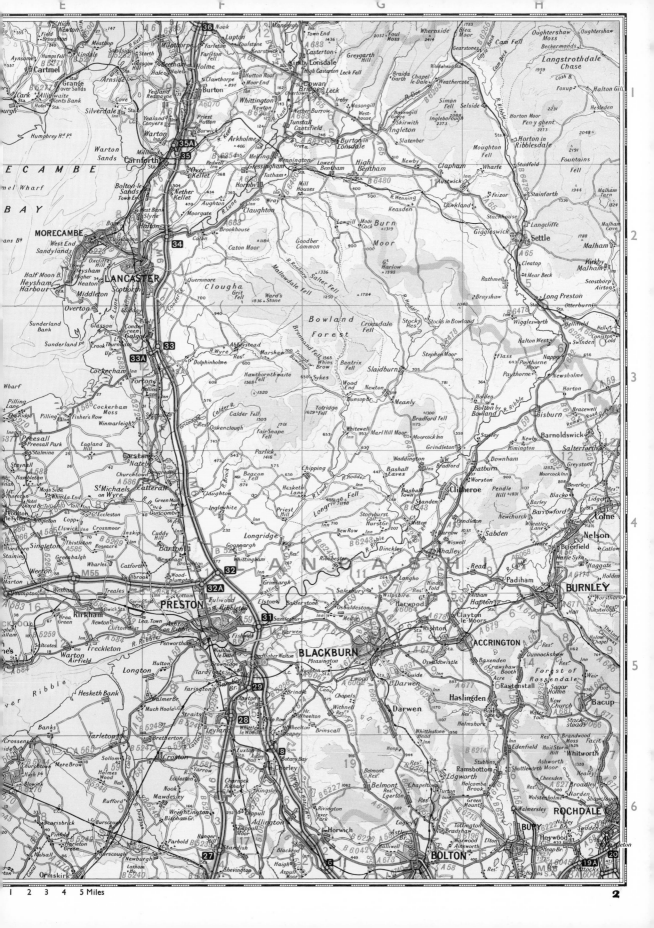

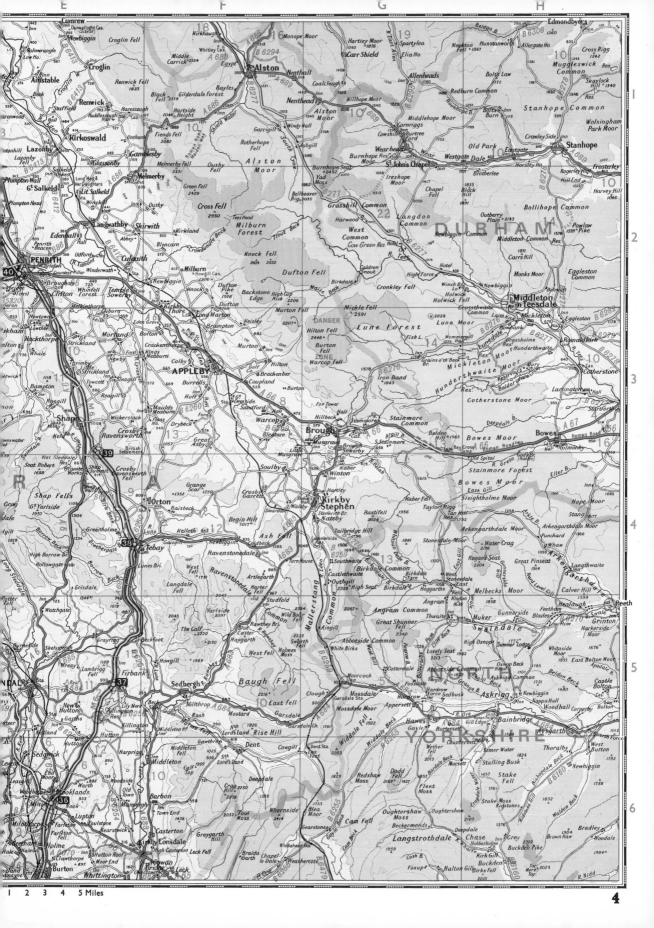

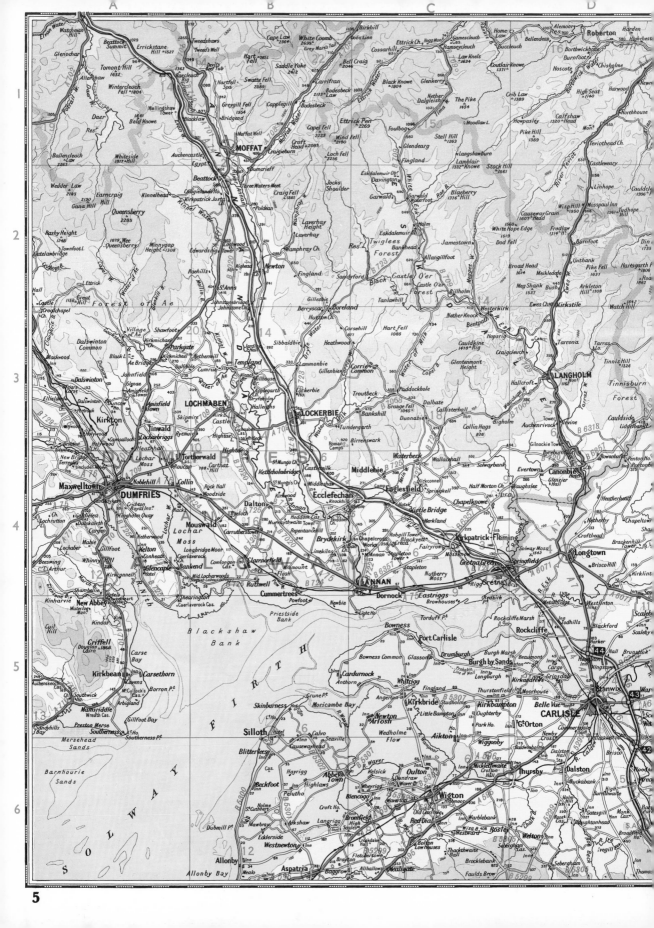

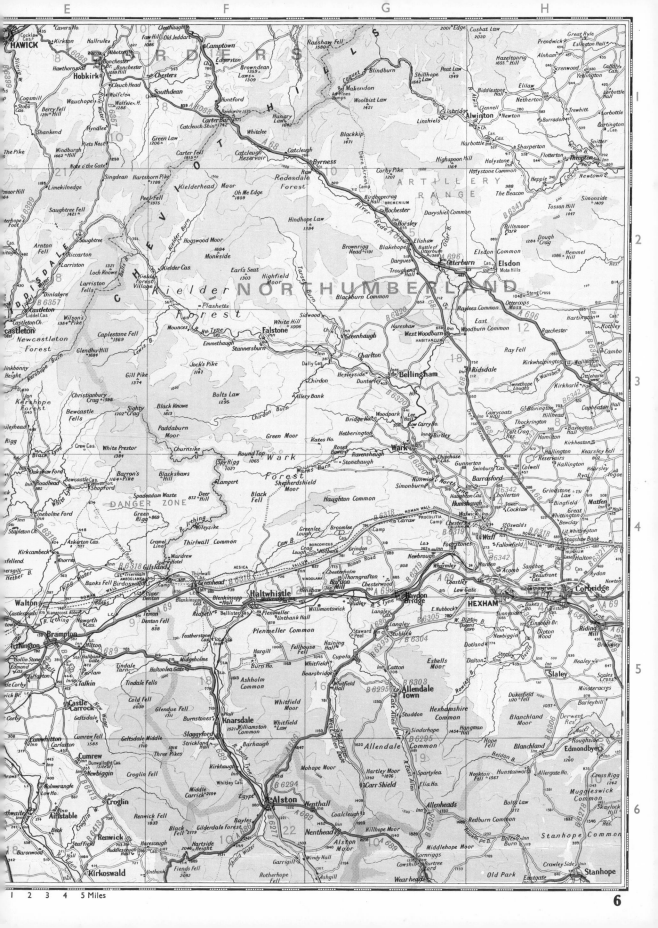

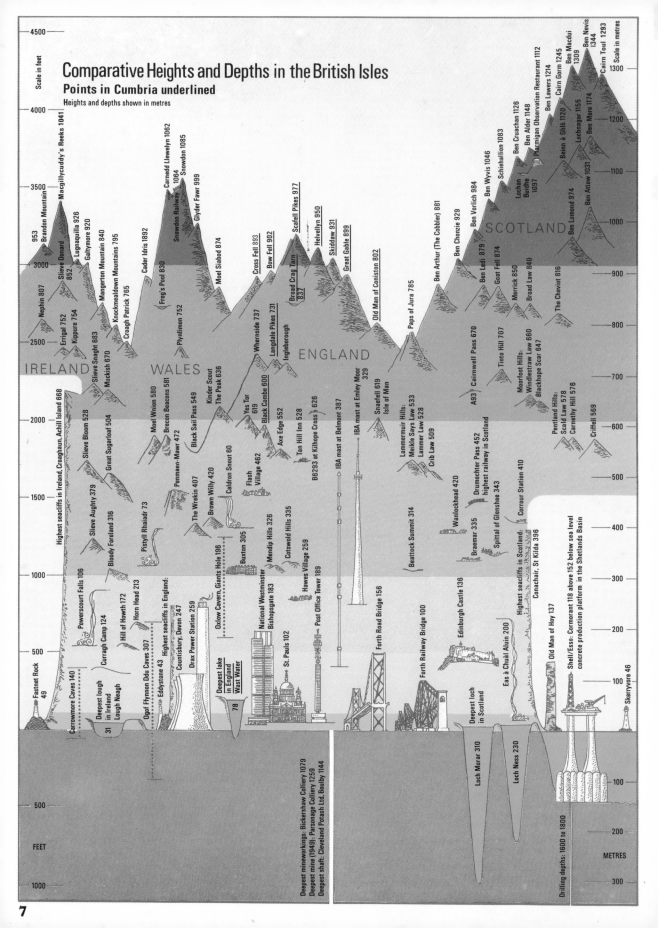

Comparative Heights and Depths in the British Isles
Points in Cumbria underlined
Heights and depths shown in metres

Scale in feet

Scale in metres

IRELAND

WALES

ENGLAND

SCOTLAND

FEET

METRES

953
Brandon Mountain
Macgillycuddy's Reeks 1041
Slieve Donard 852
Lugnaquilla 926
Galtymore 920
Nephin 807
Errigal 752
Kippure 754
Slieve Snaght 683
Mangerton Mountain 840
Knockmealdown Mountains 795
Croagh Patrick 765
Muckish 670
Slieve Aughty 379
Slieve Bloom 528
Great Sugarloaf 504
Bloody Foreland 316
Highest seacliffs in Ireland, Croaghaun, Achill Island 668
Powerscourt Falls 106
Curragh Camp 124
Hill of Howth 172
Horn Head 213
Pistyll Rhaiadr 73
Carrowmore Caves 140
Fastnet Rock 49
Deepest lough in Ireland Lough Neagh 31

Cader Idris 1892
Frog's Pool 830
Plynlimon 752
Moel Wnion 580
Brecon Beacons 581
Black Sail Pass 549
The Wrekin 407
Penmaen-Mawr 472
Kinder Scout
The Peak 636
Brown Willy 420
Caldron Snout 60
Ogof Ffynnon Ddu Caves 307
Eddystone 43
Highest seacliffs in England:
Countisbury, Devon 247
Drax Power Station 259

Carnedd Llewelyn 1062
Snowdon 1085
Snowdon Railway 1064
Glyder Fawr 999
Moel Siabod 874

Cross Fell 893
Bow Fell 902
Scafell Pikes 977
Helvellyn 950
Skiddaw 931
Great Gable 899
Broad Crag Tarn 837
Whernside 737
Langdale Pikes 731
Ingleborough
Black Combe 600
Yes Tor 619
Axe Edge 552
Tan Hill Inn 528
B6293 at Kilhope Cross 626
Flash Village 462
Mendip Hills 326
Cotswold Hills 335
Buxton 305
Hawes Village 259
Oxlow Cavern, Giants Hole 196
National Westminster Bishopsgate 183
Post Office Tower 189
St. Pauls 102
Deepest lake in England West Water 78

IBA mast at Belmont 387
IBA mast at Emley Moor 329
Snaefell 619 Isle of Man
Beattock Summit 314
Forth Road Bridge 156
Forth Railway Bridge 100

Old Man of Coniston 802
Paps of Jura 785

Ben Arthur (The Cobbler) 881
Ben Chonzie 929
Ben Vorlich 984
Cairnwell Pass 670
A93 Cairnwell Pass 670
Lammermuir Hills:
Meikle Says Law 533
Lammer Law 528
Crib Law 509
Wanlockhead 420
Drumochter Pass 452 highest railway in Scotland
Braemar 335
Spittal of Glenshee 343
Corrour Station 410
Edinburgh Castle 136
Eas à Chual Aluin 200
Deepest loch in Scotland

Ben Wyvis 1046
Ben Cruachan 1126
Ben Alder 1148
Schiehallion 1083
Ben Ledi 879
Goat Fell 874
Tinto Hill 707
Merrick 850
Broad Law 840
Moorfoot Hills:
Windlestraw Law 660
Blackhope Scar 847
The Cheviot 816
Pentland Hills:
Scald Law 578
Carnethy Hill 576
Criffel 569
Lochan Buidhe 1097
Parmigan Observation Restaurant 1112
Ben Lawers 1214
Cairn Gorm 1245
Ben Macdui 1309
Benn à Ghlò 1120
Lochnagar 1155
Ben More 1174
Ben Attow 1031
Ben Lomond 974
Highest seacliffs in Scotland:
Conachair, St Kilda 396
Old Man of Hoy 137
Shell/Esso: Cormorant 118 above 152 below sea level concrete production platform in the Shetlands Basin
Skerryvore 46

Ben Nevis 1344
Cairn Toul 1293

Loch Morar 310
Loch Ness 230

Deepest mineworkings: Bickershaw Colliery 1079
Deepest mine (1949): Parsonage Colliery 1259
Deepest shaft: Cleveland Potash Ltd, Boulby 1144

Drilling depths: 1600 to 1800

7